CATCH-UP MATH

Get your child back on track!

Counting · Place Value · Addition · Subtraction · Word Problems · Measurement · Graphs · Shapes · Fractions · Time · Money

Author
Kristin Kemp, M.A.Ed.

Consultant
Angela Gallo , M.A.Ed.
Richardson Independent School District

Publishing Credits
Corinne Burton, M.A.Ed., *President* and *Publisher*
Gabe Thibodeau, *Content Director*
Véronique Bos, *VP of Creative*
Lynette Ordoñez, *Content Manager*
Melissa Laughlin, *Editor*
Kevin Pham, *Graphic Designer*

Image Credits: all images from iStock and/or Shutterstock

Standards

A division of Teacher Created Materials

5482 Argosy Avenue
Huntington Beach, CA 92649
www.tcmpub.com/shell-education
ISBN 979-8-7659-8214-3

Printed by: 51497
Printed in: China

Contents

Contents

5. MEASUREMENT

6. DATA AND GRAPHS

7. TIME

8. MONEY

9. SHAPES

10. FRACTIONS

ANSWERS

About Catch-Up Math

The **Catch-Up Math** series enables children to start from scratch when they are struggling with grade-level math. Each book takes math back to the foundation and ensures that all basic concepts are consolidated before moving forward. Lots of revision and opportunities to practice and build confidence are provided before moving on to new topics.

Each new topic is introduced clearly with simple explanations, examples, and trial questions (with answers) before children move to the Practice section. To help students understand difficult topics, instructional videos are included throughout the book.

SCAN to watch video

A QR code on a topic page provides access to the video.

This book has 10 chapters that cover a variety of mathematical concepts. The chapters are:

1. Counting
2. Place Value
3. Addition
4. Subtraction
5. Measurement
6. Data and Graphs
7. Time
8. Money
9. Shapes
10. Fractions

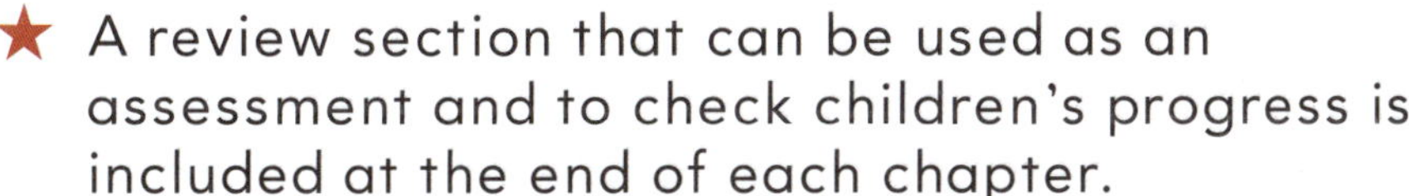

★ A review section that can be used as an assessment and to check children's progress is included at the end of each chapter.

★ Answers are at the back of the book.

Each Your Turn section contains a **SELF CHECK** for students to use for reflection and self-assessment.

How to Use This Book

Children can work through the pages from front to back or choose individual topics to reinforce areas where they are struggling.

The topics are introduced with:

- clear instructions, using simple language
- completed examples and incomplete examples for students to tackle before moving on to the **Your Turn** sections
- videos linked by QR codes to provide additional instruction and clarify difficult concepts

How to Use the QR Codes in Catch-Up Math

A unique aspect of the Catch-Up Math series is the instructional videos.

The videos further explain and clarify various mathematical concepts. The videos are simply accessed via QR codes and can be watched on a phone or tablet. Or, view all the videos by following this link: tcmpub.digital/cumath1.

Access the video by scanning the QR code with your device.

Each video shows a page from the book. An instructor talks through the concepts and examples and demonstrates what children need to do. The solutions to the examples are presented before children tackle the Your Turn sections. This careful instruction ensures that children can confidently move on to the following Practice questions. Children should be encouraged to check their Your Turn answers before moving on.

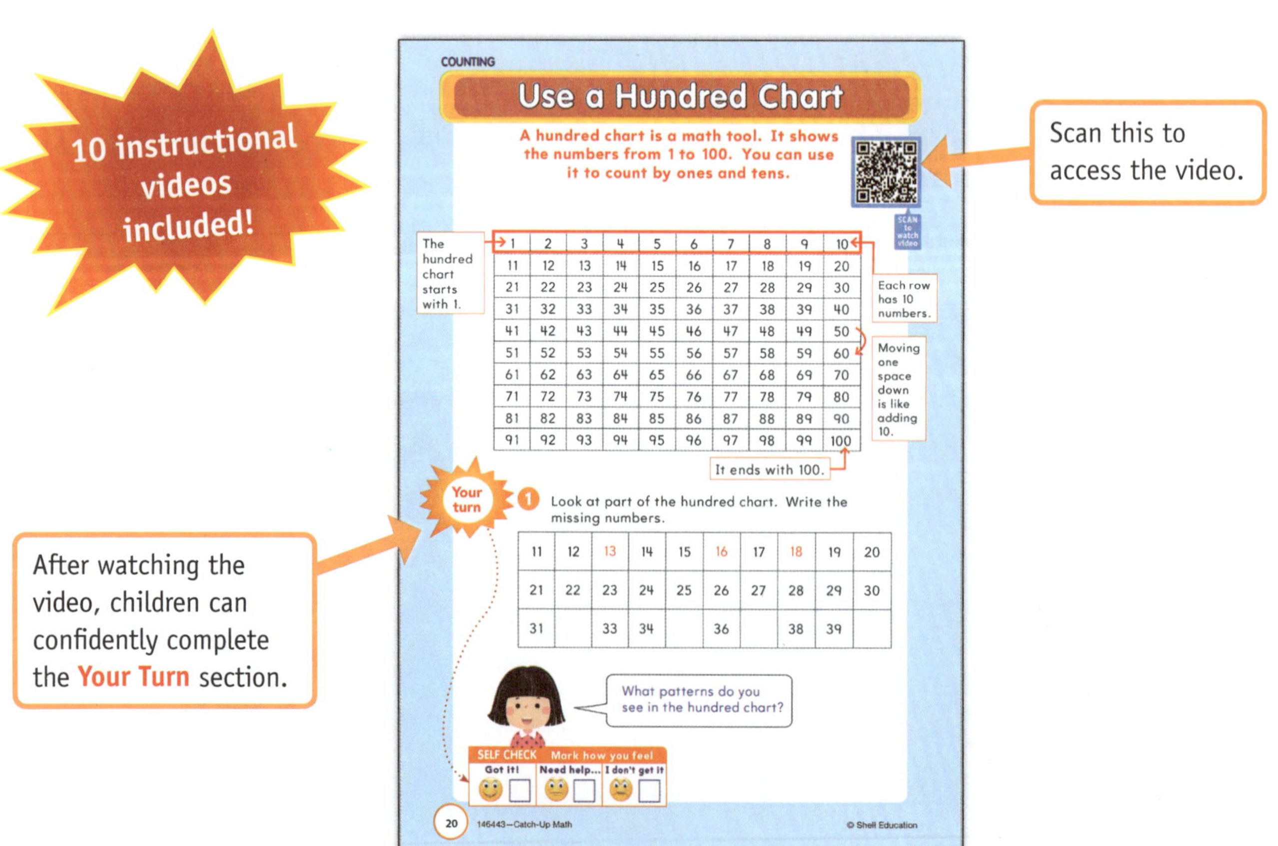

COUNTING

Use a Hundred Chart

A hundred chart is a math tool. It shows the numbers from 1 to 100. You can use it to count by ones and tens.

The hundred chart starts with 1.

1	2	3	4	5	6	7	8	9	10
11	12	13	14	15	16	17	18	19	20
21	22	23	24	25	26	27	28	29	30
31	32	33	34	35	36	37	38	39	40
41	42	43	44	45	46	47	48	49	50
51	52	53	54	55	56	57	58	59	60
61	62	63	64	65	66	67	68	69	70
71	72	73	74	75	76	77	78	79	80
81	82	83	84	85	86	87	88	89	90
91	92	93	94	95	96	97	98	99	100

Each row has 10 numbers.

Moving one space down is like adding 10.

It ends with 100.

Your turn

1 Look at part of the hundred chart. Write the missing numbers.

11	12	13	14	15	16	17	18	19	20
21	22	23	24	25	26	27	28	29	30
31		33	34		36		38	39	

What patterns do you see in the hundred chart?

SELF CHECK Mark how you feel

Got it! | Need help... | I don't get it

20 146443—Catch-Up Math © Shell Education

Math Skills

This book contains key math skills from both kindergarten and first grade to help your child catch up to grade level.

Kindergarten Math Skills	Pages
Accurately count objects in the standard order.	13–16
Write numbers from 0 to 20. Represent a number of objects with a written numeral 0–20.	9–12, 15–16
Understand the relationship between numbers and quantities.	9–16
Identify whether the number of objects in one group is greater than, less than, or equal to the number of objects in another group.	17–19, 39–52
Count to 100 by ones and by tens.	13–14, 33–35, 47–52
Represent addition and subtraction in a variety of ways, such as with objects, fingers, drawings, and equations.	59–109, 120–149
Solve addition and subtraction word problems.	106–109, 148–149
For any number from 1 to 9, find the number that makes 10 when added to it.	71–73, 97–105
Directly compare two objects, and describe the difference.	156–160
Collect, sort, and organize data into two or three categories.	169–182
Identify pennies, nickels, dimes, and quarters. Know their names and values.	200–209
Describe objects using names of shapes, and describe the relative positions of these objects.	212–214, 219–220
Identify shapes as two-dimensional (flat) or three-dimensional (solid).	217–220
Describe shapes' similarities, differences, parts, and other attributes.	215–224
Compose simple shapes to form larger shapes.	222–224

Math Skills

Grade 1 Math Skills	Pages
Count to 120, starting at any number. Represent a number of objects with a written numeral.	9–23
Understand that the two digits of a two-digit number represent amounts of tens and ones.	27–52
Compare two two-digit numbers, using the symbols >, =, and <.	39–46
Given a two-digit number, mentally find 10 more or 10 less than the number, without having to count.	47–52
Add within 100, including adding a two-digit number and a one-digit number, and adding a two-digit number and a multiple of 10.	59–109
Use strategies to add and subtract within 20, and fluently add and subtract within 10.	63–81, 97–105, 120–147
Understand the meaning of the equal sign, and determine whether addition and subtraction equations are true.	61–62, 84–86, 122–123, 141–143
Use fact families to add and subtract.	138–140
Solve addition and subtraction word problems.	106–109, 148–149
Compare and order objects by length or weight.	156–160
Use small objects (such as cubes or paper clips) to measure.	161–162
Use a ruler to measure length to the nearest inch.	163–165
Organize, represent, and interpret data. Ask and answer questions about the data.	169–182
Use data to create picture graphs and bar graphs.	171–182
Tell and write time in hours and half-hours using analog and digital clocks.	188–197
Identify the value of pennies, nickels, dimes, quarters, and dollars.	200–209
Identify defining and non-defining attributes of shapes.	215–220
Combine shapes to create a composite shape, and make new shapes from the composite shape.	222–224
Partition circles and rectangles into two and four equal shares. Describe the whole as two or four of the shares.	228–233

Write Numbers 0–20

Write numbers to show how many there are.

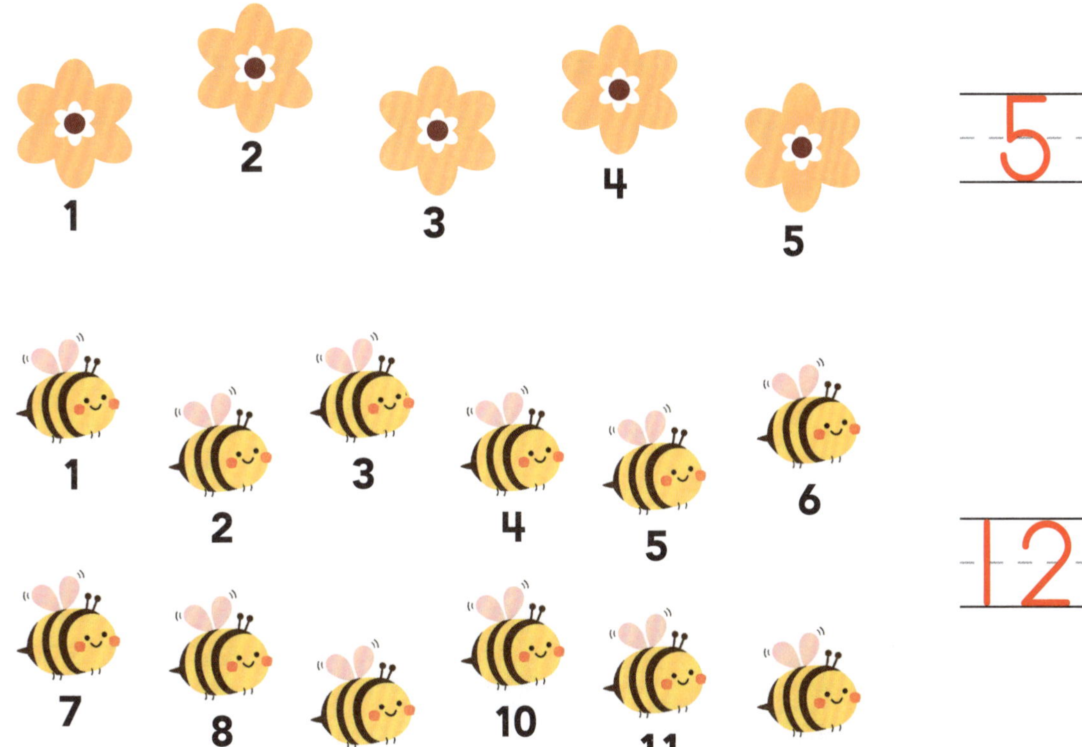

Your turn

Count each object. Write how many.

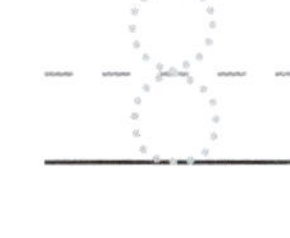

Count carefully! Each object should only be counted once.

Practice

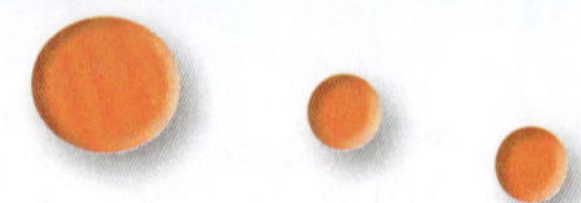

1 Count the stars. Trace the numbers. Then, write them on your own.

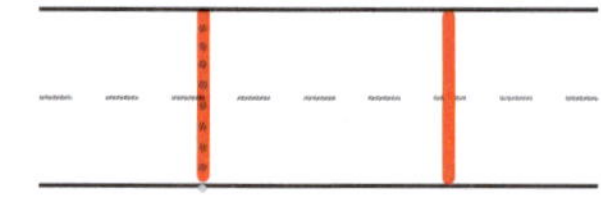

a 

b 

c 

d 

e 

f 

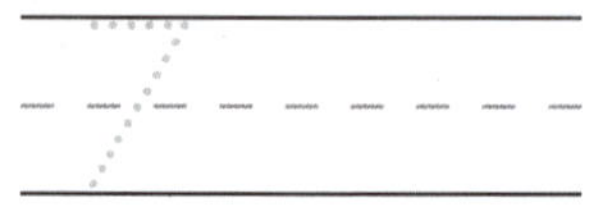

2 Count the flowers. Trace the numbers. Then, write them on your own.

a

b

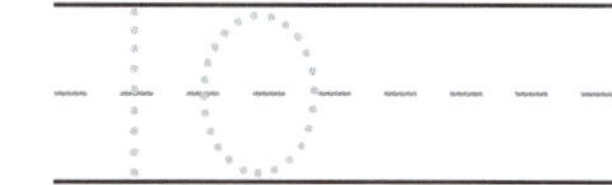

c

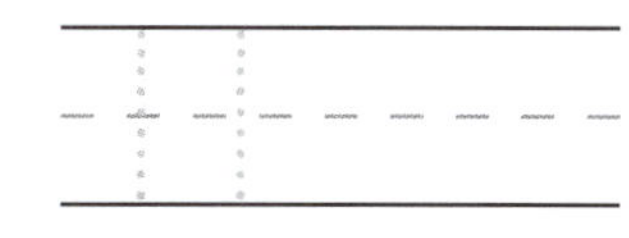

d

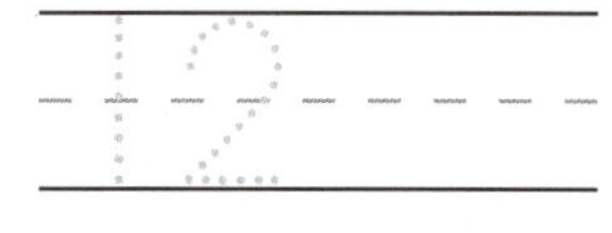

e

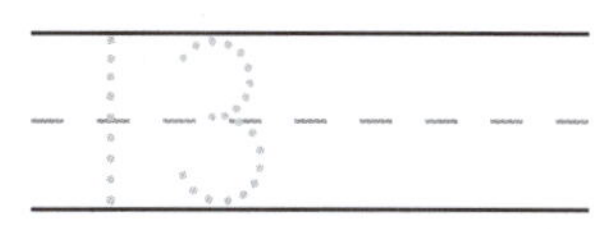

f

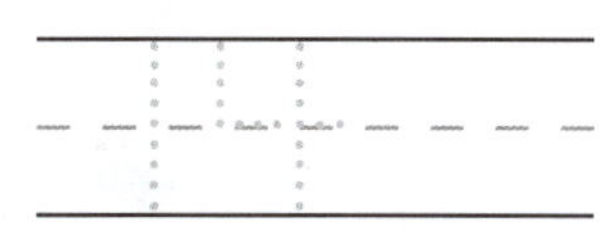

3 Count the hearts. Draw a line to the matching number.

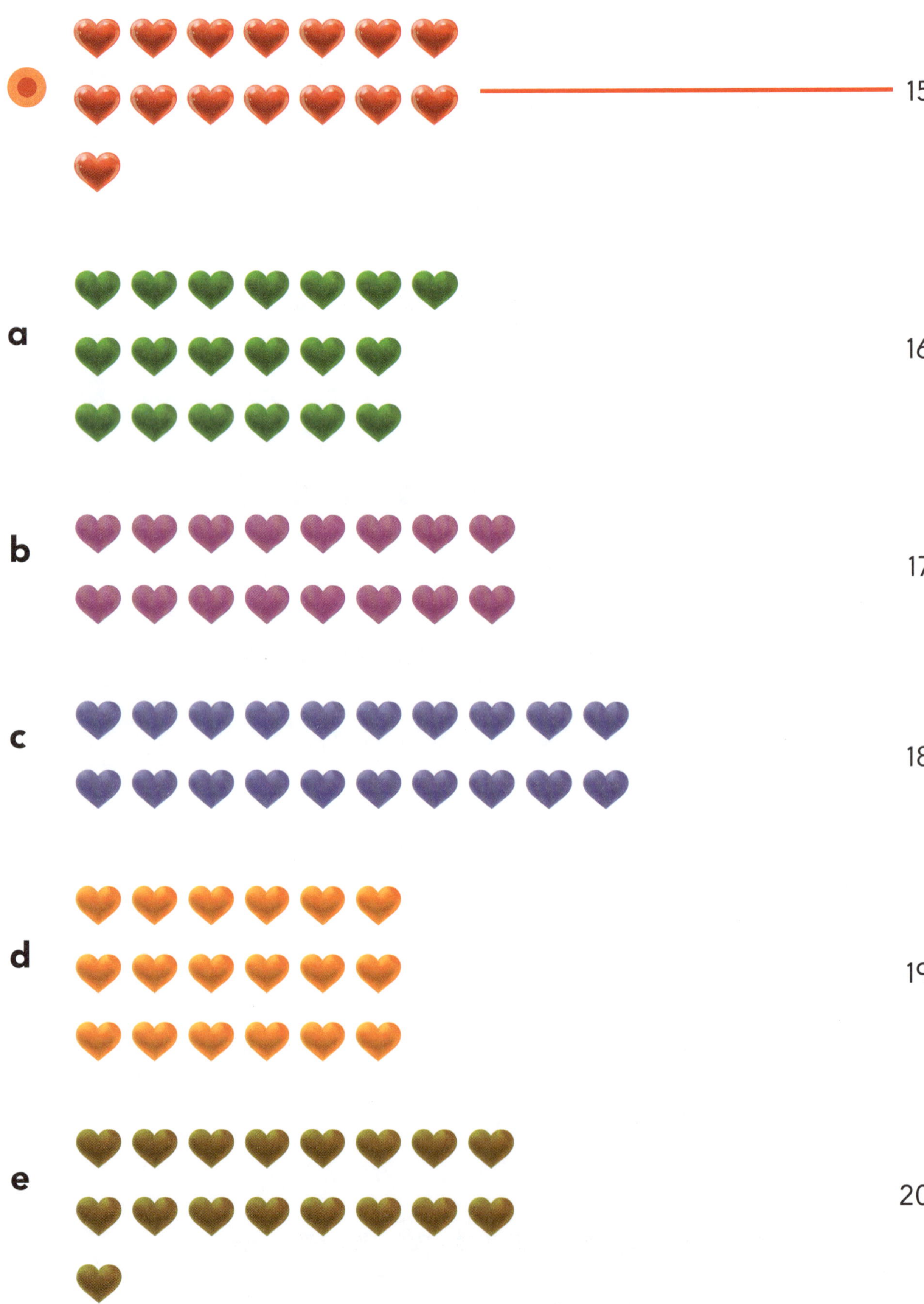

Count Forward to 120

**To count is to say or write numbers in order.
You can count by ones.**

Counting follows a pattern. Numbers go in order.

1, 2, 3, 4, 5, 6, 7, 8, 9...

Count to find the missing number. Write it.

Example 1:

7, 8, 9

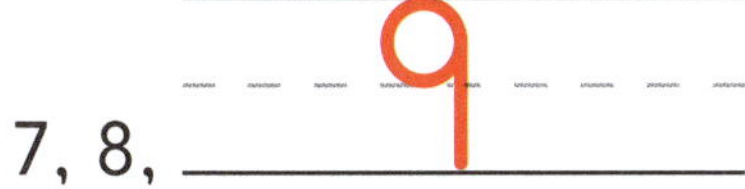

Example 2:

73, 74, 75

1 Write the missing numbers.

- 8, 9, 10

a 100, 101, ________

b 31, 32, ________

c 57, ________, 59, ________

d 83, ________, ________ 86

The pattern in the ones place repeats. After 9, comes a 0 in the ones place. For example: 28, 29, 30.

SELF CHECK Mark how you feel

Got it!	Need help...	I don't get it
 ☐	  ☐	 ☐

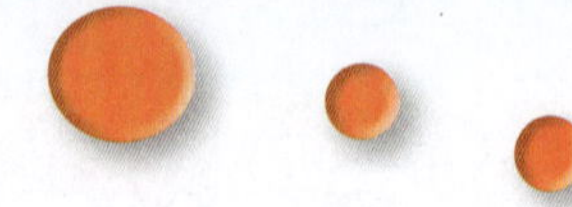

Practice

1 Write the missing numbers.

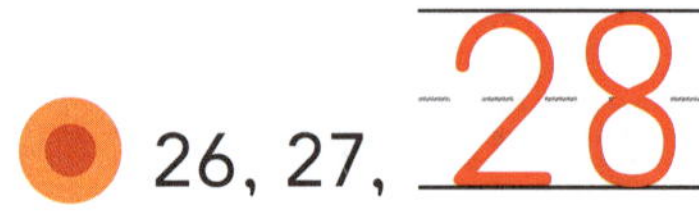

26, 27, 28

a 108, 109, ______

b 91, 92, ______

c 47, 48, ______

d 68, 69, ______

e 53, 54, ______, ______, ______

f 77, 78, ______, ______, ______

g 116, 117, ______, ______, ______

h 39, 40, ______, ______, ______

Count Objects

You can find how many objects there are. Touch and count to find the total. The last number you say is the total.

Example 1:

How many triangles are there?

Touch and count each triangle. Say the numbers in order.

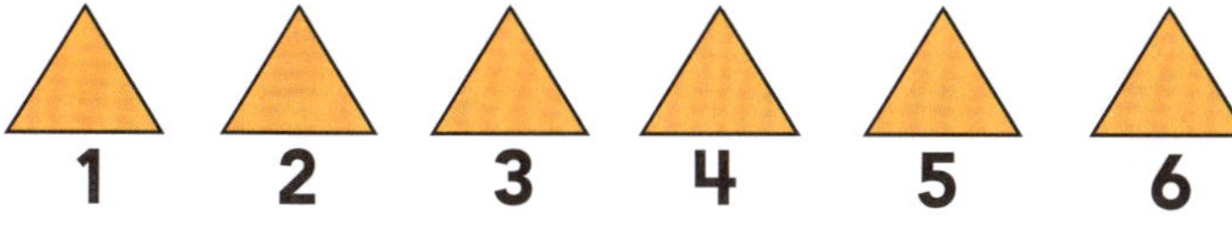

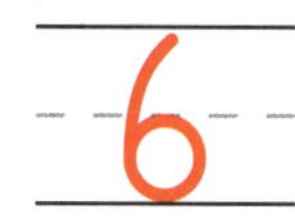

There are 6 triangles.

Example 2:

Circle 4 squares.

Circle one square for each number as you count.

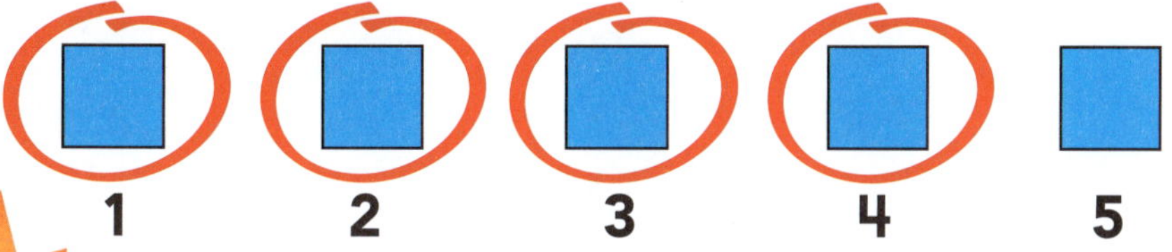

Your turn

1. Touch and count each object. Say the numbers in order. Write the total.

● How many books are there?

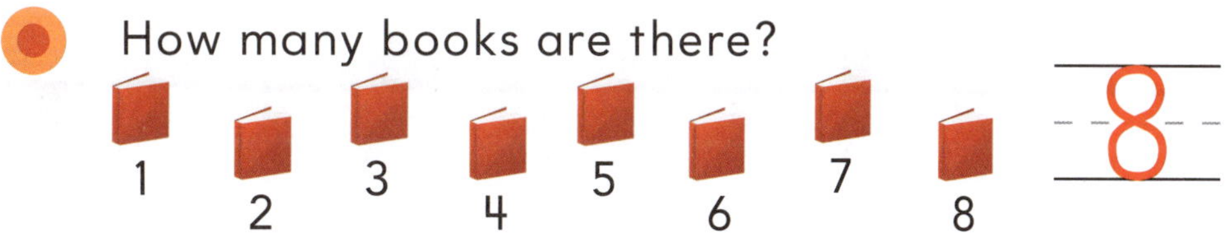

a How many bugs are there? _____

Touch each picture as you count to help stay on track.

SELF CHECK	Mark how you feel	
Got it! ☐	Need help... ☐	I don't get it ☐

Practice

1 Touch and count the objects. Write each total.

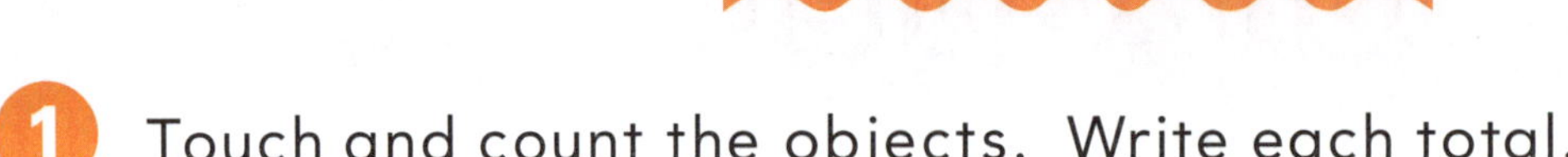

1 2 3 4 5 6 7

7

a

b

c

d

e

f

More or Less?

You can compare numbers. This means you find the bigger or smaller number.

Example 1:

Circle the group with more.

Count each side. The first group has 5 apples. The second group has 3 apples. The first group has more.

Example 2:

Circle the group with less.

Count each side. The first group has 10 flowers. The second group has 7. The second group has less.

Example 3:

Circle the bigger number.

Count each group! You can write the number so you don't forget.

2  4

1 Circle the bigger group or number.

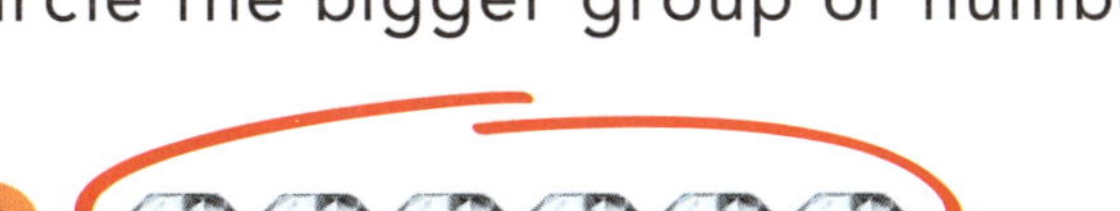

a     

b 12 10

SELF CHECK	Mark how you feel	
Got it!	Need help...	I don't get it
 ☐	 ☐	 ☐

Practice

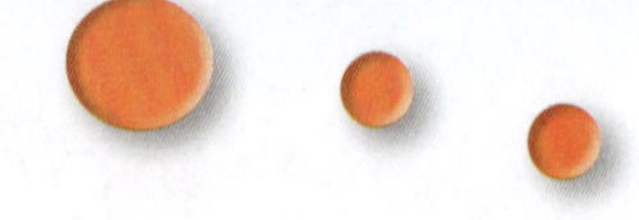

1 Circle the group with more.

a

b

c

d

2 Circle the bigger number in each set.

●	(7)	5	**c**	16	18
a	11	10	**d**	15	17
b	7	3	**e**	4	6

3 Circle the group with less triangles.

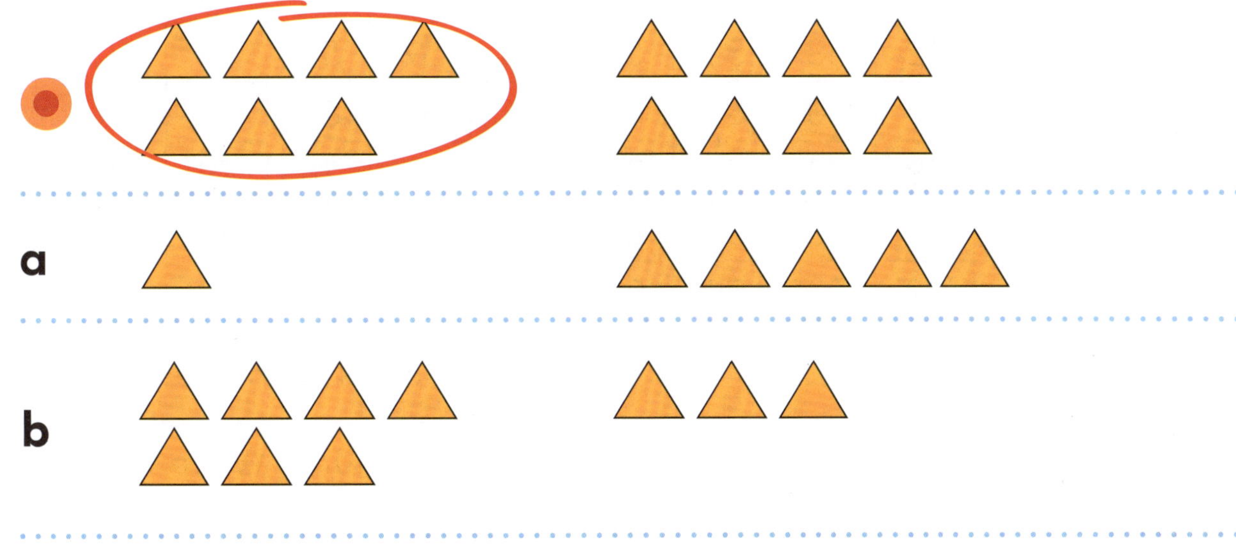

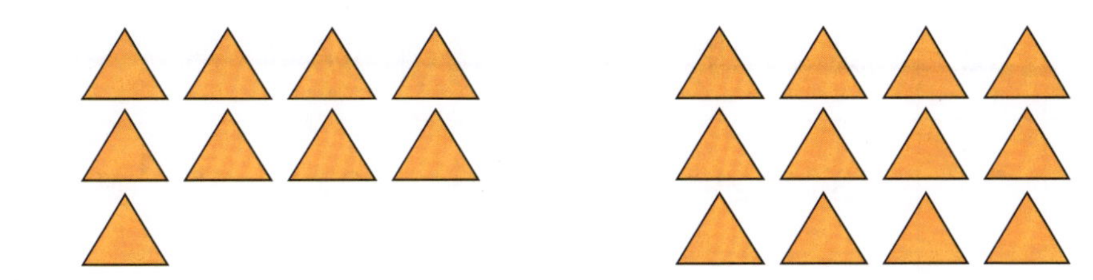

4 Circle the smaller number in each set.

●	(10)	12	**c**	3	5
a	13	9	**d**	14	16
b	8	7	**e**	20	19

Use a Hundred Chart

A hundred chart is a math tool. It shows the numbers from 1 to 100. You can use it to count by ones and tens.

SCAN to watch video

The hundred chart starts with 1.

1	2	3	4	5	6	7	8	9	10
11	12	13	14	15	16	17	18	19	20
21	22	23	24	25	26	27	28	29	30
31	32	33	34	35	36	37	38	39	40
41	42	43	44	45	46	47	48	49	50
51	52	53	54	55	56	57	58	59	60
61	62	63	64	65	66	67	68	69	70
71	72	73	74	75	76	77	78	79	80
81	82	83	84	85	86	87	88	89	90
91	92	93	94	95	96	97	98	99	100

Each row has 10 numbers.

Moving one space down is like adding 10.

It ends with 100.

1 Look at part of the hundred chart. Write the missing numbers.

11	12	13	14	15	16	17	18	19	20
21	22	23	24	25	26	27	28	29	30
31		33	34		36		38	39	

SELF CHECK Mark how you feel

Got it!	Need help...	I don't get it
 ☐	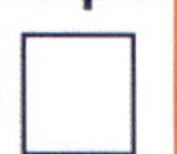  ☐	 ☐

Practice

1. Write the missing numbers.

1	2	3	4	5	6	7	8	9	10
11		13	14			17		19	
21	22		24				28		30
31				35		37	38		
		43		45	46			49	
	52	53			56			59	60
61	62		64			67	68		70
		73		75		77		79	
81	82		84		86				90
91		93		95			98		

Count by 10s

Counting by 10s follows a pattern.

Example 1:

1	2	3	4	5	6	7	8	9	(10)
11	12	13	14	15	16	17	18	19	(20)
21	22	23	24	25	26	27	28	29	(30)
31	32	33	34	35	36	37	38	39	(40)
41	42	43	44	45	46	47	48	49	(50)
51	52	53	54	55	56	57	58	59	(60)
61	62	63	64	65	66	67	68	69	(70)
71	72	73	74	75	76	77	78	79	(80)
81	82	83	84	85	86	87	88	89	(90)
91	92	93	94	95	96	97	98	99	(100)

These are the numbers you use when you count by 10s.

Example 2:

10, 20, 30, 40, 50, 60, 70, 80, 90, 100

The first part of each number gets bigger like you are counting.

The second part of each number ends in a 0.

1 Write the number that comes next.

- 10, 20, 30
- **a** 50, 60, ______
- **b** 70, 80, ______

SELF CHECK Mark how you feel

Got it!	Need help...	I don't get it
 ☐	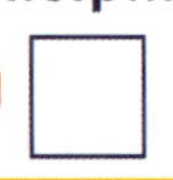 ☐	  ☐

Practice

1 Count by 10s. Write the missing numbers.

60, 70, 80

a 20, 30, ______

b 50, 60, ______

c ______, 20, 30, ______

d 40, ______, ______, ______, 80

2 Count by 10s to 100. Color each 10 as you count. The first one has been done for you.

1	2	3	4	5	6	7	8	9	10
11	12	13	14	15	16	17	18	19	20
21	22	23	24	25	26	27	28	29	30
31	32	33	34	35	36	37	38	39	40
41	42	43	44	45	46	47	48	49	50
51	52	53	54	55	56	57	58	59	60
61	62	63	64	65	66	67	68	69	70
71	72	73	74	75	76	77	78	79	80
81	82	83	84	85	86	87	88	89	90
91	92	93	94	95	96	97	98	99	100

Counting Review

1 Write the missing numbers.

1	2	3	4	5	6	7	8	9	10
	12					17	18		
21		23						29	30
	32			35			38		
41			44		46				50
		53				57			
61			64				68	69	
	72	73				77			80
81				85				89	
			94				98		

2 Count the pictures. Write the number.

a ________

b ________

c ________

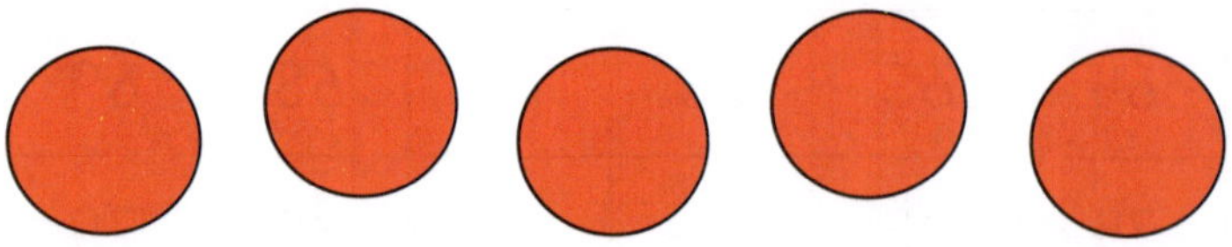

d ________

Review

3 Circle the group with more butterflies.

a

b

4 Circle the group with less rabbits.

a

b

Review

5 Circle the bigger number in each set.

a	1	4	**c**	8	5
b	12	10	**d**	9	6

6 Circle the smaller number in each set.

a	14	17	**c**	11	7
b	3	2	**d**	5	10

7 Count by 10s. Write the missing numbers.

a 50, 60, ______

b 70, ______ 90, ______

c 40, ______, ______, 70

d ______, 30, 40, ______, ______

Digits

A digit is one single number. Some numbers have only one digit. Others have more than one.

Example 1:

There are only 10 numbers with one digit. These are one-digit numbers:

0 1 2 3 4 5 6 7 8 9

Example 2:

Numbers can also have two digits. Here are some two-digit numbers:

27 80 11 55 94

1 Circle one-digit numbers in red. Circle two-digit numbers in blue.

a	3	0	76
b	97	1	44
c	8	4	19

How many digits are in your age?

Practice

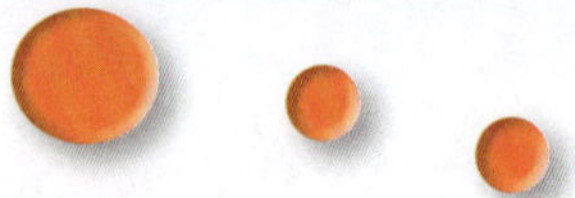

1 Circle the two-digit numbers. Put an ***X*** on the one-digit numbers.

●	(90)	~~8~~ X	(22)	**b**	0	80	40
a	88	4	1	**c**	9	46	6

2 Sort the numbers into the table.

● 19 3 35

7 88 65 17 6 20

5 0 44 8 96 1

One-Digit Numbers	Two-Digit Numbers
3	19 35

3 Write two-digit numbers using the digits.

●	3	7	37	and	73
a	1	6	____	and	____
b	2	8	____	and	____
c	4	5	____	and	____

Ones Place

Place value shows how much a digit is worth. The ones place is the place furthest to the right.

8

ones place

Example 1:

The ones place is shown with cubes.

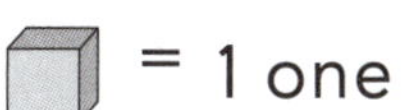 = 1 one

 = 8 ones

Example 2:

You can draw dots to show the number of ones.

5 ones = ●●●●●

1 What numbers are shown?

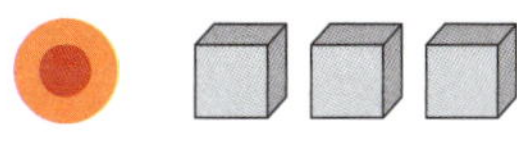 3

a 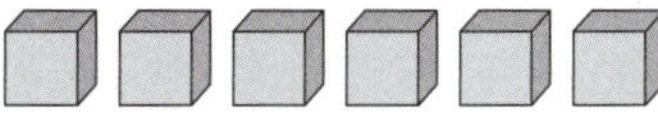 

b 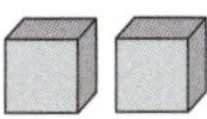 

Practice

1. Write each number.

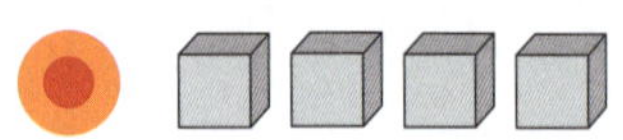

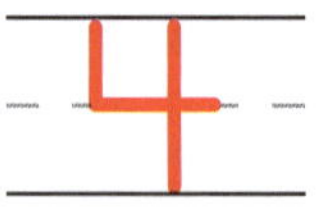

a

b

c

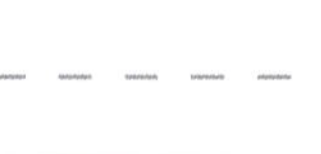

2. Draw each number using dots.

 3  

a 9

b 5

c 1

Tens Place

A two-digit number has a digit in the ones place and a digit in the tens place. The tens place is to the left of the ones place.

10

↑ tens place ↑ ones place

Example 1:

The tens place is shown with bundles.
10 ones cubes = 1 ten bundle

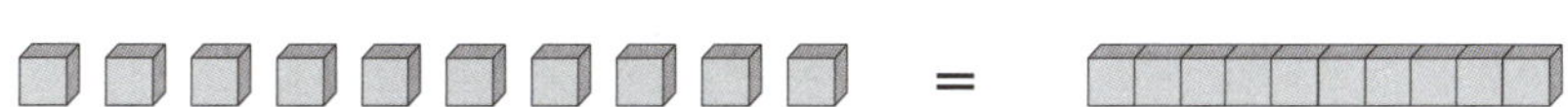

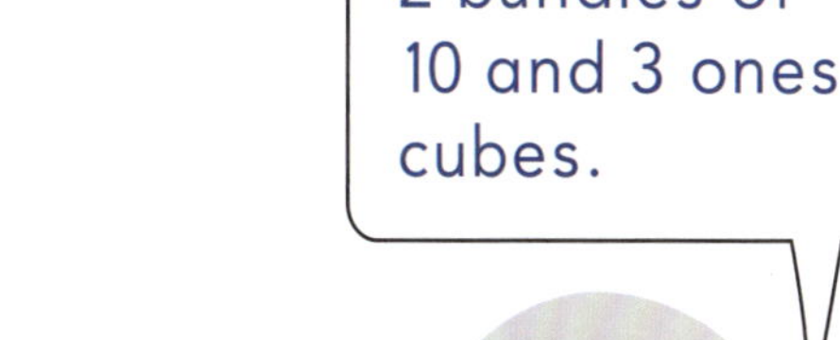

Example 2:

You can draw tens bundles easily.
Make a straight line for each bundle.

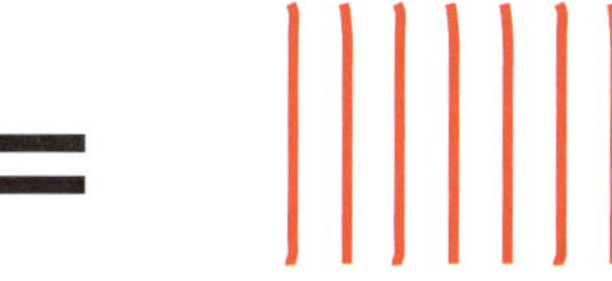

1 Count how many tens.

- (example) = 3 tens
- **a** = ____ tens
- **b** = ____ tens

SELF CHECK	Mark how you feel	
Got it! ☐	Need help... ☐	I don't get it ☐

Practice

1 Circle the number in the tens place.

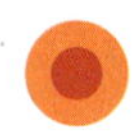 

●	64	30	28	**b**	90	44	58
a	15	87	36	**c**	72	19	50

2 Write how many tens.

  6 tens

a 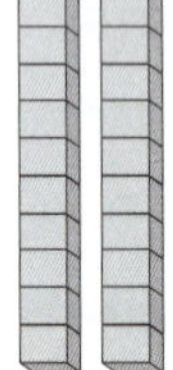 ______ tens

b  ______ tens

c 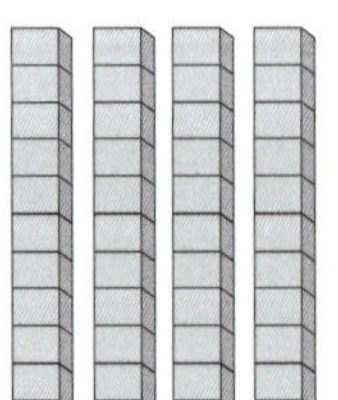 ______ tens

3 Draw the tens. Use a straight line for each bundle.

●	3 tens 	**b**	5 tens
a	1 tens	**c**	8 tens

Multiples of 10

You can make numbers using tens bundles.

Example 1:

What number does this show?

How many tens? 4

How many ones? 

How do you write that number?

tens ones

Example 2:

Draw tens bundles to make 50. Use a straight line for each bundle.

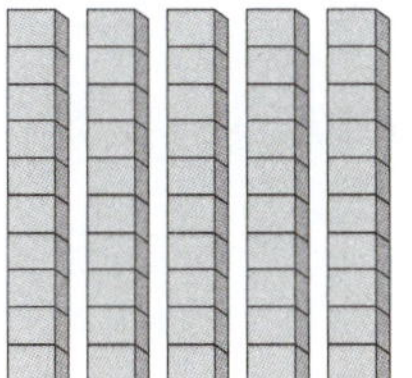

1 Write the number for each drawing.

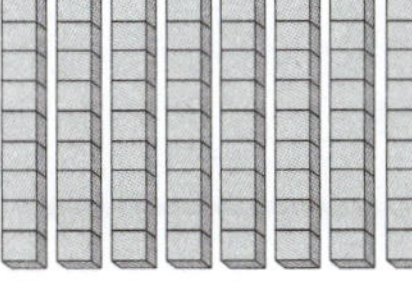

8 tens 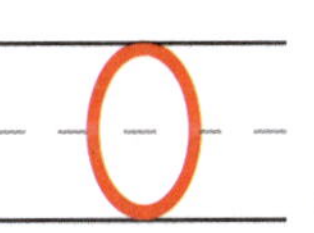 ones = 80

a 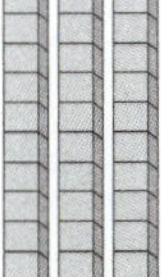 ______ tens ______ ones = ______

b 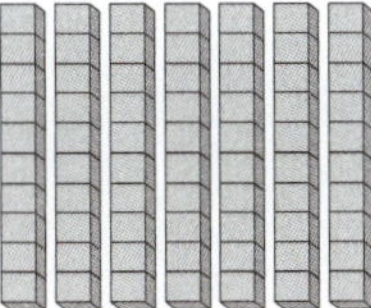 ______ tens ______ ones = ______

SELF CHECK Mark how you feel

Got it!	Need help...	I don't get it
☐	☐	☐

Practice

1 Write the digits in the tables.

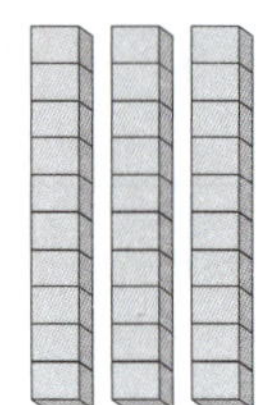

Tens	Ones
3	0

= 30

a

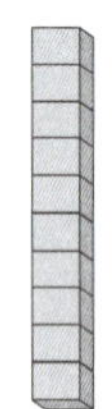

Tens	Ones

= ______

b

Tens	Ones

= ______

2 Draw tens bundles to show each number.

60 = ||||||

a 20 =

b 40 =

Tens and Ones to 99

You can create numbers using tens bundles and ones cubes.

Example 1:

What number does this show?

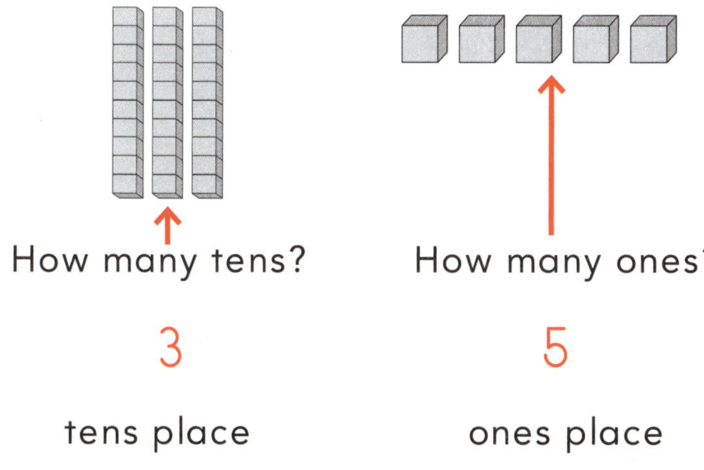

How many tens? How many ones?

3 5

tens place ones place

Remember, the tens are on the left. The ones are on the right.

Example 2:

Draw a picture to show this number.

There are 7 tens, so draw 7 bundles, or lines. → 72 ← There are 2 ones, so draw 2 cubes, or dots.

||||||| :

1 What number is shown?

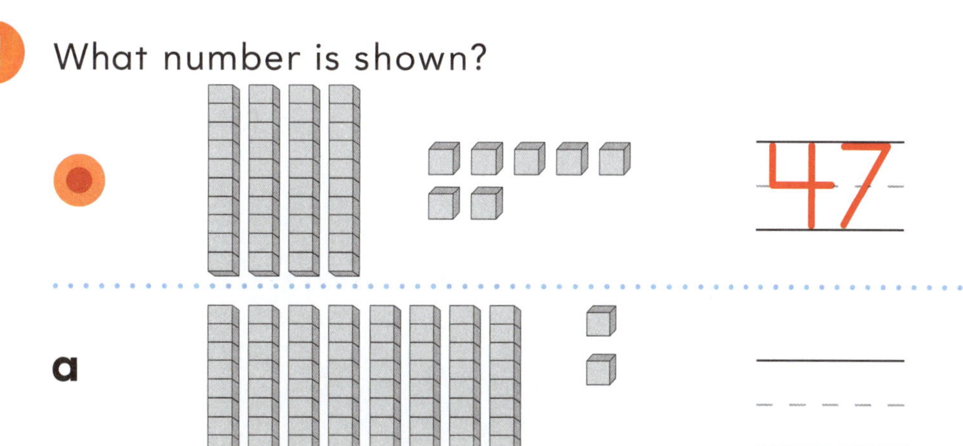

- ● 47
- a ______

SELF CHECK Mark how you feel

Got it!	Need help...	I don't get it
☐	☐	☐

Practice

1 Circle the digit in the tens place in **red**. Circle the digit in the ones place in **blue**.

● (1)(2) (8)(9) (3)(6)

a 4 5 2 9 5 5

b 3 5 6 2 4 6

c 6 7 7 5 0 7

2 Write the number shown in each row.

	Tens	Ones	Number
●	4 tens	5 ones	45
a	1 ten	6 ones	
b	2 tens	7 ones	
c	3 tens	8 ones	
d	2 tens	1 one	
e	5 tens	3 ones	

3 Draw the numbers. Use tens bundles and ones cubes.

	Tens	Ones	Number
●	|	⋮	13
a			37
b			83
c			27
d			60
e			59
f			41
g			99

4 Sort the numbers by the digit that is underlined. The first two have been done for you.

7$\underline{1}$ $\underline{1}$1 2$\underline{9}$ $\underline{7}$8 3$\underline{8}$ 3$\underline{2}$ 3$\underline{0}$

$\underline{4}$5 $\underline{2}$8 $\underline{1}$3 9$\underline{9}$ 5$\underline{9}$ 1$\underline{0}$ $\underline{8}$6

Tens Place Underlined	Ones Place Underlined
11	71

5 Write the digits in the boxes.

- 24 = 2 tens and 4 ones

a 42 = ☐ tens and ☐ ones

b 39 = ☐ tens and ☐ ones

c 18 = ☐ tens and ☐ ones

d 56 = ☐ tens and ☐ ones

e 71 = ☐ tens and ☐ ones

f 69 = ☐ tens and ☐ ones

Greater Than, Less Than, Equal To

You can compare numbers. You can see which is larger, which is smaller, or if they are equal. There are special symbols to use.

$>$ means greater than
$<$ means less than
$=$ means equal to

Imagine the symbols are alligator mouths! The gator always wants to eat the bigger number.

Example 1:

2 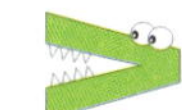 1

The first number is bigger.
2 is **greater than** 1.

Example 2:

1 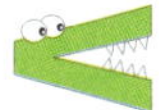 2

The first number is smaller.
1 is **less than** 2.

Example 3:

1  1

The numbers are the same. 1 is **equal to** 1.

1 Trace the correct symbol.

	2	$>$		$=$	4
a	1	$>$		$=$	0
b	2	$>$		$=$	2
c	0	$>$	$<$	$=$	1

SELF CHECK Mark how you feel

Got it!	Need help...	I don't get it

Practice

1 Make each symbol look like an alligator mouth.

 = 

b 

a 

c 

2 Draw lines to match the symbols to their names.

a	>	greater than
b	<	equal to
c	=	less than

3 Compare the numbers. Write the correct symbol in each circle.

 4  3

c 2 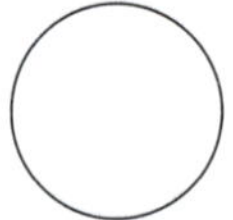 3

a 3 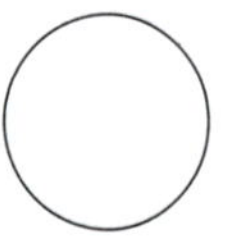 3

d  5 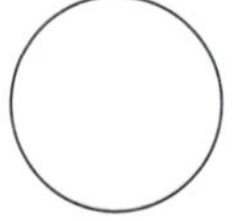 7

b 1 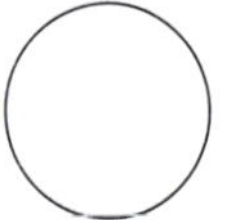 0

e 9 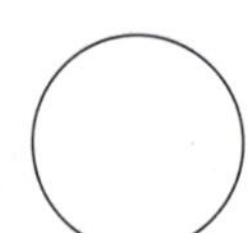 4

Compare Numbers to 19

You can compare bigger numbers. Think about the value of each number. Decide which is bigger. Then, write the symbol.

> greater than
< less than
= equal to

Don't forget! The gator wants to eat the bigger number.

Example 1:

You can draw a picture to help.

6 ? 8

There are more stars under 8. It is the bigger number.

6 < 8

Example 2:

You can use mental math to help.

10 ? 8

When counting, 8 comes before 10. That means it is smaller.
10 > 8

 1 Write >, <, or = to compare the numbers.

 8  4

a 12 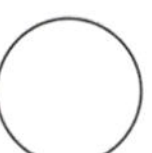 15

b 15  17

SELF CHECK	Mark how you feel	
Got it! ☐	Need help... ☐	I don't get it ☐

Practice

1 Draw circles to show each amount. Then, use >, <, or = to compare them.

Example: 6 > 4

a 14 ◯ 16

c 18 ◯ 8

b 9 ◯ 9

d 11 ◯ 10

2 Use >, <, or = to compare each set of numbers. Use mental math to help you.

Example: 17 > 8

a 3 ◯ 3

c 8 ◯ 9

b 14 ◯ 7

d 11 ◯ 11

3 Circle the number that makes each comparison true.

 $15 < ?$

12   15   (17)

a $6 > ?$

6   12   5

b $19 = ?$

19   10   9

c $? < 13$

14   13   11

d $? > 7$

5   12   7

e $3 > ?$

11   2   19

f $? = 15$

15   5   10

g $? < 14$

19   15   13

h $? < 17$

18   20   13

i $12 < ?$

14   9   12

Compare Numbers to 99

You can compare larger numbers.
Remember these symbols:

> greater than
< less than
= equal to

Example 1:

To compare two numbers, look at the tens place first.

4̲5 ? 6̲7

4 is less than 6, so...

45 < 67

Example 2:

If the tens places are the same, look at the ones.

37̲ ? 34̲

The tens are equal. So, you compare the ones. 7 is greater than 4, so...

37 > 34

1 Circle the correct symbol.

Compare the tens first because they have a greater value than the ones.

 25 ◯ 35

 >  <  =

 **a** 67 ◯ 69

 > < =

 **b** 21 ◯ 12

> < =

Practice

1 Underline the digit in the tens place. Then, use >, <, or = to compare the numbers.

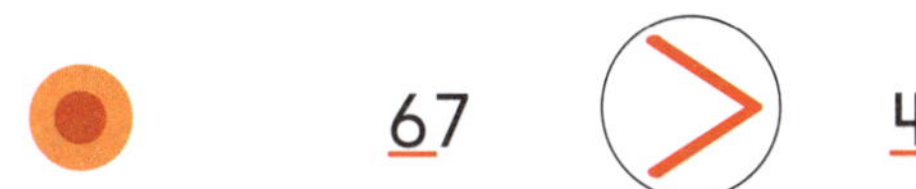

a	29 ◯ 17	**c**	76 ◯ 92
b	34 ◯ 55	**d**	61 ◯ 23

2 Underline the digit in the ones place. Then, use >, <, or = to compare the numbers.

a	89 ◯ 85	**c**	76 ◯ 79
b	35 ◯ 38	**d**	54 ◯ 51

3 Use >, <, or = to compare the numbers.

a	90 ◯ 90	**c**	39 ◯ 20
b	74 ◯ 71	**d**	58 ◯ 59

4 Circle the words to make each comparison true.

● 45 (?) 39 — is greater than (circled) / is less than / is equal to

b 16 (?) 16 — is greater than / is less than / is equal to

a 98 (?) 93 — is greater than / is less than / is equal to

c 23 (?) 38 — is greater than / is less than / is equal to

5 Write the number that makes each comparison true.

● 20 < 34 — 18, 20, 34

b ____ > 38 — 46, 33, 22

a 80 = ____ — 80, 90, 70

c 80 < ____ — 80, 67, 90

6 Write a number to make each comparison true.

● 99 > 85

b ____ > 54

a 35 < ____

c ____ = 90

10 More

You can find a number that is 10 more. Move down one row on a hundred chart. Or, just make the digit in the tens place 1 more.

Example 1:

Here is part of a hundred chart. Find 10 more than 27. Put your finger on 27. Jump down one row. Now you are on 37.

21	22	23	24	25	26	27	28	29	30
31	32	33	34	35	36	37	38	39	40

10 more than 27 is 37.

Example 2:

Find 10 more than 62. Underline the digit in the tens place. Make it 1 more.

62
+1

10 more than 62 is 72.

1 Find 10 more than each number. Draw an arrow on the chart to show your jump.

71	72	73	74	75	76	77	78	79	80
81	82	83	84	85	86	87	88	89	90

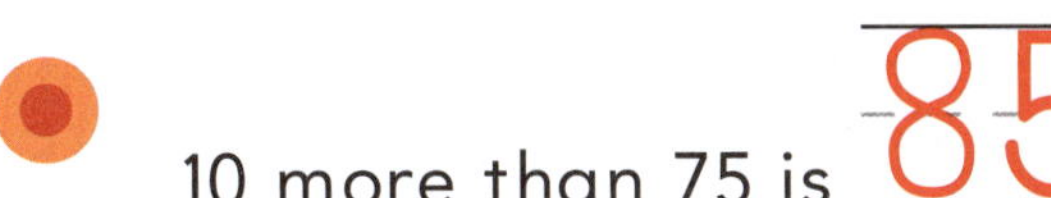

● 10 more than 75 is 85.

a 10 more than 73 is ______.

Practice

1 Find 10 more than each number. Use the hundred chart. Draw an arrow to show your jump to 10 more.

	Number	10 More
●	61	71
a	89	
b	37	
c	70	
d	22	
e	69	
f	43	

1	2	3	4	5	6	7	8	9	10
11	12	13	14	15	16	17	18	19	20
21	22	23	24	25	26	27	28	29	30
31	32	33	34	35	36	37	38	39	40
41	42	43	44	45	46	47	48	49	50
51	52	53	54	55	56	57	58	59	60
61	62	63	64	65	66	67	68	69	70
71	72	73	74	75	76	77	78	79	80
81	82	83	84	85	86	87	88	89	90
91	92	93	94	95	96	97	98	99	100

2 Underline the digit in the tens place. Then, write the number that is 10 more.

16 26

a 42

b 74

c 33

d 82

e 55

f 25

g 64

h 39

i 17

j 10

10 Less

You can find a number that is 10 less. Go up one row on a hundred chart. You can also make the digit in the tens place 1 less.

Example 1:

Here is part of a hundred chart. Find 10 less than 52. Put your finger on 52. Jump up one row. Now you are on 42.

41	42	43	44	45	46	47	48	49	50
51	52	53	54	55	56	57	58	59	60

10 less than 52 is 42.

Example 2:

Find 10 less than 75. Underline the digit in the tens place. Make it 1 less.

<u>7</u>5
−1

10 less than 75 is 65.

1 Find 10 less than each number. Draw an arrow on the chart to show your jump.

81	82	83	84	85	86	87	88	89	90
91	92	93	94	95	96	97	98	99	100

● 10 less than 96 is 86.

a 10 less than 94 is ______.

SELF CHECK	Mark how you feel	
Got it! ☐	Need help... ☐	I don't get it ☐

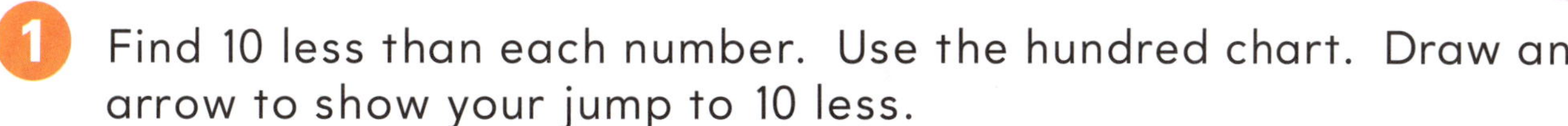

Practice

1 Find 10 less than each number. Use the hundred chart. Draw an arrow to show your jump to 10 less.

	Number	10 Less
●	45	35
a	90	
b	14	
c	66	
d	82	
e	75	
f	99	

1	2	3	4	5	6	7	8	9	10
11	12	13	14	15	16	17	18	19	20
21	22	23	24	25	26	27	28	29	30
31	32	33	34	35 ↑	36	37	38	39	40
41	42	43	44	45	46	47	48	49	50
51	52	53	54	55	56	57	58	59	60
61	62	63	64	65	66	67	68	69	70
71	72	73	74	75	76	77	78	79	80
81	82	83	84	85	86	87	88	89	90
91	92	93	94	95	96	97	98	99	100

2 Underline the digit in the tens place. Then, write the number that is 10 less.

- <u>7</u>8 68

a	44	______	**f**	24	______
b	78	______	**g**	61	______
c	39	______	**h**	39	______
d	83	______	**i**	12	______
e	50	______	**j**	97	______

Place Value Review

1 Circle the two-digit numbers. Write an ***X*** on the one-digit numbers.

a	39	10	5
b	7	18	27
c	2	3	58
d	90	9	19
e	18	28	8

2 Circle the digit in the tens place in blue. Circle the digit in the ones place in red.

a 3 4

b 1 8

c 5 6

d 9 2

e 5 5

3 Complete the tables.

a

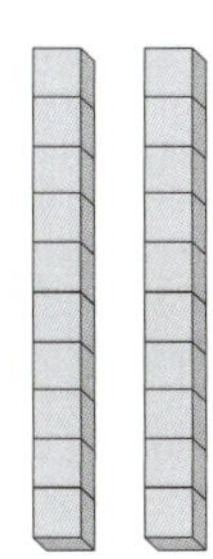

Tens	Ones

= ________

Review

b

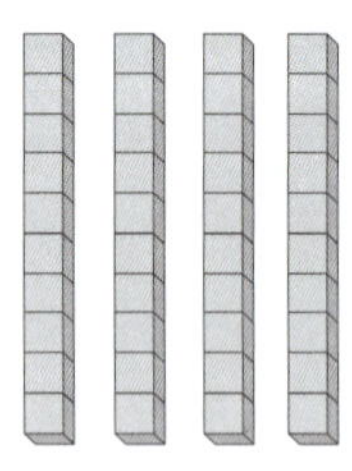

Tens	Ones

= ______

c

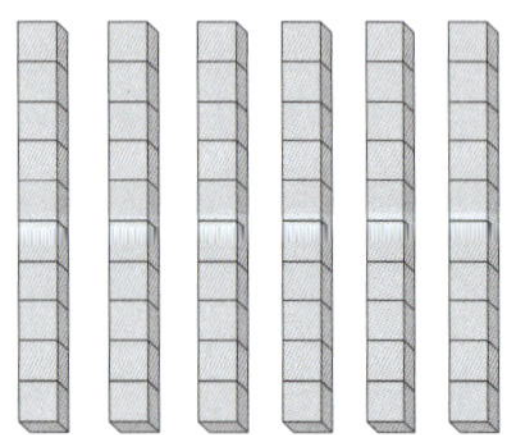

Tens	Ones

= ______

4 Write the number shown in each row.

	Tens	Ones	Number
a			______
b			______
c			______
d			______

Review

5 Draw the tens and ones to show each number.

	Number	Tens	Ones
a	17		
b	85		
c	34		
d	66		

6 Circle the number to make each comparison true.

a $60 > ?$

20
60
80

c $? < 43$

40
49
47

b $49 = ?$

59
69
49

d $? < 72$

66
81
72

Review

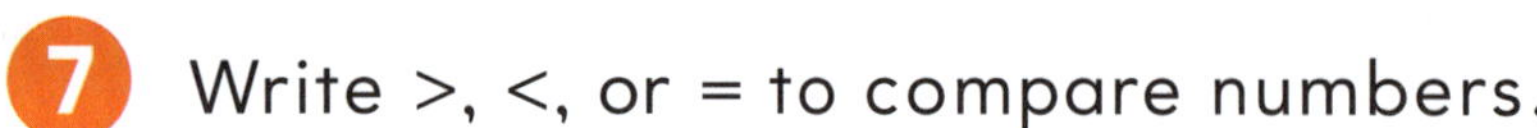

7 Write >, <, or = to compare numbers.

a 19  14

b 25  25

c 81 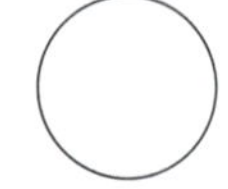 89

d 55 ◯ 45

e 31  31

f 67  70

8 Write a number to make each comparison true.

a 74 < ______

b ______ < 89

c 90 > ______

d ______ > 36

e 84 = ______

f ______ < 14

Review

9 Write 10 more and 10 less than for each number. Show the jumps on the hundred chart.

	10 Less	Number	10 More
a		80	
b		62	
c		58	
d		45	
e		19	
f		84	

1	2	3	4	5	6	7	8	9	10
11	12	13	14	15	16	17	18	19	20
21	22	23	24	25	26	27	28	29	30
31	32	33	34	35	36	37	38	39	40
41	42	43	44	45	46	47	48	49	50
51	52	53	54	55	56	57	58	59	60
61	62	63	64	65	66	67	68	69	70
71	72	73	74	75	76	77	78	79	80
81	82	83	84	85	86	87	88	89	90
91	92	93	94	95	96	97	98	99	100

Review

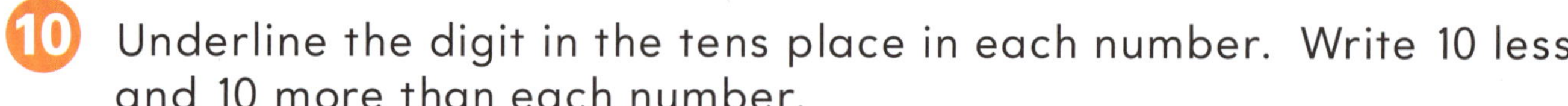

10 Underline the digit in the tens place in each number. Write 10 less and 10 more than each number.

	10 Less	Number	10 More
a		69	
b		21	
c		72	
d		17	
e		50	
f		75	
g		33	
h		85	
i		48	
j		36	

Addition Within 10

Adding is putting numbers together. Count how many in each group. Using pictures can help you find the total.

Example 1:

There are 6 bananas. There are 3 apples. How many fruits are there in all? Draw pictures to help you solve.

Remember to count on when you reach the second group!

1 2 3 7 8 9

4 5 6

Start counting bananas. When you get to the apples, keep counting.

There are 9 fruits in all.

Your turn

1 Count the items to find how many there are in all.

There are 10 insects in all.

a 

There are ______ objects in all.

b    

There are ______ shapes in all.

SELF CHECK Mark how you feel		
Got it! ☐	Need help... ☐	I don't get it ☐

Practice

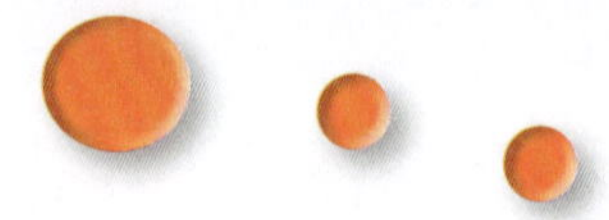

1 Read each problem. Count the groups. Then, write the total.

There are 2 roses. There are 2 daisies. How many flowers are there in all?

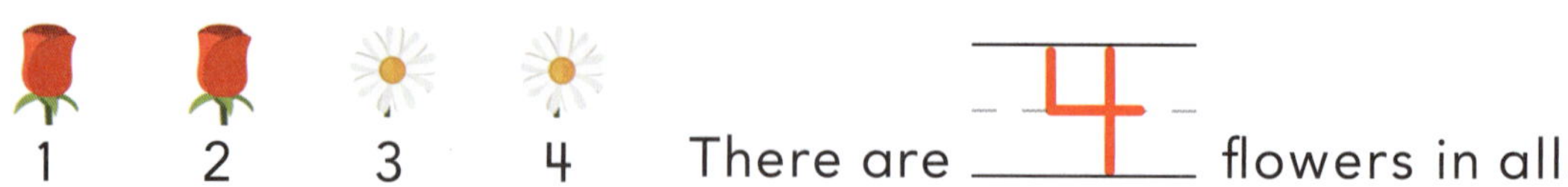

1 2 3 4 There are 4 flowers in all.

a There are 3 red books. There are 6 green books. How many books are there in all?

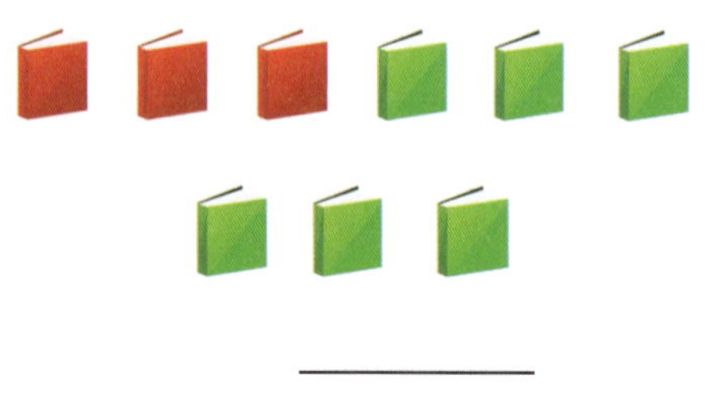

There are ________ books in all.

b There is 1 pair of reading glasses. There are 5 pairs of sunglasses. How many pairs of glasses are there in all?

There are ________ pairs of glasses in all.

2 Count to find how many shapes in all. Then, write the total.

There are 5 objects in all.

a

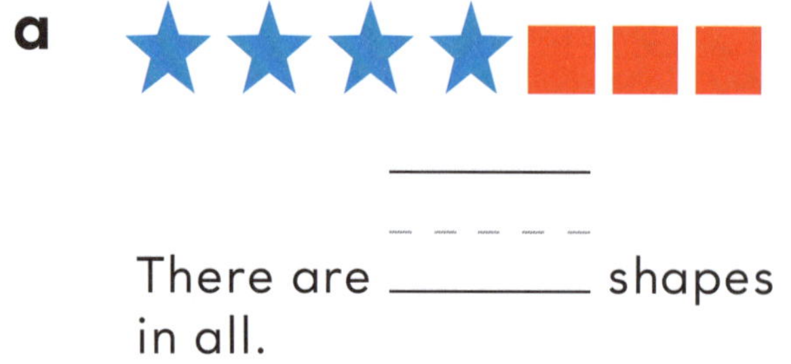

There are ________ shapes in all.

b

There are ________ shapes in all.

Equal Sign and Plus Sign

When you put groups together, it is called adding. There are special symbols to use to make an addition equation.

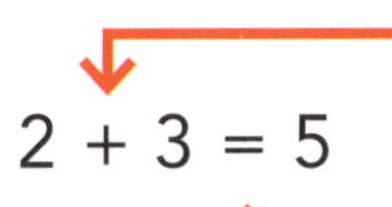

2 + 3 = 5

The plus sign goes between the numbers you are adding.

Both sides of the equal sign have the same value.

Example 1:

Is this equation true? 3 + 4 = 7
Use stars to show if they are equal.

3	+	4	=	7

Both sides have 7.

Is the equation true? yes no

The equal sign goes between the numbers you're adding and their total.

Your turn

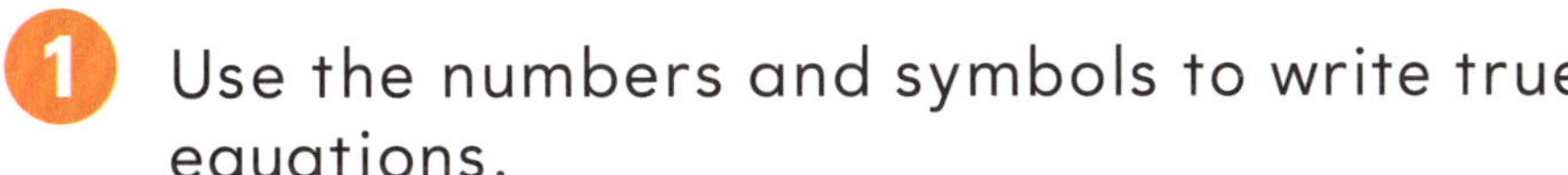

1 Use the numbers and symbols to write true equations.

9 3 6 + =

a + = 8 1 7

____ ____ ____ ____ ____

b 3 4 1 = +

____ ____ ____ ____ ____

Practice

1 Are the number sentences true? Draw shapes to show each problem. Circle the answer.

	3	+	5	=	9	
●	★★★		★★★★★		★★★★★ ★★★★	yes / (no)
a	4	+	0	=	4	yes / no
b	5	+	2	=	7	yes / no
c	6	+	1	=	8	yes / no

2 Use the numbers and symbols to write true equations.

● 1 4 3 = +

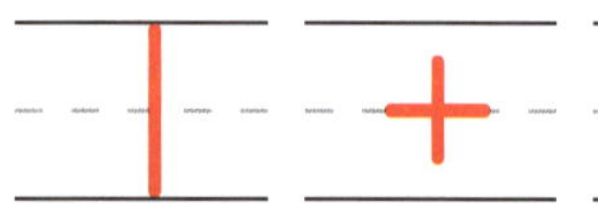

1 + 3 = 4

a 8 3 5 + =

____ ____ ____ ____ ____

b 7 3 4 = +

____ ____ ____ ____ ____

Draw a Picture

You can draw pictures to help you add. Draw each amount you are adding. Then, write the total.

Example 1:

Draw a picture to help you add. Then, write the total. 4 + 5 = ?

Draw 4 circles.	Draw 5 circles.	Count them all.
●●●●	+ ●●●●●	= 9

Example 2:

Draw number cubes to match the number sentence. Then, write the total.

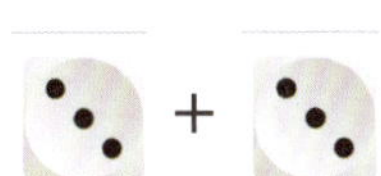

3 + 3 = 6

1 Draw a picture to help you add. Then, write the total.

● 9 + 4 = ?

Draw 9 stars.	Draw 4 stars.	Count them all.
★★★★★ ★★★★	+ ★★★★	= 13

a 6 + 4 = ?

Draw 6 squares.	Draw 4 squares.	Count them all.
	+	=

SELF CHECK Mark how you feel

Got it!	Need help...	I don't get it
☐	☐	☐

Practice

1 Draw number cubes to match the equation. Then, write the total.

Example number cubes:     

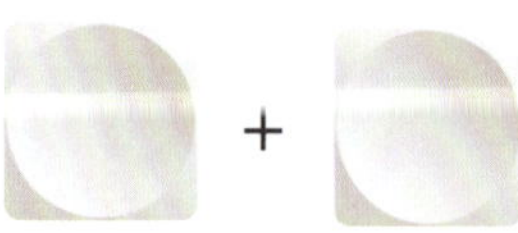 6 + 6 = 12

a  +  4 + 3 = ______

b  + 2 + 6 = ______

c + 5 + 1 = ______

2 Add apples to the trees to match the equations. Then, write the total.

 5 + 7 = 12

a  +  8 + 3 = ______

3 Draw your own pictures for each equation. Then, write the total.

● 4 + 3 = 7

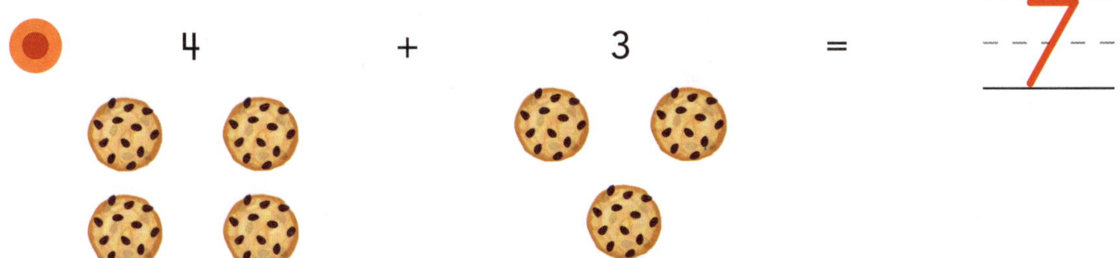

a 8 + 2 = ____

b 9 + 7 = ____

c 3 + 2 = ____

d 5 + 6 = ____

e 4 + 4 = ____

Use Your Fingers

You can use your fingers to add up to 10.

Example 1:

Use your fingers to add 3 + 2.
Hold up 3 fingers on one hand. Hold up 2 fingers on the other. Count them.

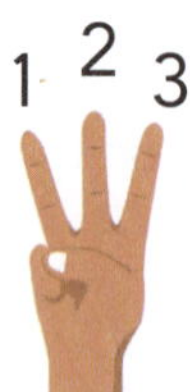

3 + 2 = 5

Example 2:

Add 6 + 2 using your fingers.
Hold up 6 fingers. Then, hold up 2 more. Count them.

6 + 2 = 8

Your turn

1 Use your fingers to add.

4 + 5 = 9

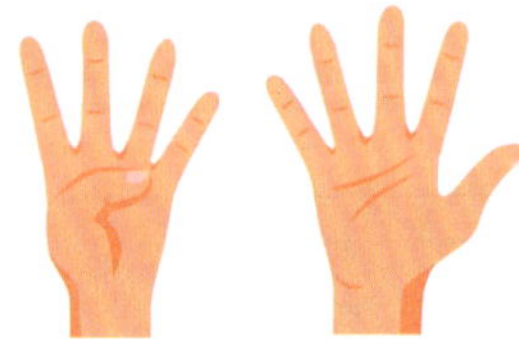

a 3 + 3 = ____

b 4 + 1 = ____

SELF CHECK Mark how you feel

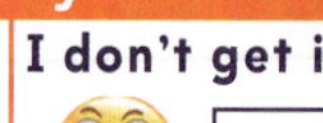

Got it!	Need help...	I don't get it

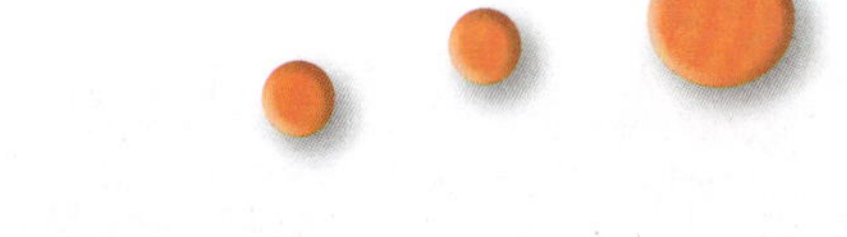

Practice

 Use your fingers to add. Circle the fingertips to show which fingers you used.

1 + 4 = 5

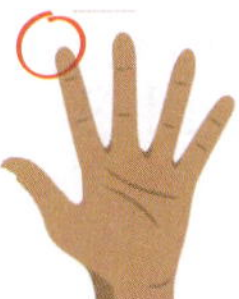 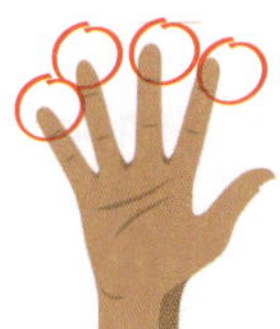

b 5 + 1 = ______

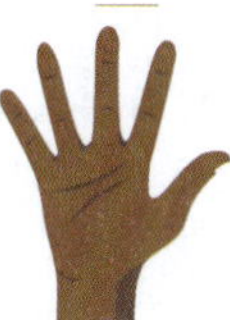

a 3 + 5 = ______

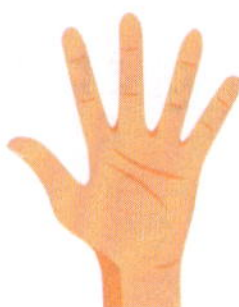 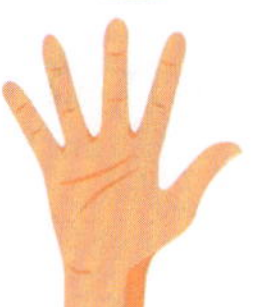

c 6 + 2 = ______

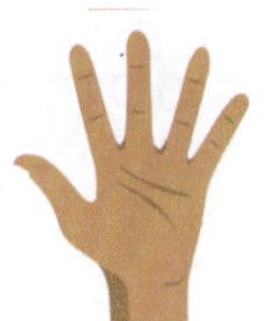 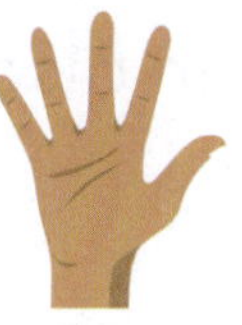

 Use your fingers to add.

6 + 3 = ______

c 1 + 7 = ______

a 5 + 5 = ______

d 2 + 4 = ______

b 7 + 2 = ______

e 8 + 2 = ______

Count On

You can count on to add. Begin with the larger number. Then, count on with the second number.

Example 1:

4 + 3

4 is larger, so say the number 4 to yourself. Then, hold up 3 fingers. Count on from 4 until you have counted all 3 fingers.

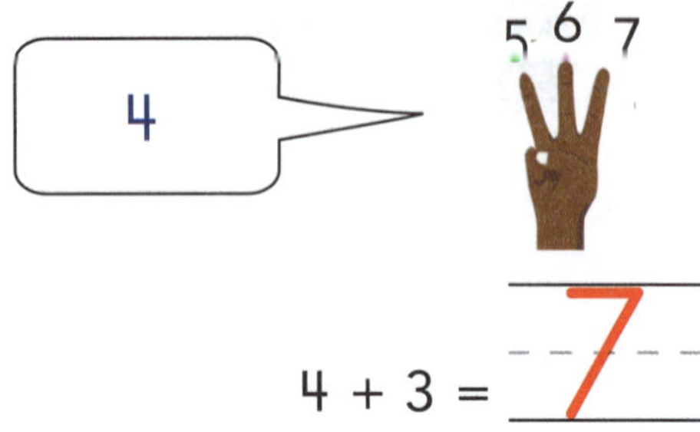

4 + 3 = 7

Example 2:

You can also put dots on a paper and count on using those.

9 + 4

Begin with 9. Make 4 dots. Count on from 9 until you have counted each dot.

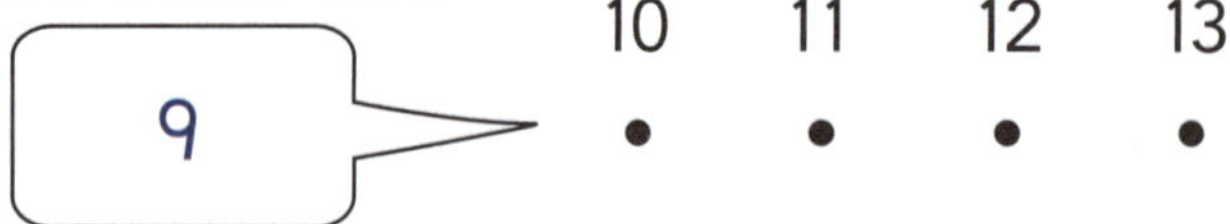

9 + 4 = 13

1 Add by counting on.

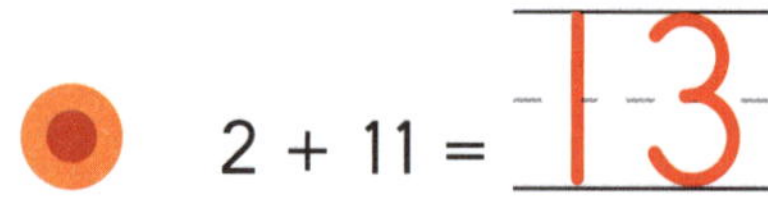

2 + 11 = 13

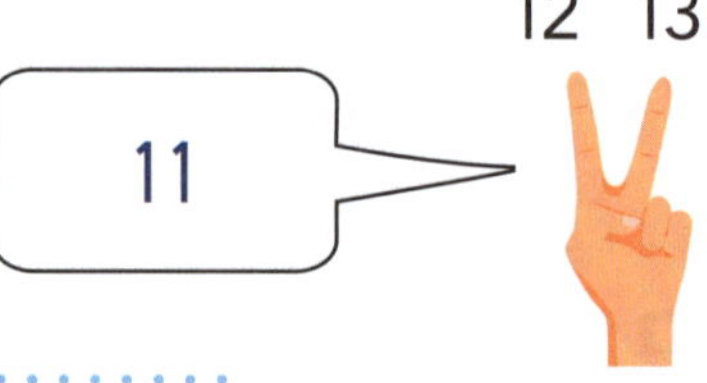

a 9 + 7 = ______

SELF CHECK Mark how you feel		
Got it! ☐	Need help... ☐	I don't get it ☐

Practice

1 Add by counting on.

7 + 10 = 17

10

11 12 13 14 15

a 8 + 3 = ______

b 4 + 5 = ______

c 8 + 9 = ______

d 6 + 4 = ______

e 3 + 13 = ______

f 6 + 11 = ______

g 12 + 5 = ______

h 4 + 4 = ______

2 Add. Count on using the dots.

● 13 + 3 = 16 — 13 • • • (14 15 16)

a 4 + 2 = ____ — 4 • •

b 6 + 8 = ____ — 8 • • • • • •

c 11 + 4 = ____ — 11 • • • •

d 8 + 8 = ____ — 8 • • • • • • • •

e 3 + 4 = ____ — 4 • • •

f 10 + 2 = ____ — 10 • •

g 5 + 4 = ____ — 5 • • • •

Make a 10

Knowing numbers that add to make 10 is helpful. You can use a ten frame or your fingers to practice. This is a ten frame filled in.

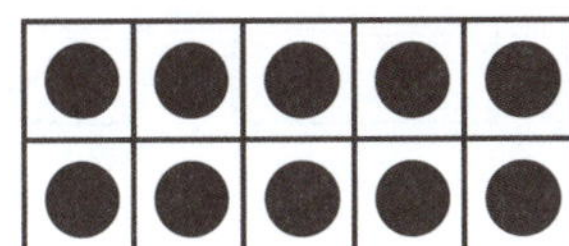

Example 1:

A ten frame has 10 spaces. This ten frame has 7 spaces filled in. There are 3 empty spaces.

So, 7 + 3 = 10.

Example 2:

There are 10 fingers. Some are down, and some are up. These hands have 4 fingers down. There are 6 fingers up.

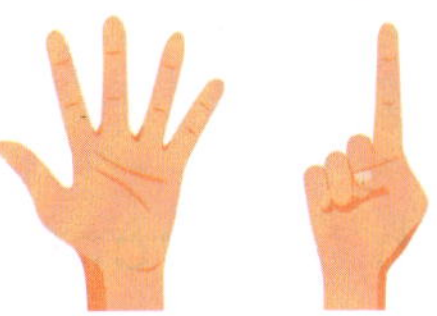

So, 6 + 4 = 10.

1 Study each ten frame. Write an equation to make 10.

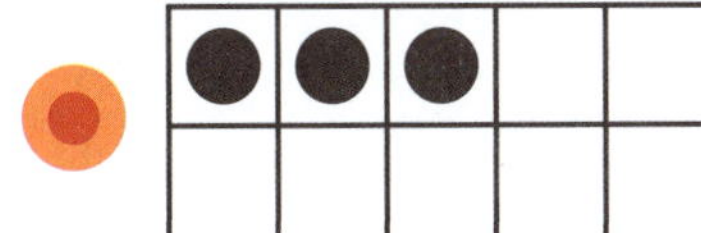

● 3 + 7 = 10

a

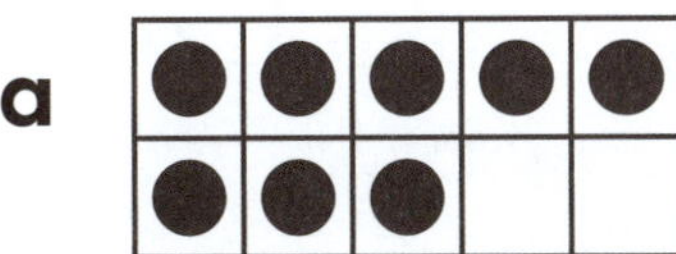

☐ + ☐ = 10

SELF CHECK	Mark how you feel	
Got it! ☐	Need help... ☐	I don't get it ☐

Practice

1 Study each ten frame. Write an equation to make 10.

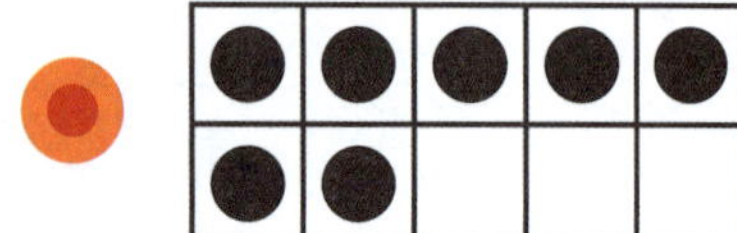

7 + 3 = 10

a

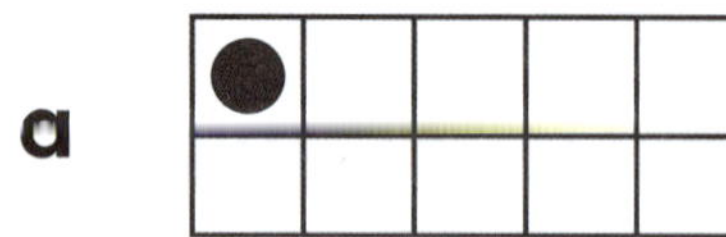

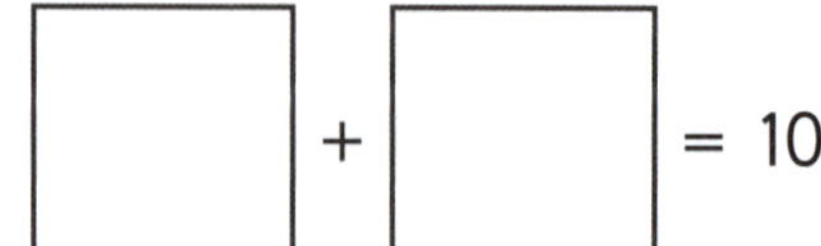

☐ + ☐ = 10

b

☐ + ☐ = 10

2 Fill in each ten frame to match the number sentence.

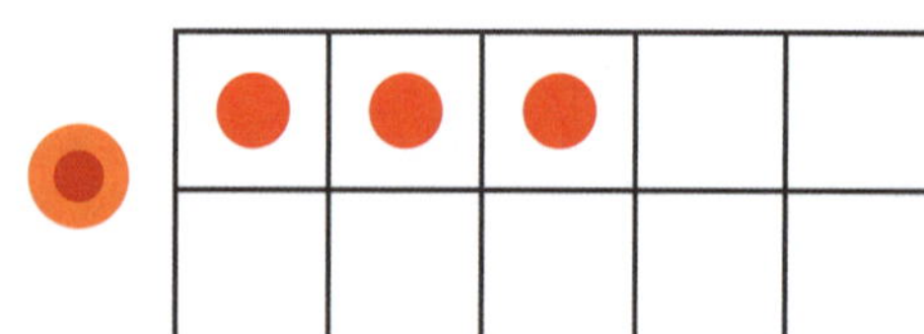

3 + 7 = 10

a

5 + 5 = 10

b

6 + 4 = 10

3 Study the hands. Write equations to make 10.

 3 + 7 = 10 

a ☐ + ☐ = 10 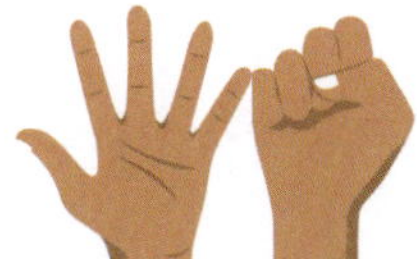

b ☐ + ☐ = 10  

c ☐ + ☐ = 10 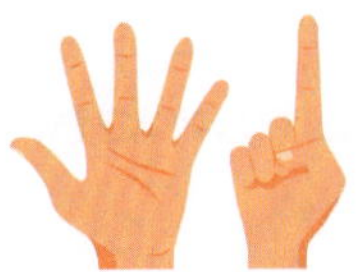

d ☐ + ☐ = 10 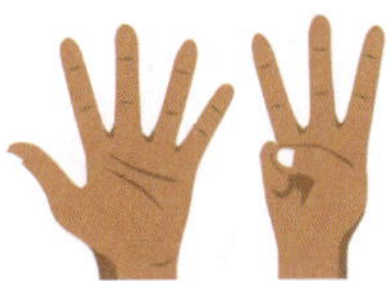

4 Write the missing number to make 10. Use any strategy.

9 + 1 = 10

a 4 + ☐ = 10

b ☐ + 9 = 10

c 7 + ☐ = 10

d ☐ + 1 = 10

Use a Number Line

You can use a number line to add.
Jump or move to the right to add.

Example 1:

Solve 5 + 3 using the number line.

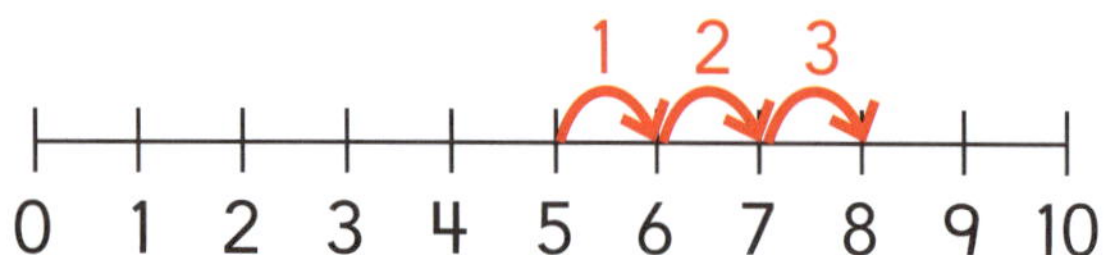

Start on 5. Jump ahead 3 spaces.

You land on 8, so 8 is the answer. 5 + 3 = 8

1 Use the number line to add. Show your jumps.

1 + 4 = 5

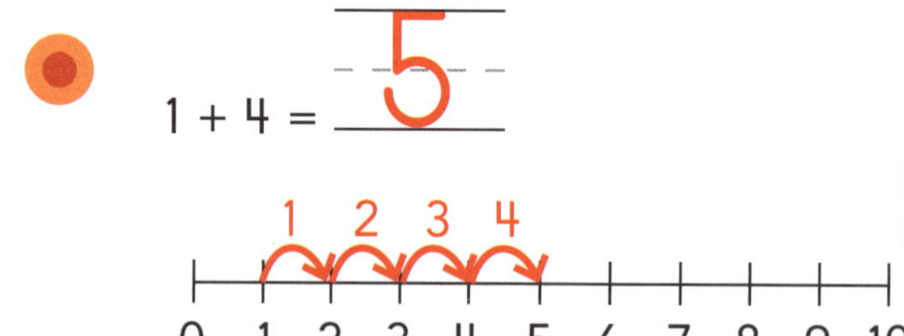

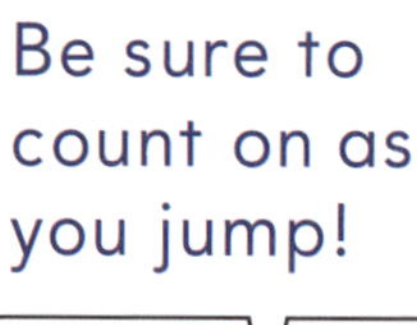

a 5 + 2 = ______

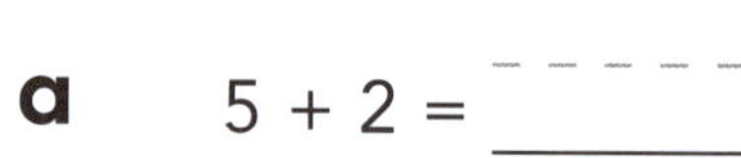

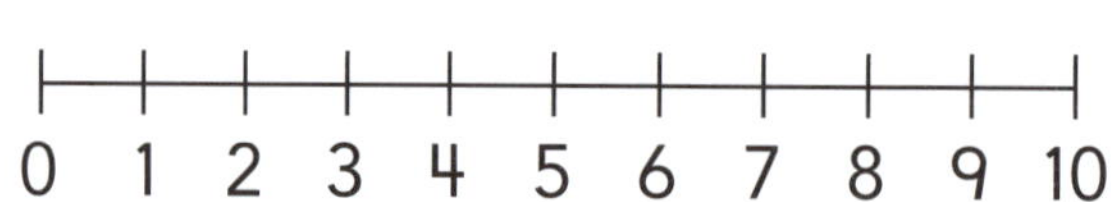

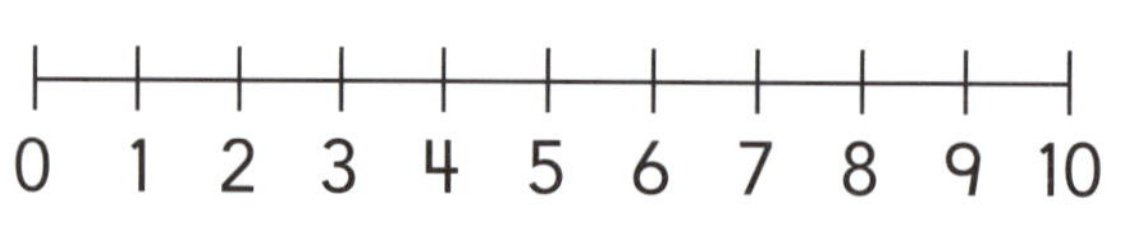

b 9 + 4 = ______

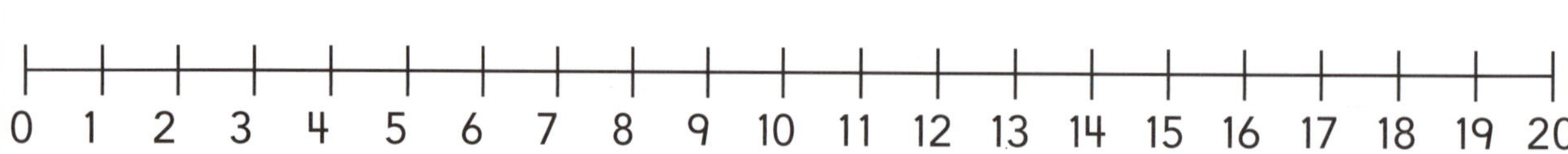

Practice

1 Use the number lines to add. Show your jumps.

3 + 3 = 6

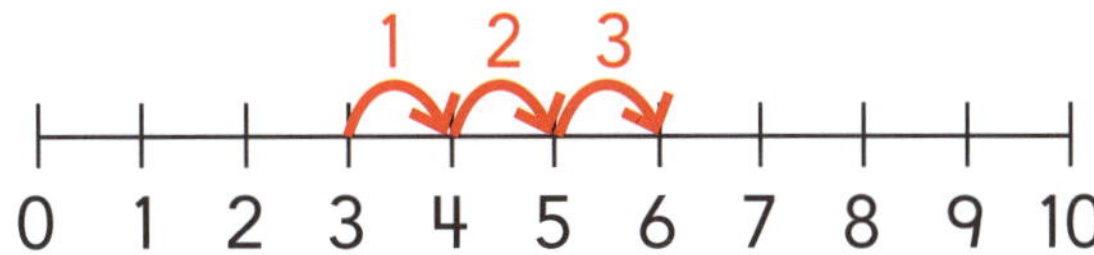

a 1 + 6 = ______

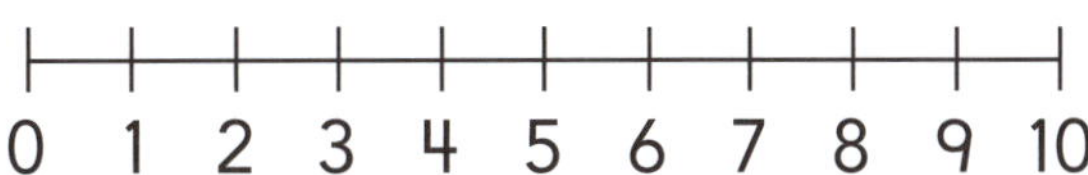

b 4 + 1 = ______

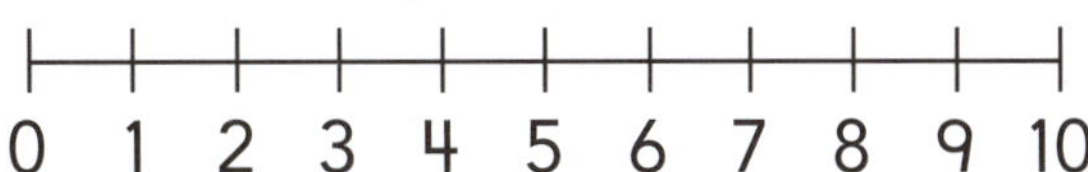

c 7 + 2 = ______

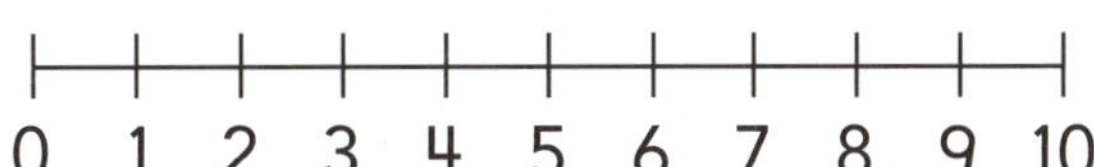

d 2 + 5 = ______

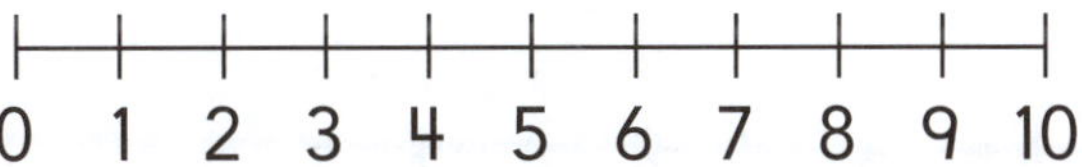

e 5 + 5 = ______

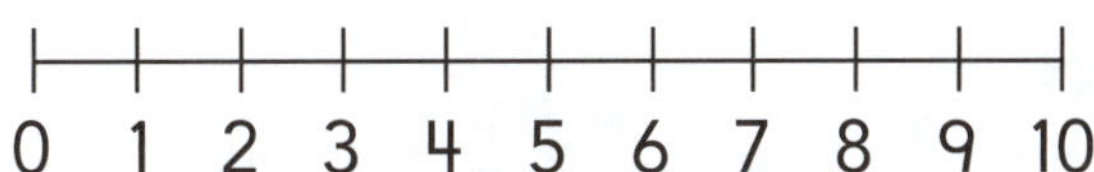

f 6 + 3 = ______

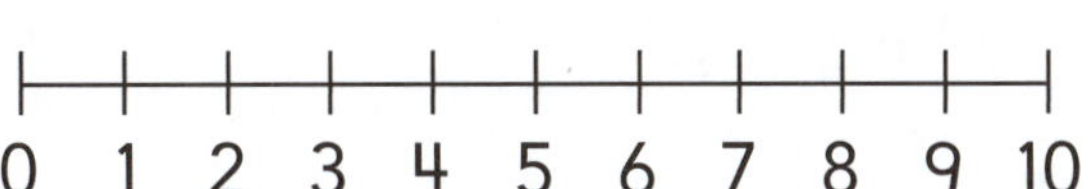

2 Use the number lines to add. Show your jumps.

8 + 4 = 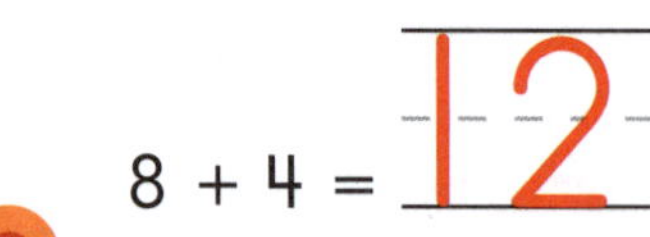

a 3 + 9 = ______

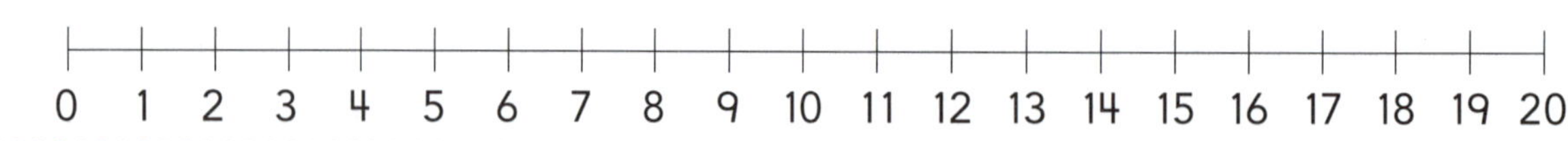

b 7 + 6 = ______

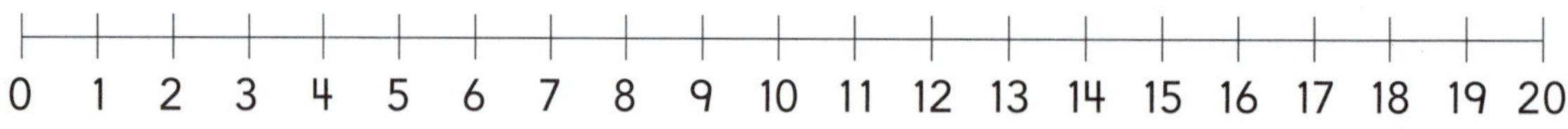

c 8 + 8 = ______

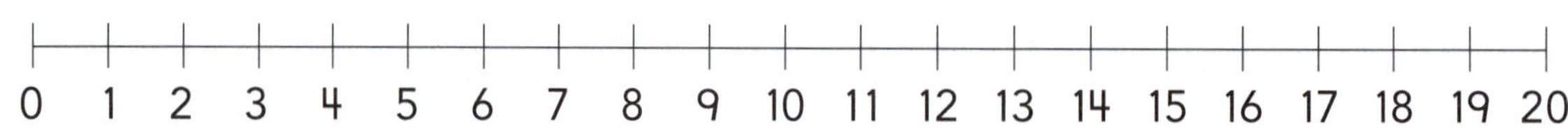

d 9 + 6 = ______

0 1 2 3 4 5 6 7 8 9 10 11 12 13 14 15 16 17 18 19 20

e 5 + 7 = ______

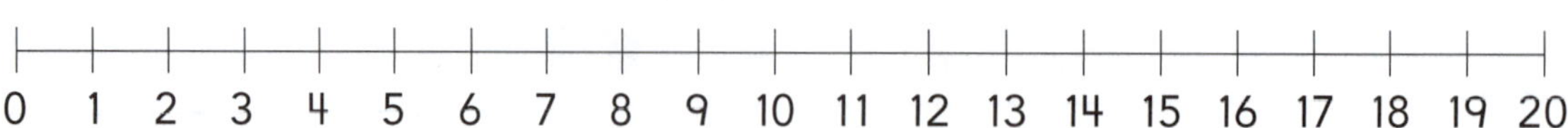

Tally Marks

Making tally marks can help you add. Tally marks are straight lines. They are made in groups of 5.

1	I	6	~~IIII~~ I	11	~~IIII~~ ~~IIII~~ I
2	II	7	~~IIII~~ II	12	~~IIII~~ ~~IIII~~ II
3	III	8	~~IIII~~ III	13	~~IIII~~ ~~IIII~~ III
4	IIII	9	~~IIII~~ IIII	14	~~IIII~~ ~~IIII~~ IIII
5	~~IIII~~	10	~~IIII~~ ~~IIII~~	15	~~IIII~~ ~~IIII~~ ~~IIII~~

Example 1:

You can use tallies to count on. Solve 4 + 3. Start with 4 tally marks. Then, add 3 more.

~~IIII~~ II 4 + 3 = 7

The tally groups are skip counting by 5s. They go 5, 10, 15, and so on.

1 Draw tally marks to count on. Write the total.

● 3 + 5 = 8 ~~IIII~~ III

a 3 + 3 = ______ III

b 7 + 2 = ______ ~~IIII~~ II

c 4 + 8 = ______ IIII

SELF CHECK Mark how you feel

Got it!	Need help...	I don't get it
 ☐	  ☐	  ☐

Practice

1 Draw tally marks to show each number.

●	3 |||	6 卌 |	11 卌 卌 |
a	9	15	5
b	13	1	14
c	4	7	10

2 Draw tally marks to count on. Write the total.

● 7 + 7 = 14 卌 卌 ||||

a 5 + 8 = ______ 卌

b 6 + 1 = ______ 卌 |

c 2 + 2 = ______ ||

d 8 + 3 = ______ 卌 |||

e 9 + 3 = ______ 卌 ||||

3 Draw tally marks to add. Write the total.

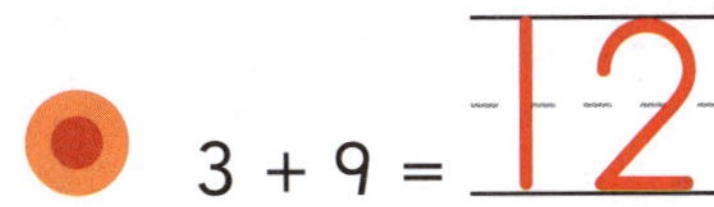 

a 7 + 1 = ______

b 1 + 5 = ______

c 4 + 3 = ______

d 2 + 7 = ______

e 6 + 4 = ______

f 5 + 8 = ______

4 Add. Use any strategy.

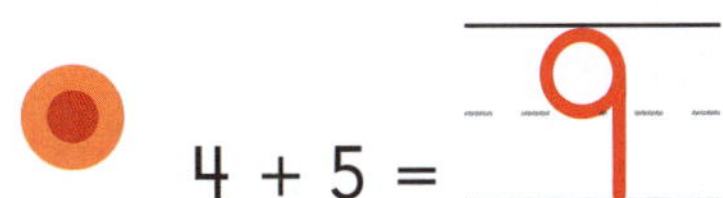

a 3 + 6 = ______

b 5 + 7 = ______

c 8 + 1 = ______

d 9 + 4 = ______

e 1 + 8 = ______

Doubles

Sometimes both numbers being added are the same. This is called a double.

Dominoes are a fun way to practice doubles. You can count the dots.

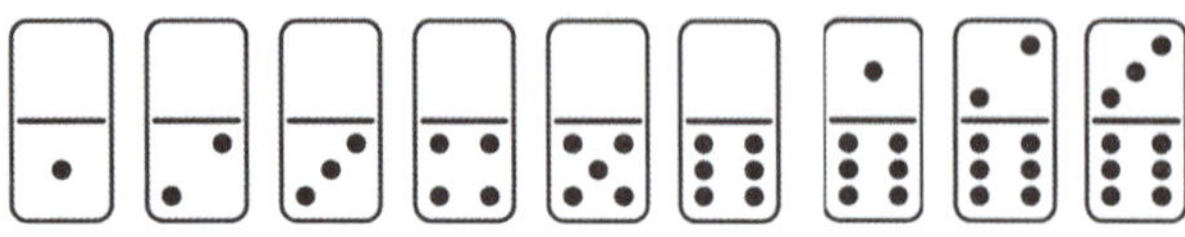

Example 1:

3 + 3 = 6

Example 2:

7 + 7 = 14

1 Use the dominoes to add doubles. Count the dots. Then, write the total.

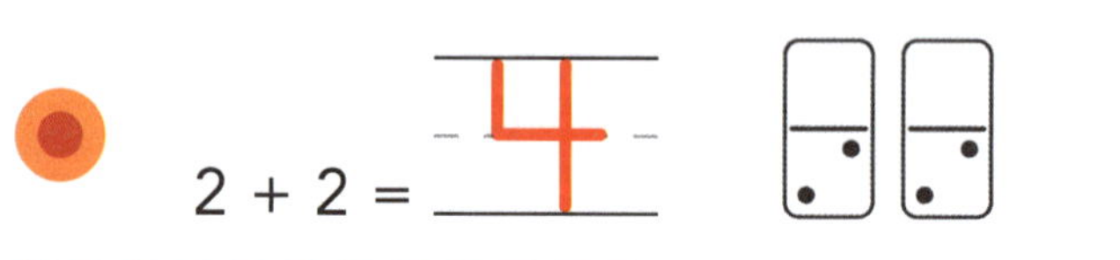

2 + 2 = 4

a 5 + 5 = ______

b 8 + 8 = ______

c 4 + 4 = ______

Practice

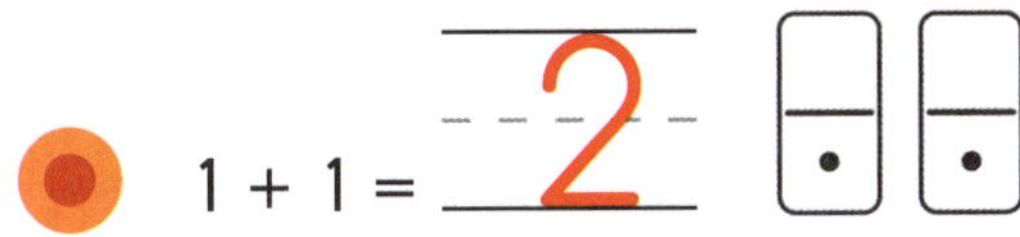

1 Use the dominoes to add. Write the total.

● 1 + 1 = 2

e 9 + 9 = ______

a 4 + 4 = ______

f 2 + 2 = ______

b 7 + 7 = ______

g 6 + 6 = ______

c 3 + 3 = ______

h 8 + 8 = ______

d 8 + 8 = ______

i 5 + 5 = ______

Add in Any Order

Numbers can be added in any order. It does not matter which one goes first.

Example 1:

Draw a picture to help solve the problem. 3 + 6 = ?

9 triangles

Draw a picture to help solve the problem. 6 + 3 = ?

The numbers you are adding are the same.
So, the answer is the same.

1 Add. Write the total.

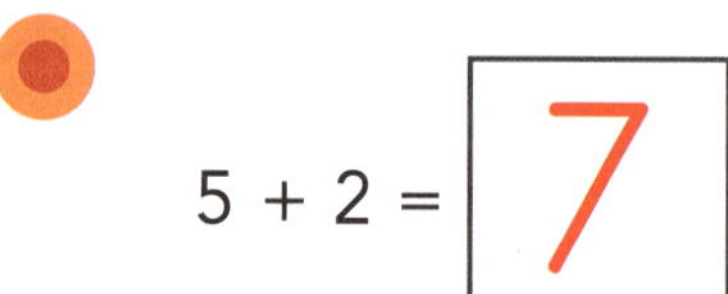

● 5 + 2 = 7 2 + 5 = 7

a 2 + 6 = ☐ 6 + 2 = ☐

b 5 + 1 = ☐ 1 + 5 = ☐

SELF CHECK Mark how you feel

Got it!	Need help...	I don't get it
☐	☐	☐

Practice

1 Add. Write the total.

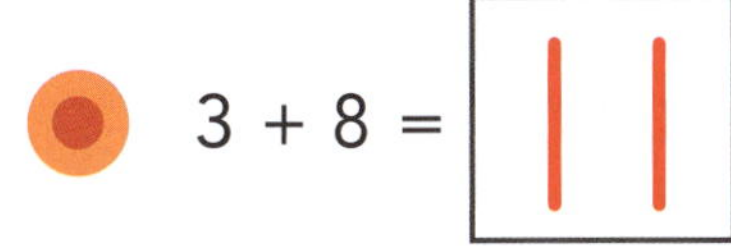

●	3 + 8 = 11	8 + 3 = 11
a	4 + 1 = ☐	1 + 4 = ☐
b	7 + 4 = ☐	4 + 7 = ☐
c	1 + 5 = ☐	5 + 1 = ☐
d	9 + 2 = ☐	2 + 9 = ☐
e	6 + 7 = ☐	7 + 6 = ☐
f	2 + 6 = ☐	6 + 2 = ☐
g	8 + 3 = ☐	3 + 8 = ☐
h	5 + 4 = ☐	4 + 5 = ☐
i	8 + 7 = ☐	7 + 8 = ☐

Addition: True or False?

You can find equal addition problems. Add on both sides of the equal sign. If the problems have the same value, they are equal.

Example 1:

Are these addition problems equal?  Yes No

5 + 3 = 4 + 4

8 8

Both sides have the same value.

Example 2:

Are these addition problems equal? Yes   No

4 + 2 = 1 + 6

6 7

The sides have different values.

1 Circle the addition problem that has the same value.

9 + 1 = ?

7 + 4 5 + 5 3 + 6

11 10 9

a 4 + 4 = ?

7 + 2 6 + 4 3 + 5

b 8 + 5 = ?

10 + 3 9 + 7 5 + 6

SELF CHECK Mark how you feel

Got it!   Need help... 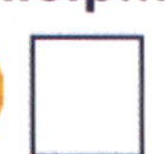  I don't get it 

Practice

1. Are the addition problems equal? Circle yes or no.

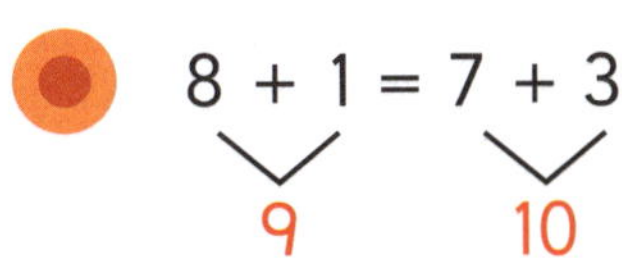

● 8 + 1 = 7 + 3 Yes **No** (9, 10)

c 10 + 2 = 8 + 3 Yes No

a 9 + 2 = 5 + 6 Yes No

d 6 + 7 = 10 + 3 Yes No

b 5 + 5 = 6 + 4 Yes No

e 12 + 2 = 7 + 6 Yes No

2. Circle the addition problems that equal the answer.

● Answer: 9

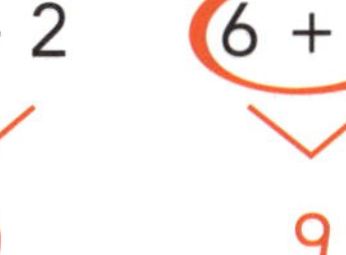

(5 + 4) 8 + 2 (6 + 3) (8 + 1)

9 10 9 9

a Answer: 14

11 + 1 7 + 7 8 + 8 10 + 4

b Answer: 7

3 + 4 5 + 2 5 + 3 8 + 2

c Answer: 10

10 + 0 5 + 7 9 + 1 7 + 3

Addition

3 Write an addition problem with the same value. Use different digits.

● 5 + 4 = 6 + 3

a 8 + 6 = ____ + ____

b 1 + 5 = ____ + ____

c 3 + 9 = ____ + ____

d 5 + 0 = ____ + ____

e 9 + 2 = ____ + ____

4 Write two equal addition problems.

● 5 + 5 = 9 + 1

a ____ + ____ = ____ + ____

b ____ + ____ = ____ + ____

c ____ + ____ = ____ + ____

Add 3 Numbers

You can add three numbers together. The same strategies for adding two numbers will work.

Example 1:

You can draw pictures. 3 + 2 + 5 = 10

Example 2:

You can use a number line. 4 + 1 + 4 = 9

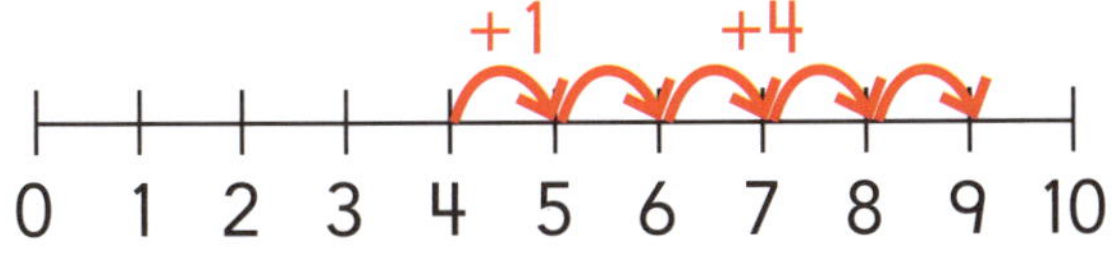

Don't forget! You can add the numbers in any order.

Example 3:

You can make a 10. 8 + 4 + 2 = 14

8 and 2 make a 10.

8 + 4 + 2

10 + 4 = 14

Your turn

1. Draw pictures to add. Write the answer.

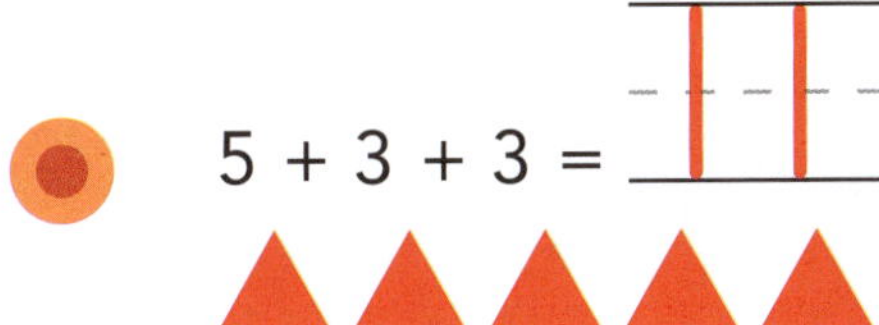

● 5 + 3 + 3 = 11

a 4 + 3 + 7 = ____

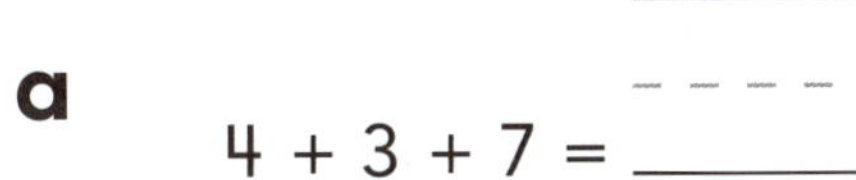

Practice

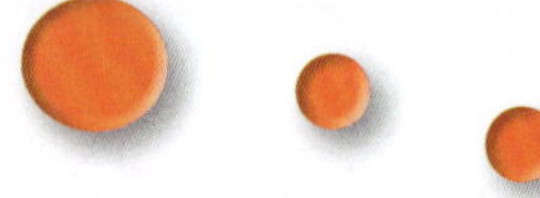

1 Draw pictures to add.

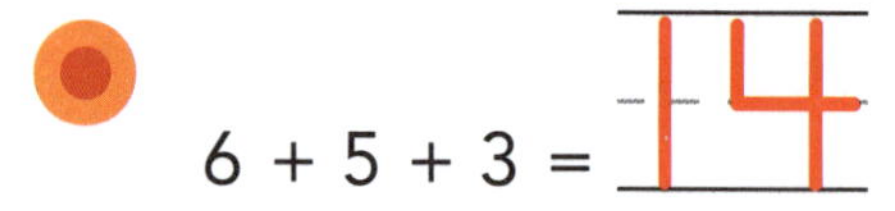

a 3 + 2 + 7 = ______

b 8 + 4 + 2 = ______

c 4 + 4 + 2 = ______

2 Use the number lines to add.

7 + 4 + 2 = 13

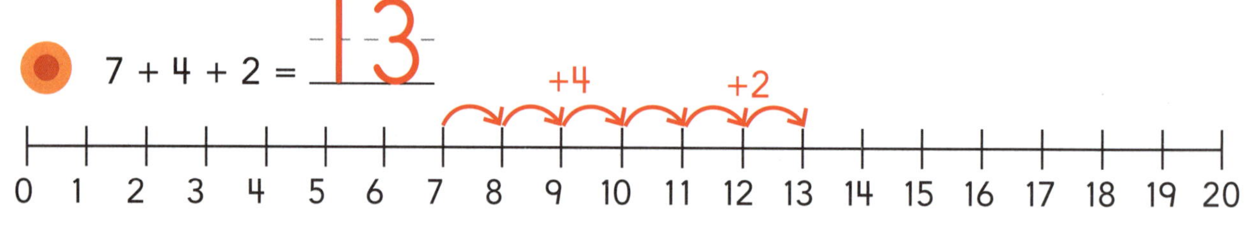

a 2 + 7 + 4 = ______

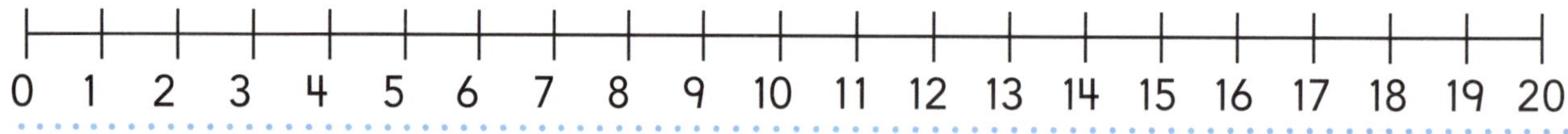

b 6 + 3 + 8 = ______

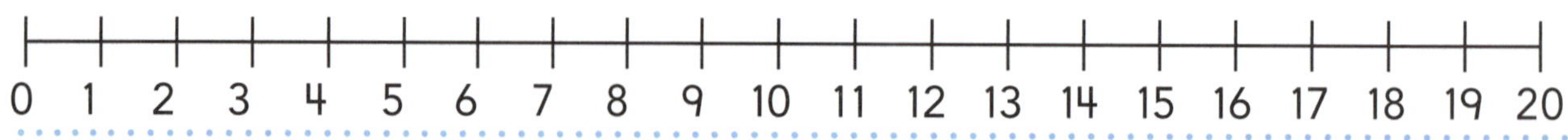

c 5 + 6 + 1 = ______

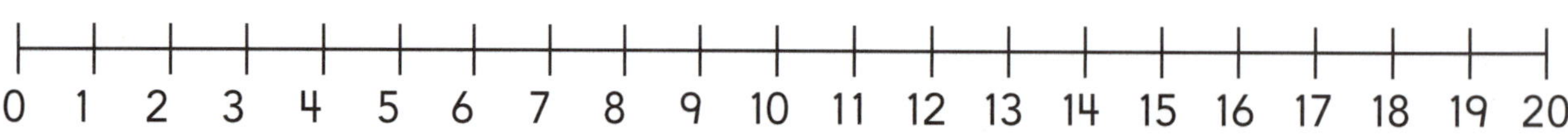

3 Make 10s to add. Circle the digits that equal 10. Complete the equations.

● 6 + 4 + 3

10 + 3 = 13

b 9 + 3 + 1

10 + ______ = ______

a 5 + 5 + 6

10 + ______ = ______

c 2 + 8 + 1

10 + ______ = ______

4 Choose any strategy to solve each problem.

● 6 + 4 + 4 = 14

a 4 + 1 + 2 = ______

c 2 + 8 + 3 = ______

b 9 + 3 + 4 = ______

d 5 + 2 + 5 = ______

2 Digits Plus 1 Digit

You can add a two-digit number and a one-digit number. You can count on. You can also use a hundred chart.

Example 1:

Use your fingers to count on. Solve 26 + 3.

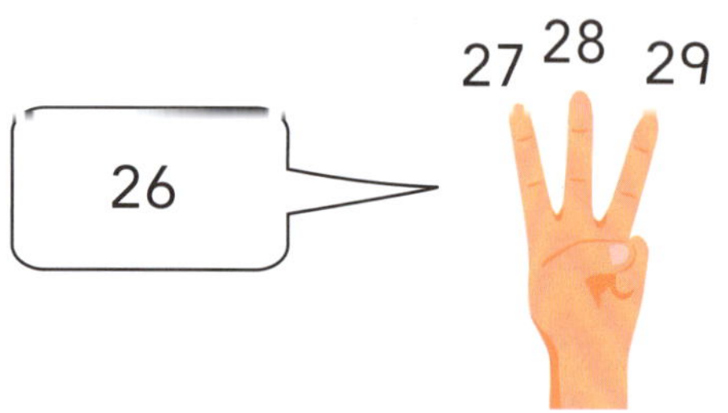

26 + 3 = 29

Example 2:

Use part of a hundred chart. Solve 42 + 6.

41	42	43	44	45	46	47	48	49	50

42 + 6 = 48

1 Add using tallies. Count on. Write the answer.

84 + 3 = 87   84 |||

a 71 + 8 = ______   71

SELF CHECK Mark how you feel		
Got it! ☐	Need help... ☐	I don't get it ☐

Practice

Add. Use your fingers to count on.

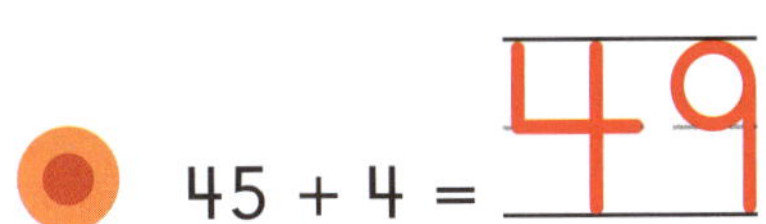

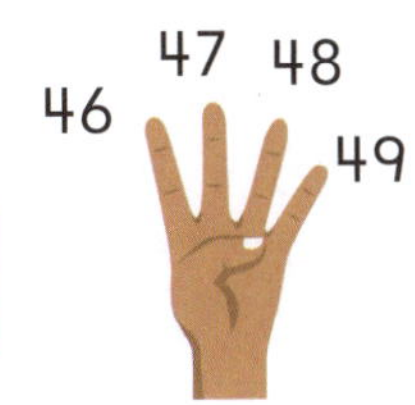

c 91 + 8 = ____

a 81 + 6 = ____

d 32 + 3 = ____

b 70 + 9 = ____

e 63 + 5 = ____

2 Add. Use tallies to count on.

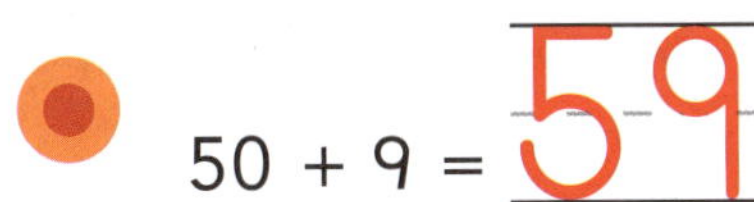

50

b 86 + 2 = ____

86

a 95 + 3 = ____

95

c 77 + 1 = ____

77

3 Use the hundred chart to add.

1	2	3	4	5	6	7	8	9	10
11	12	13	14	15	16	17	18	19	20
21	22	23	24	25	26	27	28	29	30
31	32	33	34	35	36	37	38	39	40
41	42	43	44	45	46	47	48	49	50
51	52	53	54	55	56	57	58	59	60
61	62	63	64	65	66	67	68	69	70
71	72	73	74	75	76	77	78	79	80
81	82	83	84	85	86	87	88	89	90
91	92	93	94	95	96	97	98	99	100

- 27 + 2 = 29

a 64 + 4 = ______

c 30 + 6 = ______

b 48 + 1 = ______

d 51 + 7 = ______

4 Add. Use any strategy.

- 43 + 4 = 47

a 24 + 5 = ______

c 72 + 5 = ______

b 61 + 8 = ______

d 55 + 3 = ______

2 Digits Plus Multiples of 10

You can add two-digit numbers to numbers that have a 0 in the ones place.

10 20 30 40 50 60 70 80 90

Numbers that have a 0 in the ones place are multiples of 10.

Example 1:

You can use a hundred chart. Every time you move down one row, you add a ten.

1	2	3	4	5	6	7	8	9	10
11	12	13	14	15	16	17	18	19	20
21	22	23	24	25	26	27	28	29	30
31	32	33	34	35	36	37	38	39	40
41	42	43	44	45	46	47	48	49	50
51	52	53	54	55	56	57	58	59	60
61	62	63	64	65	66	67	68	69	70
71	72	73	74	75	76	77	78	79	80
81	82	83	84	85	86	87	88	89	90
91	92	93	94	95	96	97	98	99	100

21 + 10 = 31

21 + 20 = 41

1 Use the hundred chart to add. Show your jumps.

- 16 + 30 = 46
- 16 + 40 = 56
- 16 + 50 = 66

a
- 35 + 10 = ______
- 35 + 20 = ______
- 35 + 30 = ______

SELF CHECK Mark how you feel		
Got it! ☐	Need help... ☐	I don't get it ☐

Practice

1 Use the hundred chart to add. Show your jumps.

1	2	3	4	5	6	7	8	9	10
11	12	13	14	15	16	17	18	19	20
21	22	23	24	25	26	27	28	29	30
31	32	33	34	35	36	37	38	39	40
41	42	43	44	45	46	47	48	49	50
51	52	53	54	55	56	57	58	59	60
61	62	63	64	65	66	67	68	69	70
71	72	73	74	75	76	77	78	79	80
81	82	83	84	85	86	87	88	89	90
91	92	93	94	95	96	97	98	99	100

● 57 + 10 = 67 57 + 20 = 77 57 + 30 = 87

a 24 + 40 = ______ 24 + 50 = ______ 24 + 60 = ______

b 11 + 20 = ______ 11 + 30 = ______ 11 + 40 = ______

c 66 + 10 = ______ 66 + 20 = ______ 66 + 30 = ______

d 38 + 20 = ______ 38 + 30 = ______ 38 + 40 = ______

e 43 + 10 = ______ 43 + 20 = ______ 43 + 30 = ______

Vertical Addition

Addition problems can be written up and down. This is called *vertical*. The digits in the ones place must line up. The digits in the tens place must also line up. The answer goes beneath.

Example 1:

Here is another way to write 32 + 5.

The 3 does not have anything below it. The 5 does not have a digit in the tens place.

The 2 in 32 and the 5 are lined up. They are both in the ones place.

	3	2
+		5
	3	7

Add the ones first. 2 + 5 = 7

Add the tens second. 3 + 0 = 3

Your turn

1 Add to solve each problem.

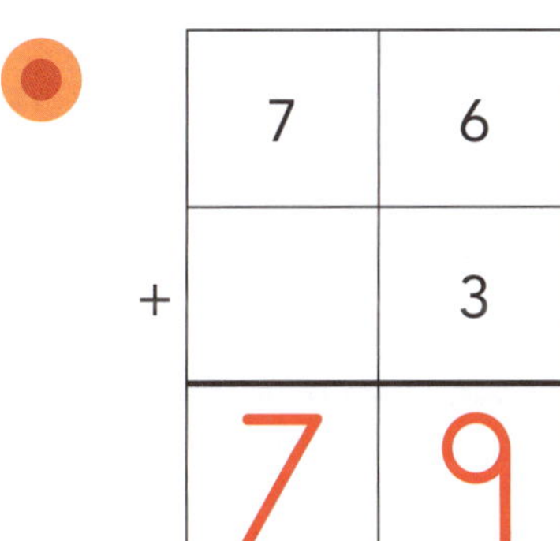

a

	4	0
+		7

b

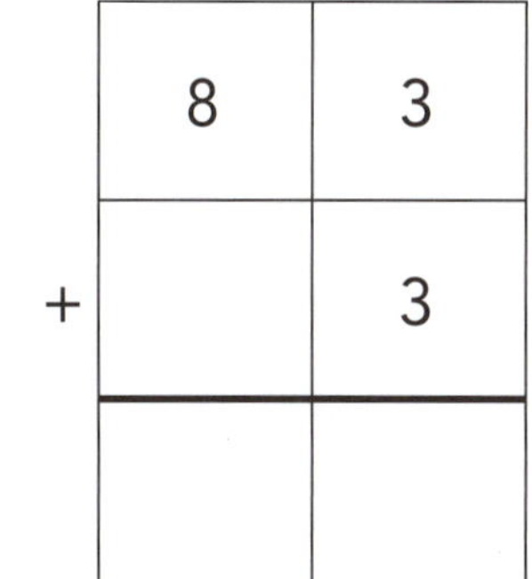

SELF CHECK	Mark how you feel	
Got it! ☐	Need help... ☐	I don't get it ☐

Practice

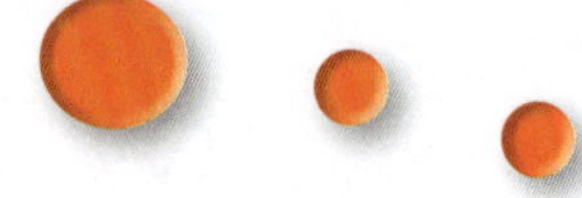

1 Solve each problem. First, add the ones. Then, add the tens.

Example:

	9	2
+		6
	9	8

b

	3	0
+		9

a

	6	4
+		2

c

	5	1
+		7

2 Write each problem in the table. Then, solve the problem.

Example: 42 + 6

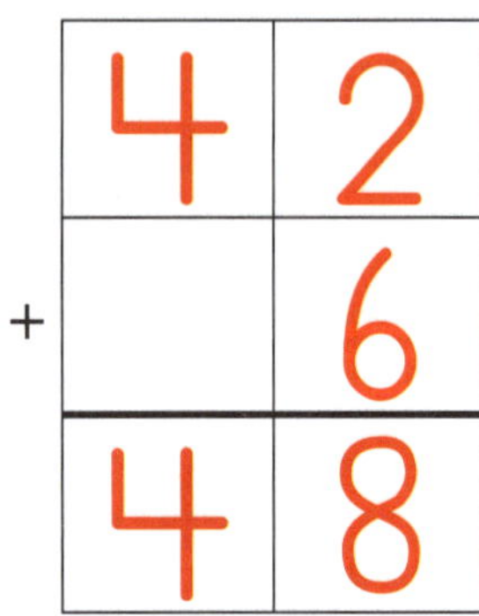

b 70 + 7

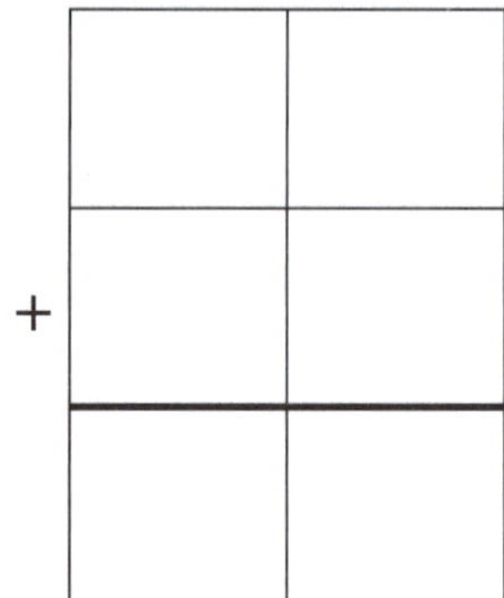

a 36 + 1

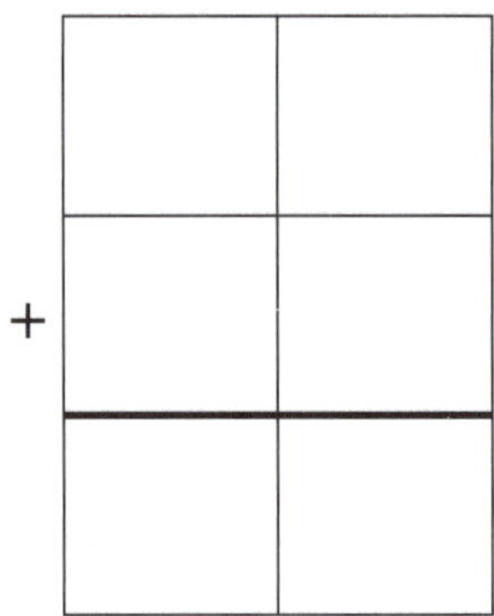

c 55 + 4

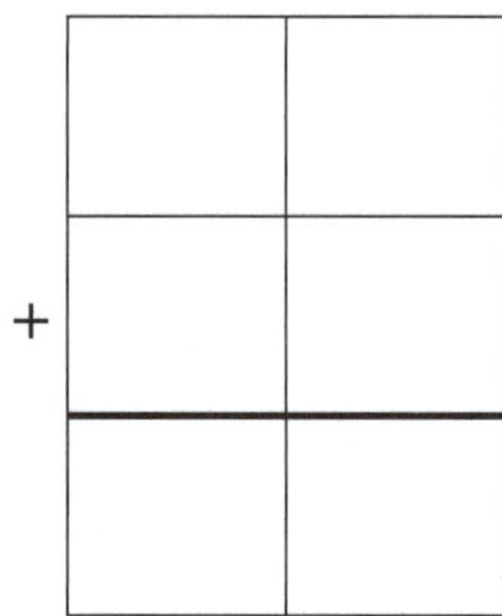

Make a 10 with 2-Digit Numbers

The largest number you can have in the ones place is 9. If there are more than 9 ones, you make a 10. This means you regroup 10 ones for 1 ten.

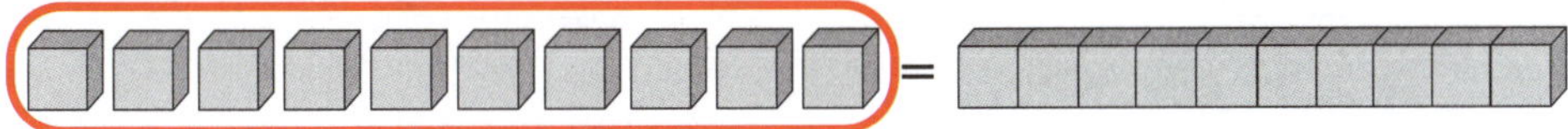

After you make a 10, you might still have ones left over.

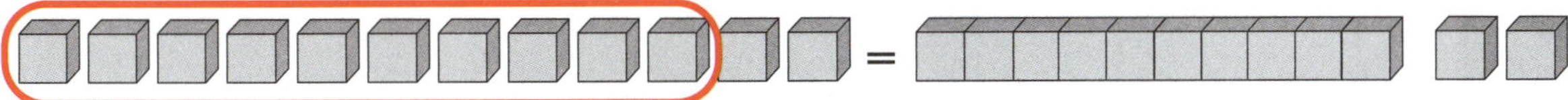

Example 1:

Circle a group of 10 ones.	Regroup.

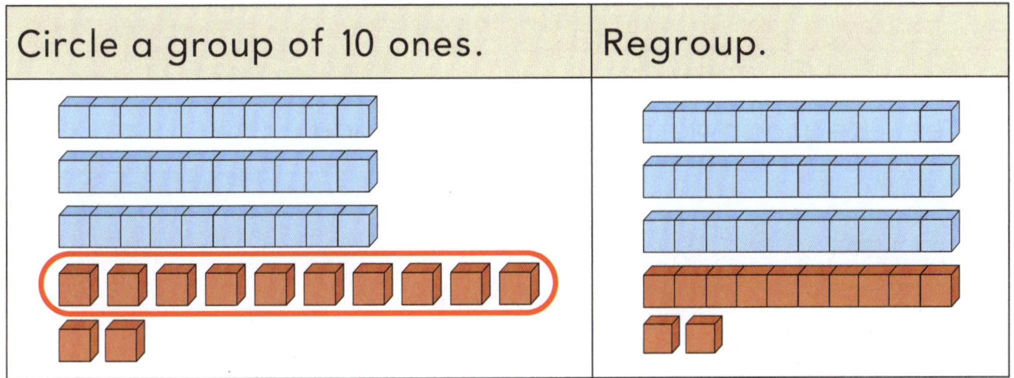

There were 3 tens. A new 10 was made. Now there are 4 tens. Two ones are left over.

1 Regroup to make a 10. Draw it.

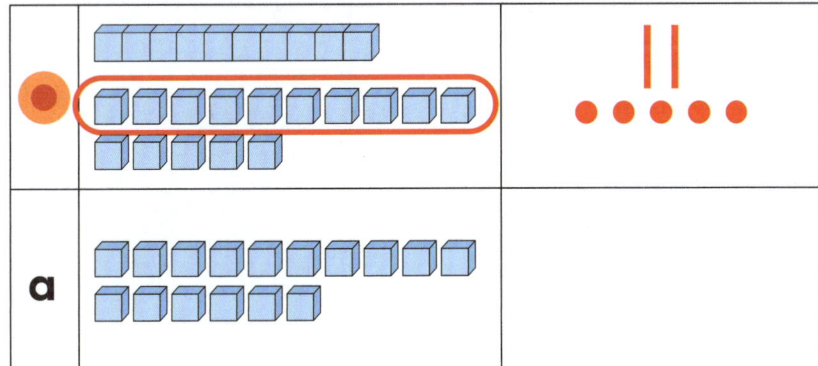

SELF CHECK Mark how you feel

Got it!	Need help...	I don't get it
☐	☐	☐

1 Circle 10 ones. Regroup to make a 10. Draw it.

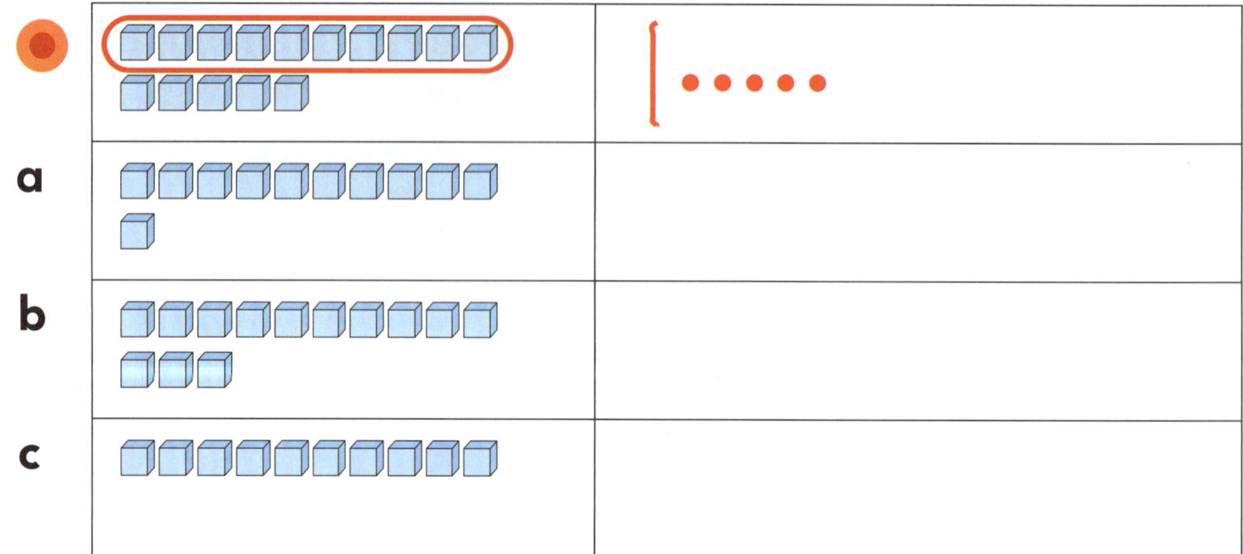

●		
a		
b		
c		

2 Circle 10 ones. Regroup to make a 10. Draw it.

●		
a		
b		
c		

3 Regroup to make a 10. Draw it. Write the number.

	Picture	Regroup	Number
●	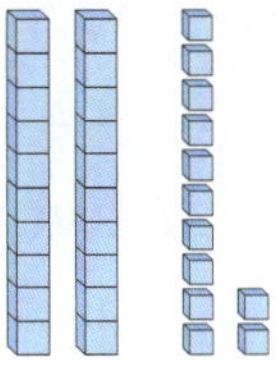	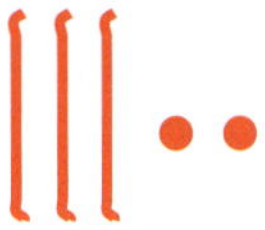 |||··	32
a	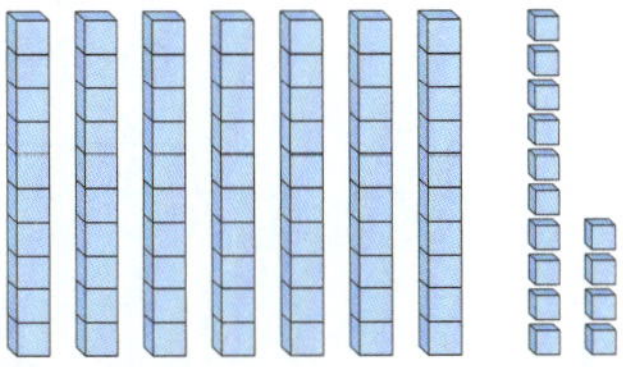		
b	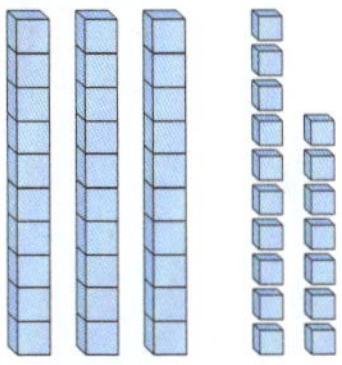		
c	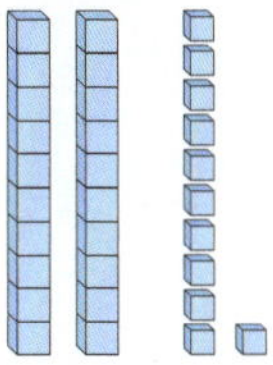		
d	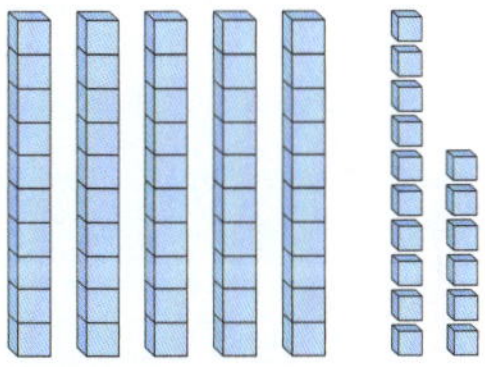		
e	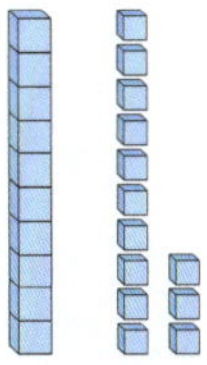		
f	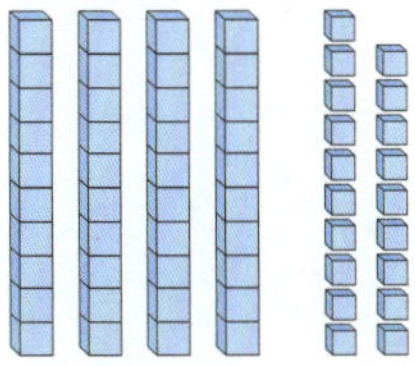		

Use Pictures to Make a 10

You have practiced adding two-digit and one-digit numbers. Sometimes there are 10 or more ones. So, you must regroup and make a 10.

Example 1:

Draw tens and ones to show the addition problem. Make a 10 and add.
68 + 3

Always add the ones first! If they equal 10 or more, make a 10.

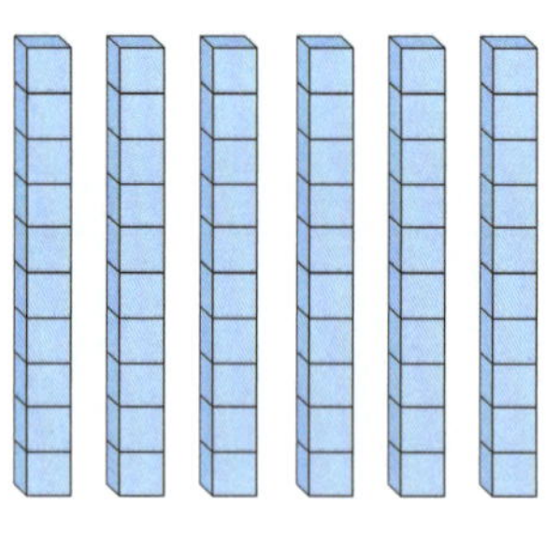

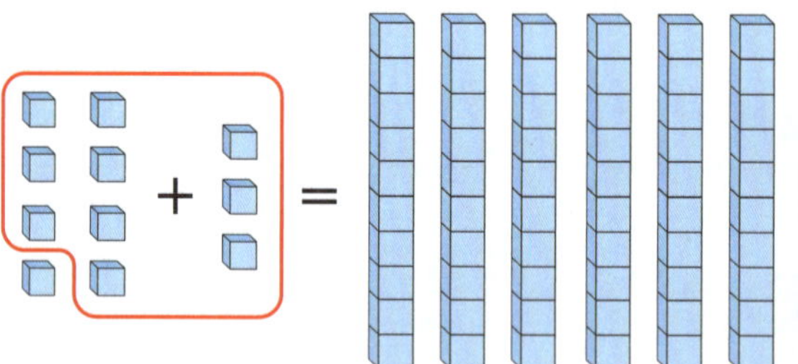

68 + 3 = 71

1 Make a 10. Then add. Draw the total.

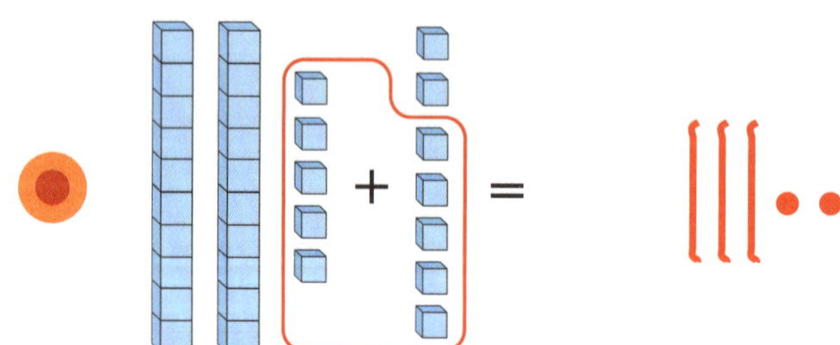

a

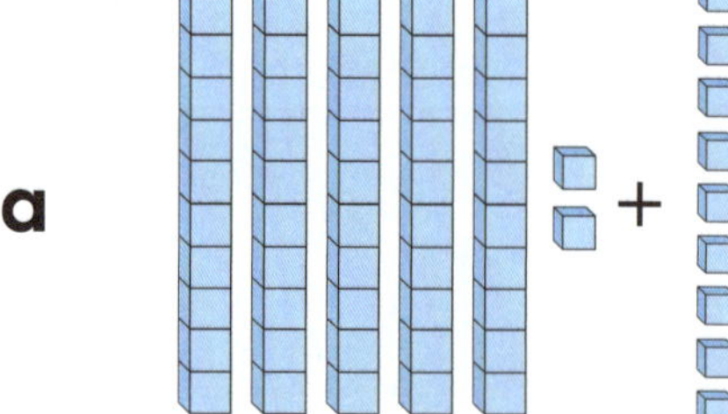

SELF CHECK Mark how you feel

Got it!	Need help...	I don't get it
☐	☐	☐

Practice

1 Make a 10. Then add. Draw the total.

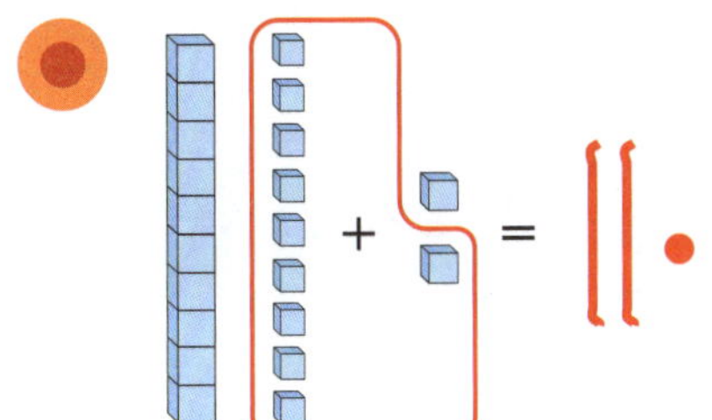

c 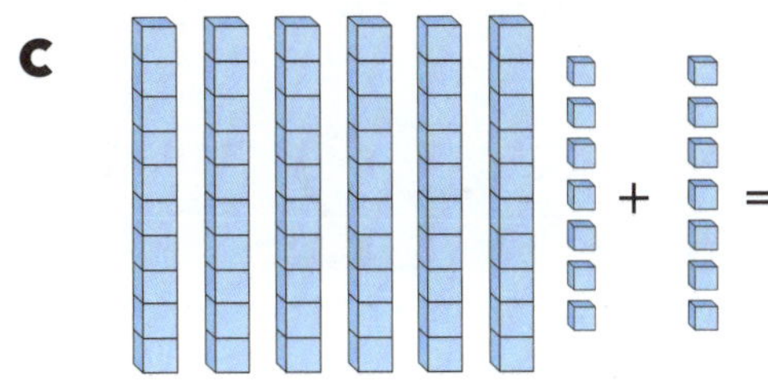

a 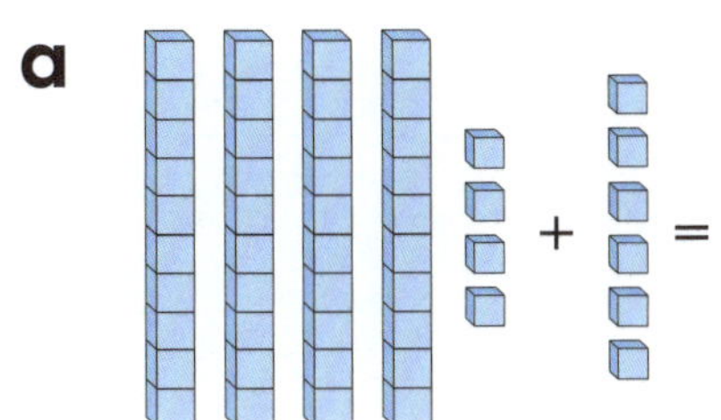

d 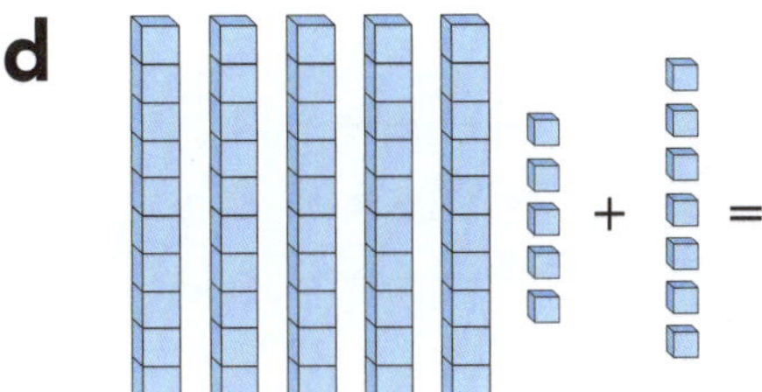

b 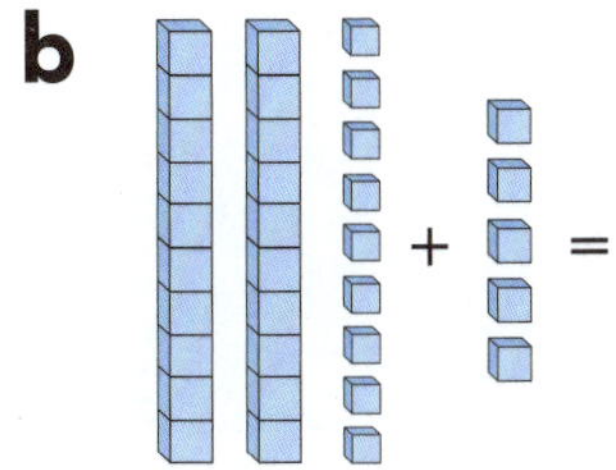

e 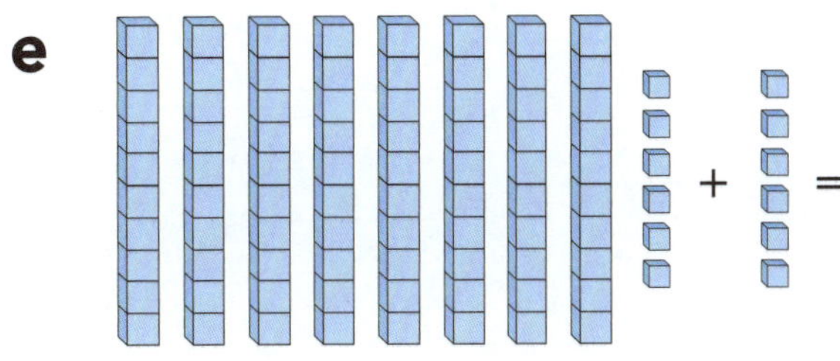

2 Draw tens and ones to show each addition problem. Make a 10 and add. Draw the total. Write the answer.

36 + 6 = 42

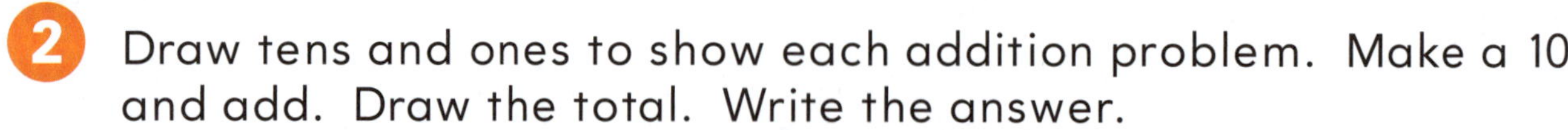

a 27 + 3 = ______

b 82 + 9 = ______

c 15 + 6 = ______

d 71 + 9 = ______

e 53 + 8 = ______

f 39 + 2 = ______

g 48 + 4 = ______

h 64 + 7 = ______

Use Numbers to Make a 10

You can make a 10 when adding. You don't have to draw a picture. You can write the numbers and show your thinking.

Compare drawing a picture and writing the numbers.

Picture	Number
	Put the 1 ten here in the tens place. → (1) Add the ones first. 6 + 7 = 1 ten and 3 ones. Add the tens. 1 + 2 = 3 tens. Put the 3 ones here in the ones place.

	(1)	
	2	6
+		7
	3	3

1 Add with pictures. Then, add with numbers. Write the answer.

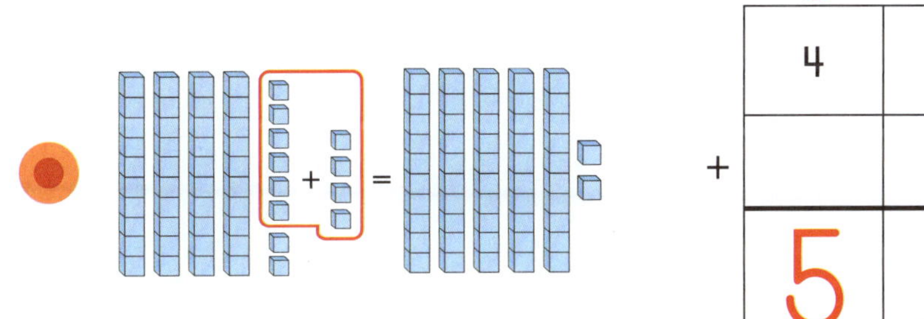

	(1)	
	4	8
+		4
	5	2

a

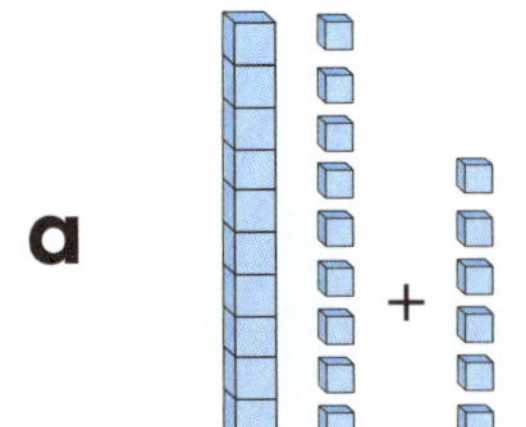

	1	9
+		6

SELF CHECK Mark how you feel

Got it!	Need help...	I don't get it
☐	☐	☐

Practice

1 Add with pictures. Then, add with numbers.

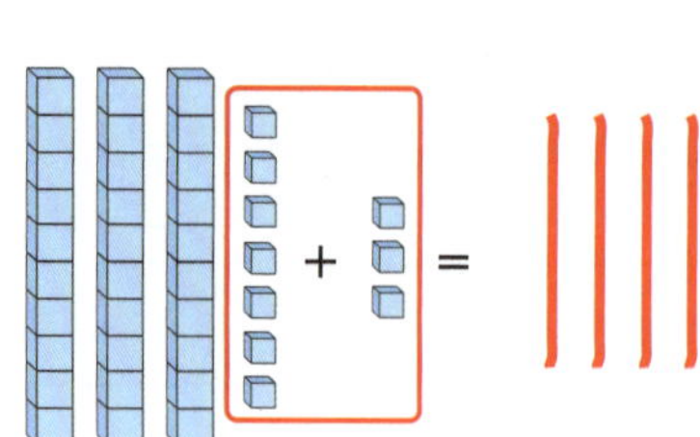

	1	
	3	7
+		3
	4	0

a

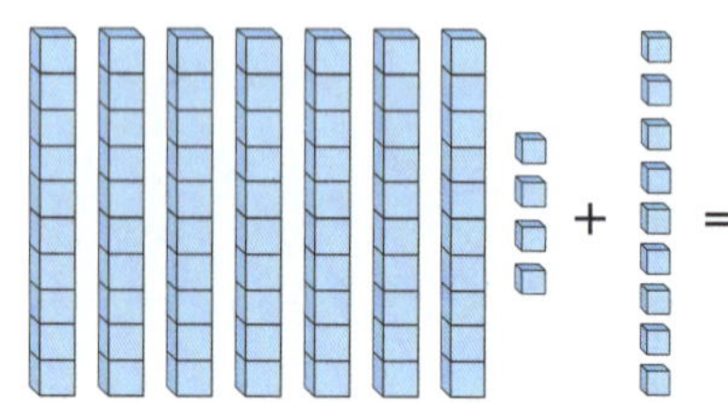

	7	4
+		9

b

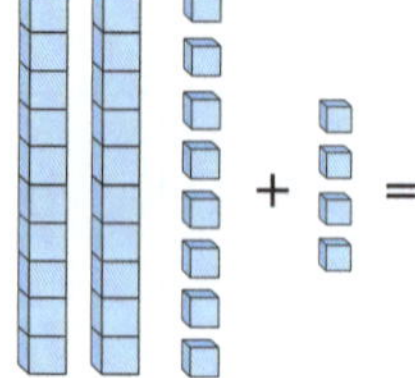

	2	8
+		4

c

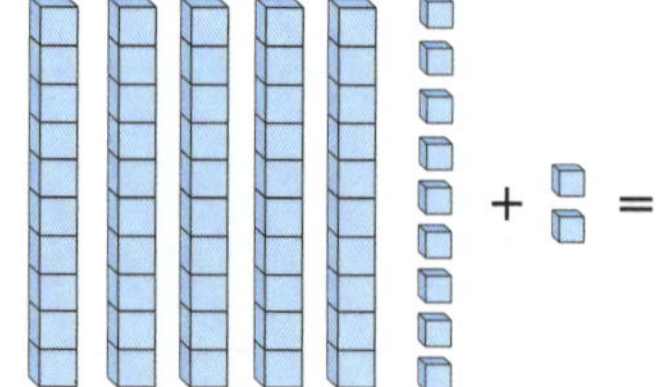

	5	9
+		2

2 Add. Then, draw pictures to show the addition.

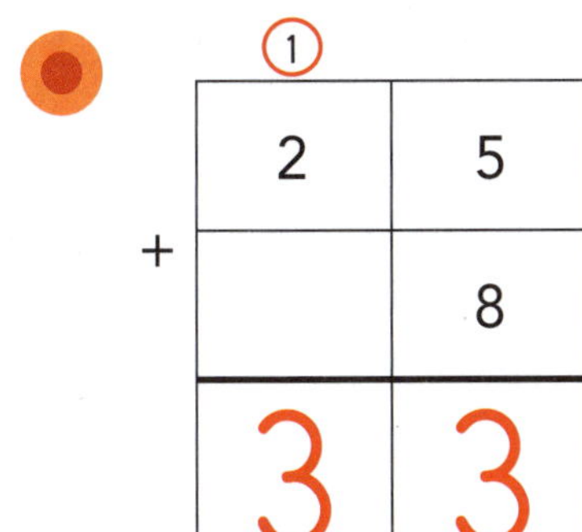

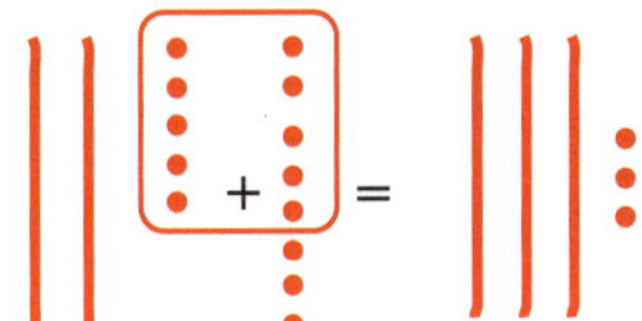

a

	7	1
+		9

3 Add. Show your regrouping with numbers.

	①	
	2	3
+		8
	3	1

a

	1	8
+		2

b

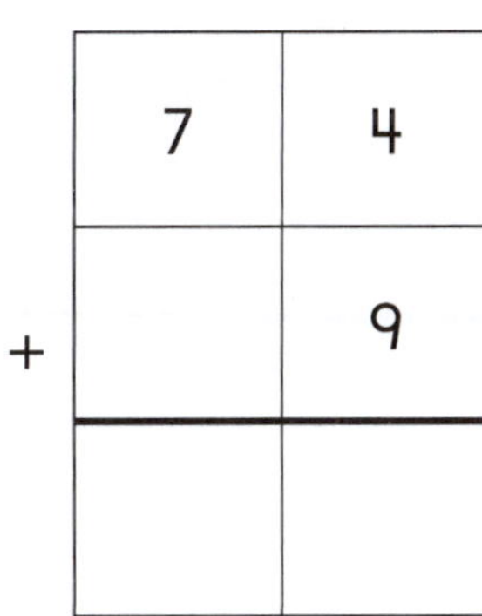

	7	4
+		9

c

	3	9
+		6

Addition Word Problems

Sometimes math is written as a story. You can look for the numbers. Look for an addition clue. Then, you can add.

Example 1:

Mateo has 6 dog stickers. He has 2 cat stickers. How many stickers does he have in all?

Circle the numbers.
Look for an addition clue.
In all means to add.

Equation: $6 + 2 = 8$ stickers

The words *all together* are another clue to add.

1 Circle the numbers and clues. Solve each word problem.

- One drawer has 8 glue sticks. The other has 5. How many glue sticks are there all together?

  Equation: $8 + 5 = 13$ glue sticks

a There are 5 cars in the parking lot. Then, 4 more come and park. How many cars are there in all?

Equation: ______________ cars

SELF CHECK	Mark how you feel	
Got it! ☐	Need help... ☐	I don't get it ☐

Practice

1 Circle the numbers and clues. Solve each word problem.

- There are 4 squirrels in one tree. There are 9 in another. How many squirrels are there in all?

  Equation: 4+9=13 squirrels

a There are 8 cookies on Ava's plate. There are 6 on Diego's plate. How many cookies are there in all?

Equation: ____________ cookies

b There are 9 books on one shelf. There are 8 books on the other. How many books are there all together?

Equation: ____________ books

c Jade has 6 feathers. She found 6 more. How many feathers are there in all?

Equation: ____________ feathers

d There are 3 fish in one bowl. There are 5 fish in another. How many fish are there all together?

Equation: ____________ fish

e The bike rack has 7 red bikes. It has 4 yellow bikes. How many bikes are there all together?

Equation: ____________ bikes

Word Problems with 3 Numbers

Word problems can have 3 numbers to add. Look for numbers and addition clues.

Example 1:

The table has 4 candles on the left and 4 candles on the right. There is 1 candle in the middle. How many candles are there all together?

Circle the numbers and clue words. Use the number line to add.

What other strategies could you use to add three numbers?

Equation: 4 + 4 + 1 = 9 candles

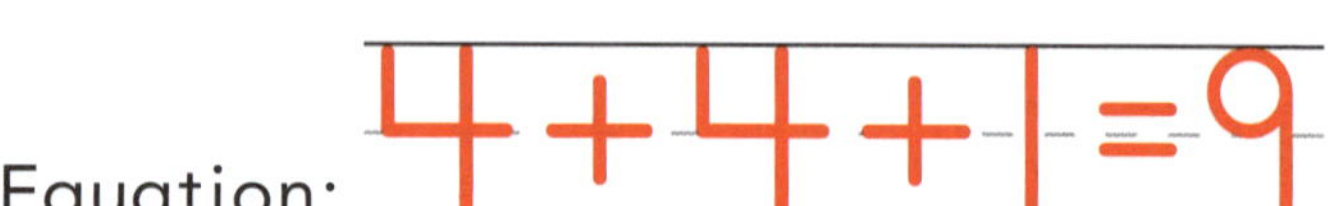

1 Circle the numbers and clues. Write the equation and the answer.

- The first flower has 6 petals. The second has 4 petals. The third has 8 petals. How many petals are there in all? Draw a picture.

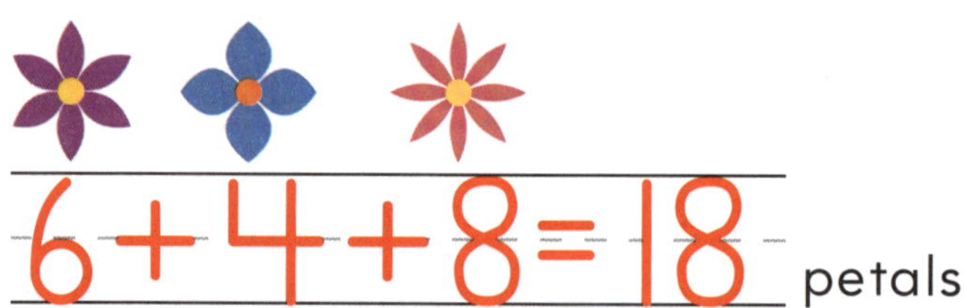

6 + 4 + 8 = 18 petals

a Jasmine found 8 short straws. She found 2 long straws. She found 6 bendy straws. How many straws are there all together? Draw a picture.

Equation: ____________________ straws

Practice

1 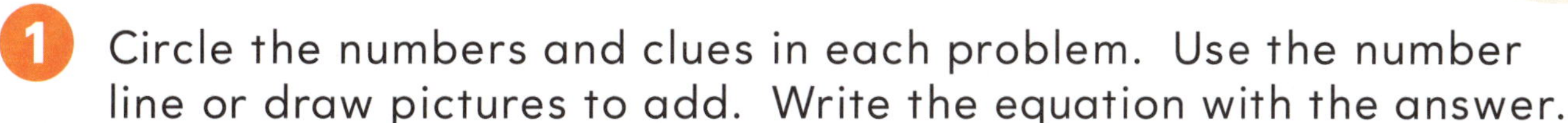
Circle the numbers and clues in each problem. Use the number line or draw pictures to add. Write the equation with the answer.

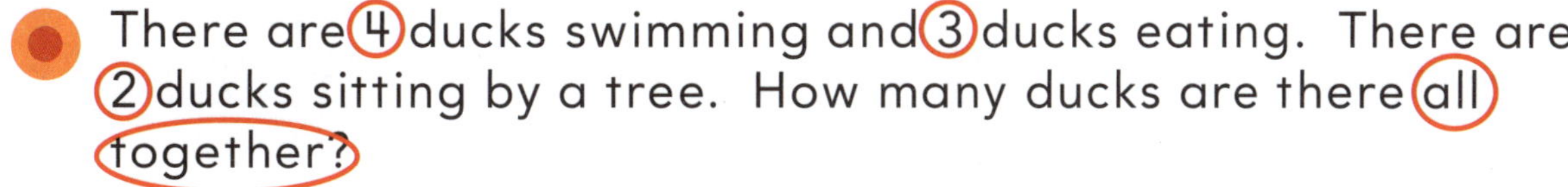
● There are 4 ducks swimming and 3 ducks eating. There are 2 ducks sitting by a tree. How many ducks are there all together?

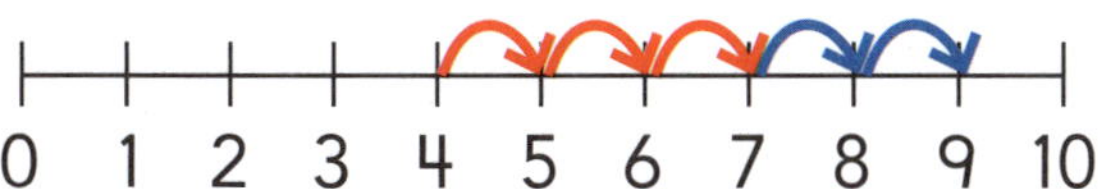

Equation: ______ ducks

a Owen listened to 3 pop songs and 5 rock songs. Then, he listened to 1 country song. How many songs did he listen to all together?

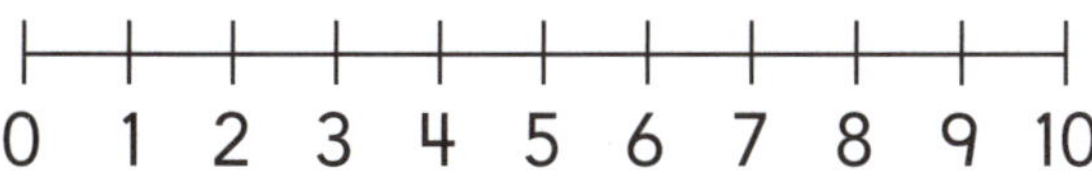

Equation: ______ songs

b There are 3 red balloons, 3 yellow balloons, and 5 blue balloons. How many balloons are there all together?

Equation: ______ balloons

c There were 6 plates in the cabinet and 5 on the counter. There were 3 on the table. How many plates were there in all?

Equation: ______ plates

Addition Review

1 Count to find how many in all.

a There are ______ in all.

b There are ______ in all.

c There are ______ in all.

2 Use the numbers and symbols to write true equations.

a 11 7 4 = + ______________________

b + = 1 8 7 ______________________

3 Draw pictures to help you add.

a 9 + 3 = ?

Draw 9 circles.	Draw 3 circles.	How many all together?

b 6 + 5 = ?

Draw 6 triangles.	Draw 5 triangles.	How many all together?

Review

4 Add. Circle the fingertips to show which fingers you used.

a 6 + 2 = ______

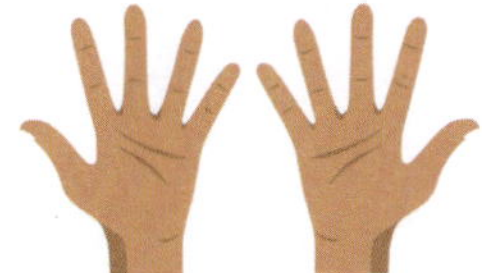

b 1 + 4 = ______

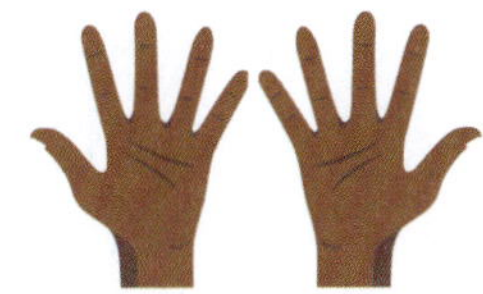

5 Count on using fingers.

a 7 + 2 = ______

c 6 + 4 = ______

b 8 + 8 = ______

d 9 + 5 = ______

6 Count on using the dots.

a 6 + 7 = ______

c 12 + 3 = ______

12 ● ● ●

b 8 + 4 = ______

8 ● ● ● ●

d 5 + 14 = ______

14 ● ● ● ● ●

Review

7 Use the ten frames to write number sentences.

a

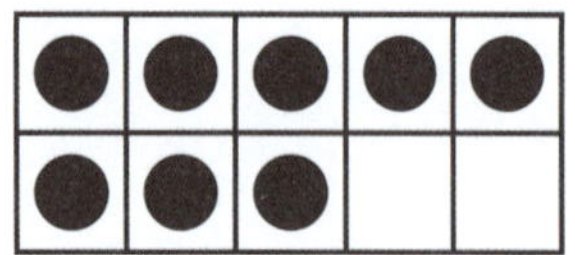

☐ + ☐ = 10

b

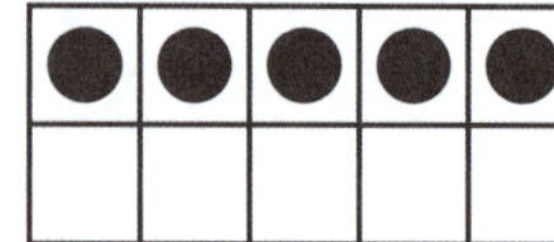

☐ + ☐ = 10

8 Write the missing number to make 10.

a 1 + ☐ = 10

b ☐ + 5 = 10

c 7 + ☐ = 10

d 2 + ☐ = 10

9 Use the number line to add. Show your jumps.

a 5 + 4 = ______

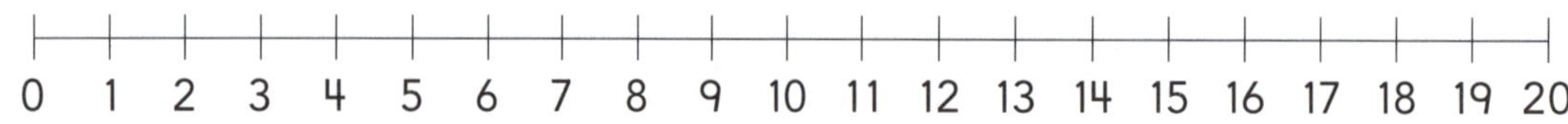

0 1 2 3 4 5 6 7 8 9 10 11 12 13 14 15 16 17 18 19 20

b 8 + 7 = ______

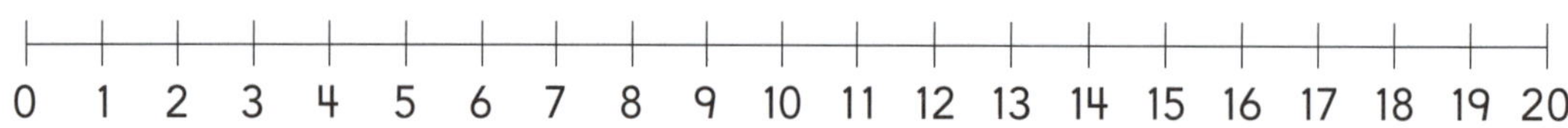

0 1 2 3 4 5 6 7 8 9 10 11 12 13 14 15 16 17 18 19 20

c 6 + 9 = ______

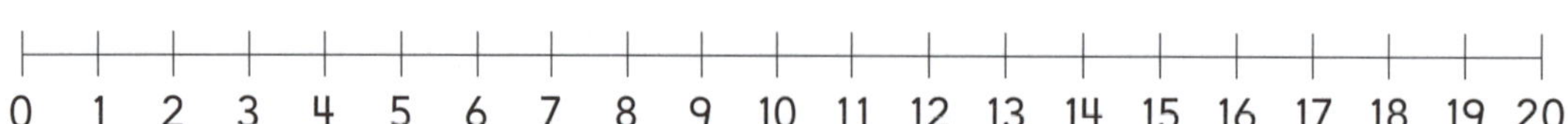

0 1 2 3 4 5 6 7 8 9 10 11 12 13 14 15 16 17 18 19 20

Review

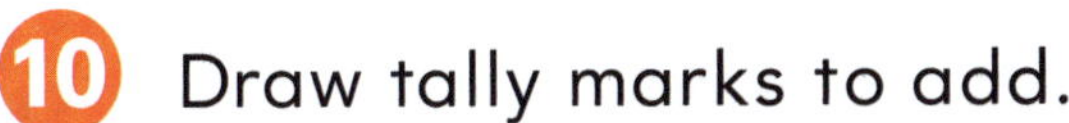

10 Draw tally marks to add.

a 3 + 3 = ______

b 7 + 9 = ______

c 3 + 6 = ______

11 Use the dominoes to add.

a 6 + 6 = ______

b 7 + 7 = ______

12 Write addition problems with the same values. Use different digits.

a 4 + 7 = ______ + ______

b 2 + 4 = ______ + ______

c 7 + 3 = ______ + ______

Review

13 Draw pictures to solve each problem.

a 1 + 7 + 6 = ______

b 4 + 2 + 5 = ______

14 Use a number line to solve each problem. Show your jumps.

a 3 + 5 + 6 = ______

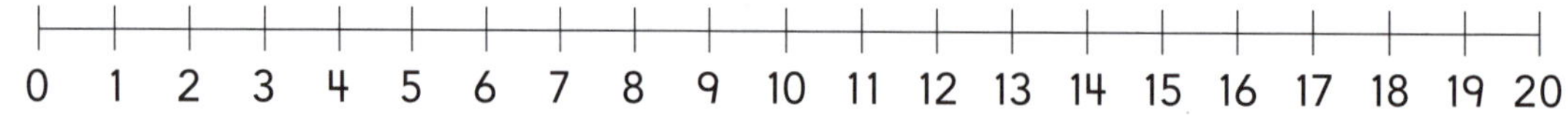

b 4 + 4 + 8 = ______

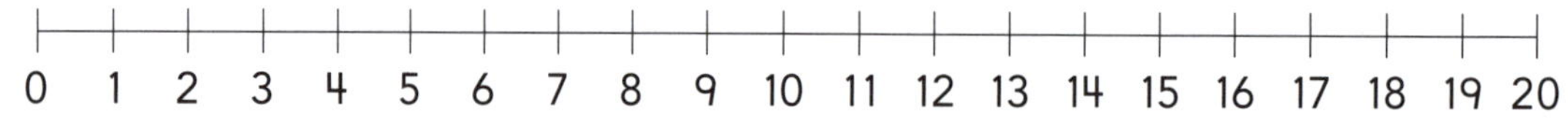

15 Make a 10 to solve each problem. Circle the digits that equal 10. Complete the new equation.

a 9 + 1 + 6

10 + ______ = ______

b 6 + 3 + 4

10 + ______ = ______

Review

16 Use your fingers to count on.

a 51 + 7 = ______

b 30 + 4 = ______

c 90 + 5 = ______

d 44 + 8 = ______

17 Use the hundred chart to add.

1	2	3	4	5	6	7	8	9	10
11	12	13	14	15	16	17	18	19	20
21	22	23	24	25	26	27	28	29	30
31	32	33	34	35	36	37	38	39	40
41	42	43	44	45	46	47	48	49	50
51	52	53	54	55	56	57	58	59	60
61	62	63	64	65	66	67	68	69	70
71	72	73	74	75	76	77	78	79	80
81	82	83	84	85	86	87	88	89	90
91	92	93	94	95	96	97	98	99	100

a 36 + 2 = ______

b 15 + 4 = ______

c 82 + 7 = ______

d 74 + 9 = ______

Review

18 Use the hundred chart on page 115 to add.

a

26 + 40 = ______

26 + 50 = ______

b

47 + 20 = ______

47 + 30 = ______

c

51 + 10 = ______

51 + 20 = ______

d

68 + 20 = ______

68 + 30 = ______

19 Write each problem vertically. Write the answer.

a 71 + 7

b 35 + 2

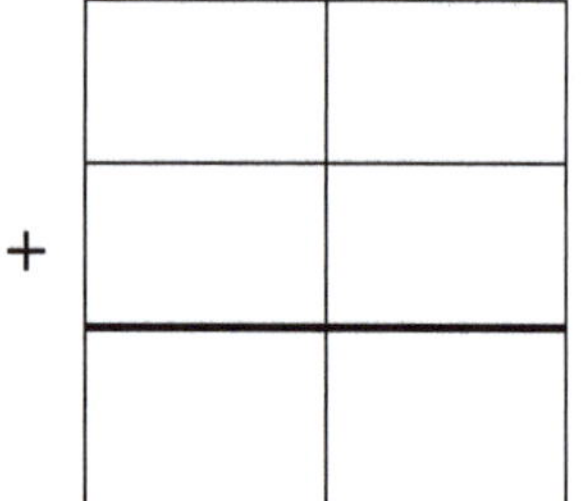

c 93 + 3

d 64 + 5

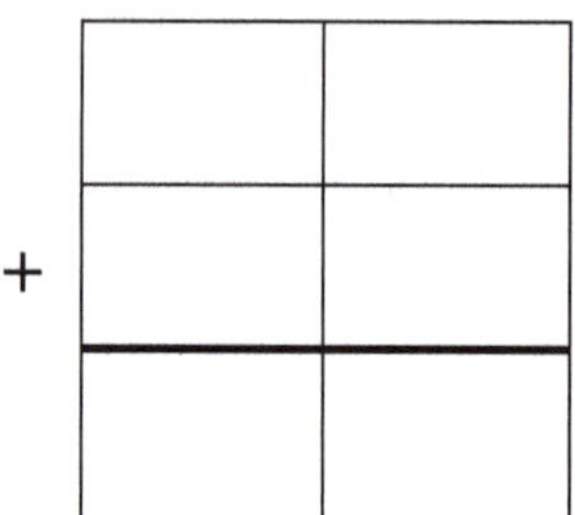

Review

20 Circle a 10. Draw the regrouped number. Then, write the number.

	Picture	Regroup	Number
a			
b	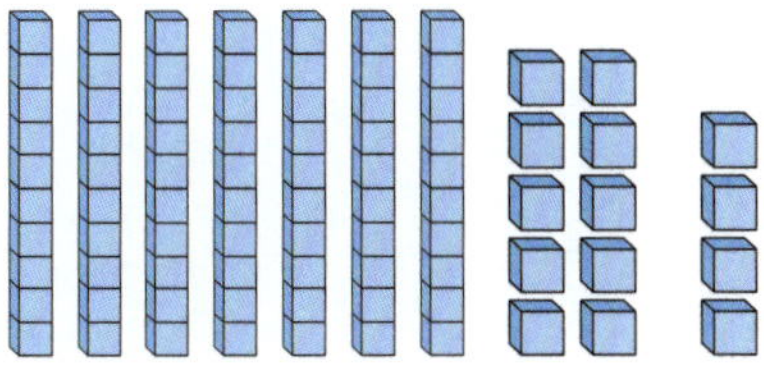		
c	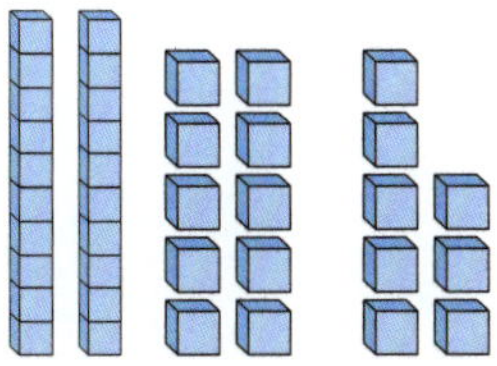		

21 Draw tens and ones to show each problem. Make a 10 and regroup. Write the answer.

a 57 + 4 = ______

b 89 + 3 = ______

c 19 + 5 = ______

Review

22 Draw the answer with pictures. Then, write the addition problem vertically. Write the answer.

a

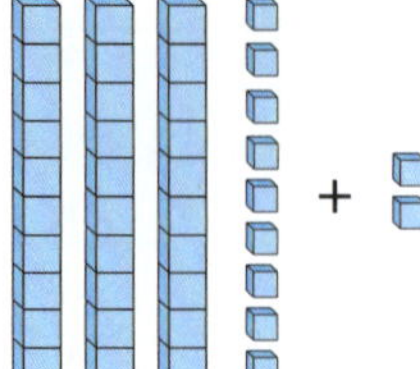

	3	9
+		2

b

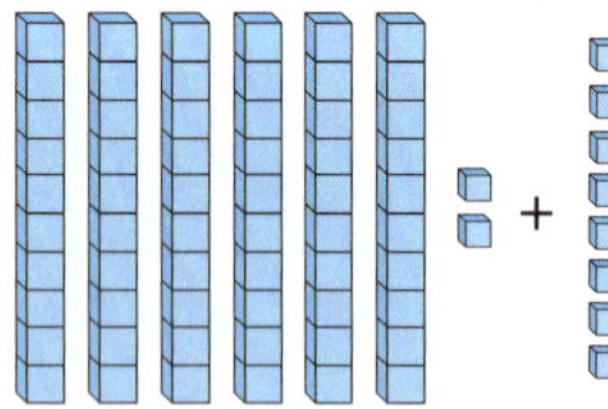

	6	2
+		8

c

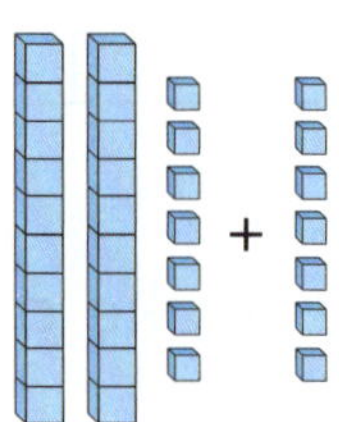

	2	7
+		7

23 Add.

a

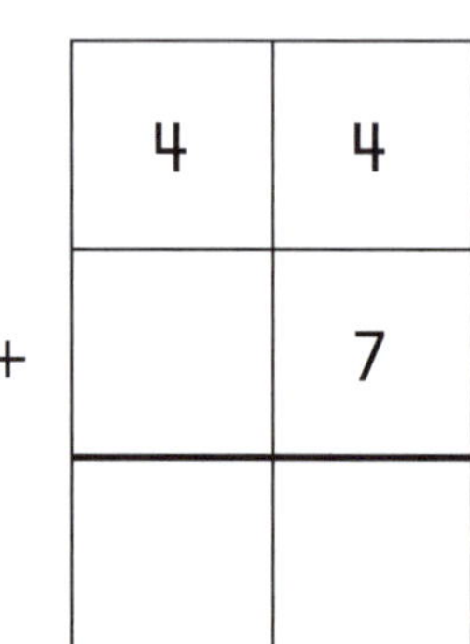

	4	4
+		7

b

	6	7
+		3

c

	7	6
+		8

d

	2	8
+		5

Review

24 Circle the numbers and clues. Write the equation with the answer.

a Lucia has 8 pieces of candy. Kobe has 5. How many pieces of candy do they have in all?

______________ pieces of candy

b There are 5 people waiting in line. Then, 3 more people join the line. How many people are there all together?

______________ people

c There are 8 green apples and 6 red apples. How many apples are there in all?

______________ apples

d Jasmine has 4 blue pens and 4 black pens. She also has 1 red pen. How many pens does she have all together?

______________ pens

e There are 6 daisies. There are also 2 roses and 4 sunflowers. How many flowers are there in all?

______________ flowers

Model Subtraction

Subtract **means to take away. You find out how many are left. You can use pictures to help you subtract.**

Example:

6 – 2 = ?

It starts with a large group. Then, some are taken away.

How many birds are left? Count them.

6 – 2 = 4 birds

When you subtract, the group gets smaller. The answer is less than you started with.

1 Use the pictures to find out how many are left.

4 – 1 = ?

3 vases are left.

a 8 – 2 = ?

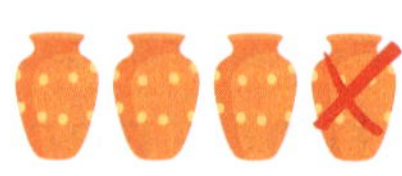

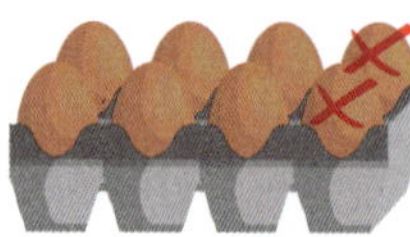

_____ eggs are left.

b 7 – 3 = ?

_____ buttons are left.

SELF CHECK	Mark how you feel	
Got it!	Need help...	I don't get it

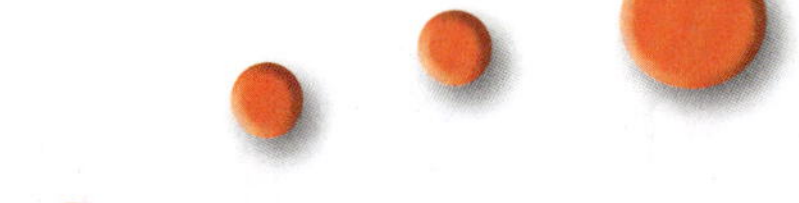

Practice

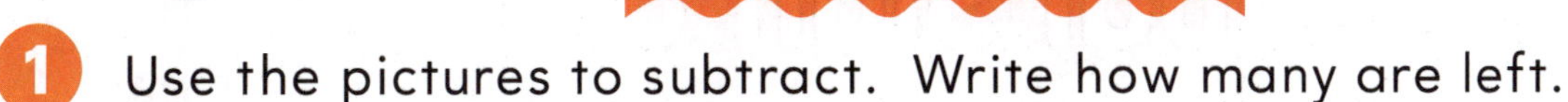

1 Use the pictures to subtract. Write how many are left.

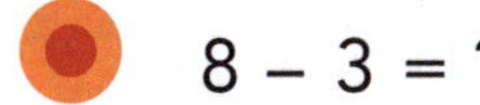

8 – 3 = ?

5 ice cubes are left.

a 4 – 2 = ?

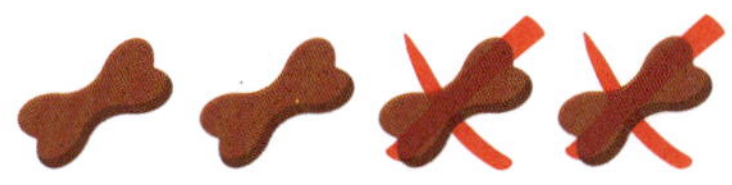

_____ treats are left.

b 5 – 1 = ?

_____ flowers are left.

c 9 – 2 = ?

_____ hot dogs are left.

d 12 – 6 = ?

_____ treees are left.

e 15 – 7 = ?

_____ papers are left.

Equal Sign and Subtraction Sign

There are symbols to use to make a subtraction equation.

The number you start with goes first.

5 – 2 = 3

The subtraction sign goes next. It is also called a ***minus sign***.

Both sides of the equal sign should have the same value.

Example 1:

Putting the numbers in the right order is important.

8 – 5 = 3

Start with the total number in the group.

This is how many are taken away.

This is how many are left.

1 Circle the subtraction equation that is true.

●	(9 – 8 = 1)	8 – 1 = 9	1 – 9 = 8
a	1 – 3 = 4	4 – 3 = 1	3 – 1 = 4
b	4 – 5 = 9	4 – 9 = 5	9 – 5 = 4

When you subtract, the largest number goes first.

SELF CHECK	Mark how you feel	
Got it!  	Need help...  	I don't get it 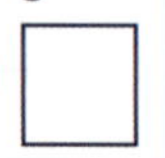

Practice

1 Circle the subtraction equation that is true.

●	7 – 2 = 5 (circled)	5 – 2 = 7	2 – 5 = 7
a	4 – 1 = 3	3 – 1 = 4	1 – 3 = 4
b	6 – 2 = 8	8 – 2 = 6	2 – 6 = 8
c	4 – 5 = 1	1 – 5 = 4	5 – 4 = 1
d	9 – 1 = 8	8 – 1 = 9	1 – 9 = 8
e	1 – 2 = 3	3 – 1 = 2	2 – 1 = 3

2 Use the numbers and symbols to write a true subtraction equation.

● 3 1 2 – =  

3 – 1 = 2

a 2 7 9 – = ______ ______ ______ ______ ______

b – = 0 6 6 ______ ______ ______ ______ ______

c 5 1 4 – = ______ ______ ______ ______ ______

d – = 5 8 3 ______ ______ ______ ______ ______

Draw a Picture

You can draw pictures to show subtraction.

Example 1:

Use pictures to solve 5 – 2.

Draw the whole group. This is the largest number.

Draw simple pictures. It will save you time and effort!

Now take 2 away. You can show this by crossing them off.

There are 3 left, so 5 – 2 = 3.

Example 2:

Draw a picture to show 9 – 5.

Draw the whole group. Cross off the ones you take away.

9 – 5 = 4

1. Use the pictures to subtract. Cross off the number you take away.

-  5 – 4 = 1

a 8 – 5 = ______

b 12 – 8 = ______

SELF CHECK	Mark how you feel	
Got it! ☐	Need help... ☐	I don't get it ☐

Practice

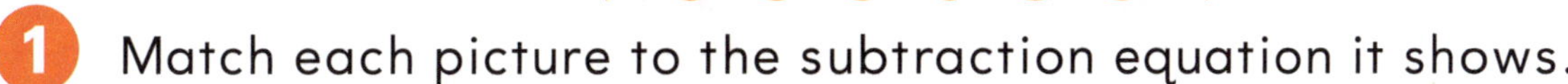

1 Match each picture to the subtraction equation it shows.

 9 – 3 = 6

a  5 – 2 = 3

b  15 – 9 = 6

c  14 – 7 = 7

2 Use the pictures to subtract. Cross off the number you take away.

  8 – 4 = 4

a  12 – 5 = ______

b  6 – 2 = ______

c  13 – 8 = ______

d  11 – 2 = ______

3 Use the pictures to subtract. Cross off the number you take away.

●  10 – 5 = 5

a 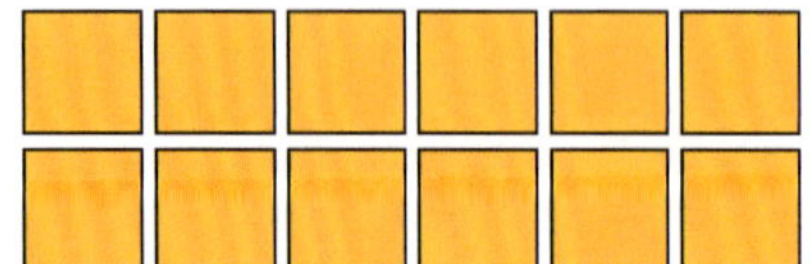 12 – 8 = ______

b  7 – 5 = ______

c  9 – 3 = ______

d 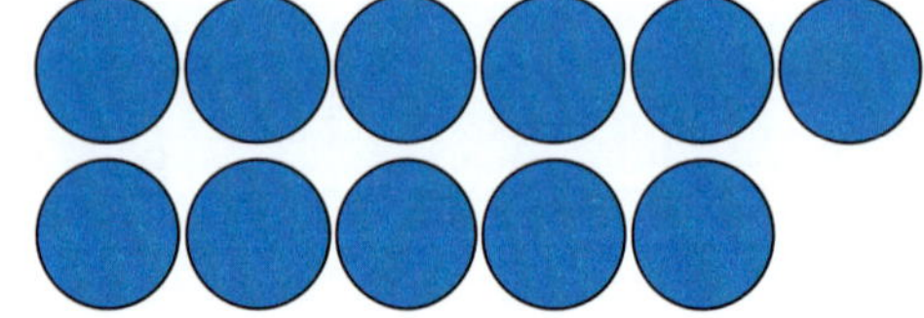 11 – 6 = ______

e  10 – 2 = ______

f  8 – 5 = ______

g  6 – 5 = ______

Use Your Fingers

You can use your fingers to subtract. Fingers work best when you are starting with 10 or less.

Example 1:

Use your fingers to solve 5 – 3.

5 is the number you are starting with.

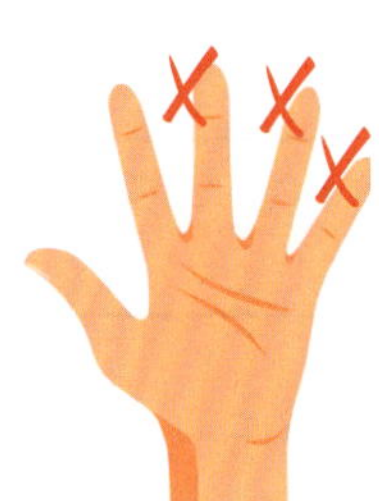

Since 3 were taken away, put 3 fingers down. Now there are 2.

5 – 3 = 2

Your turn

1 Use your fingers to subtract.

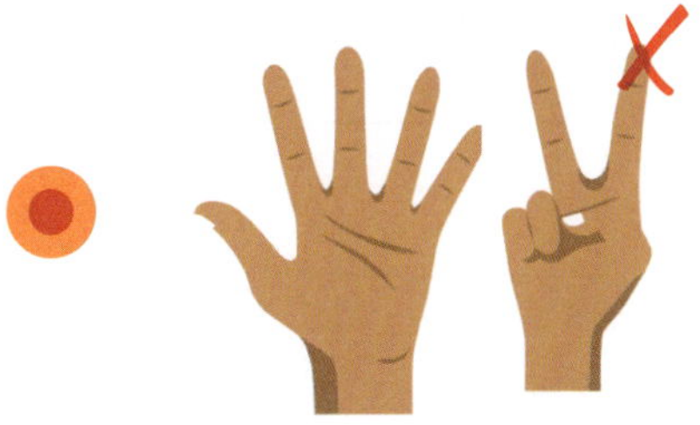

7 – 1 = 6

a

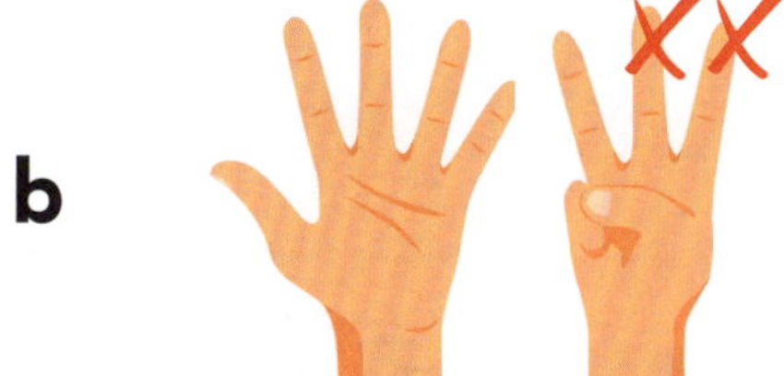

10 – 7 = ______

b

8 – 2 = ______

SELF CHECK Mark how you feel

Got it! ☐ Need help... ☐ I don't get it ☐

Practice

1 Cross off the fingers that are subtracted. Write the answer.

 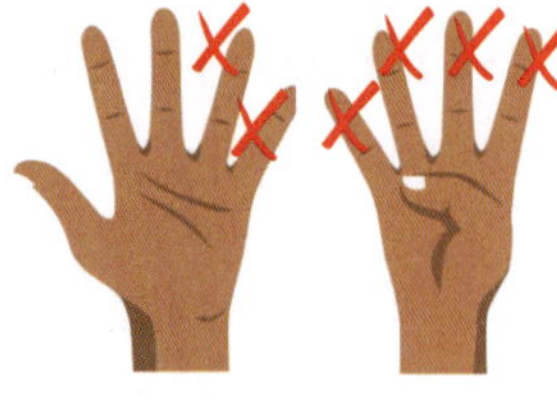 9 – 6 = 3

a 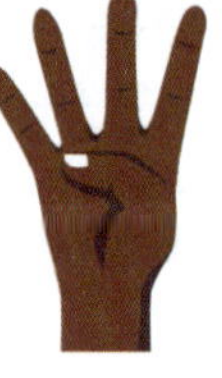 4 – 3 = ______

b 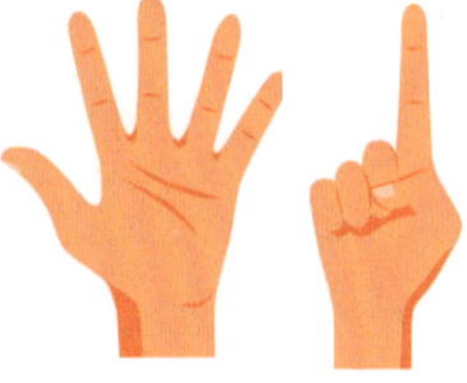 6 – 3 = ______

c 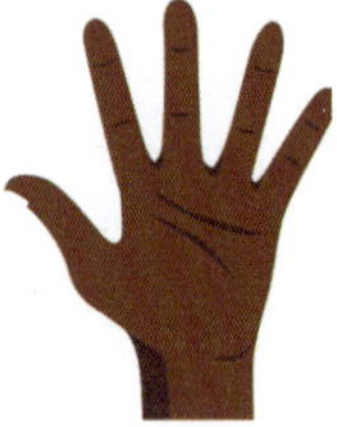 5 – 1 = ______

2 Use your fingers to subtract.

 9 – 1 = 8

a 8 – 4 = ______

b 3 – 3 = ______

c 10 – 2 = ______

d 7 – 5 = ______

e 4 – 1 = ______

Count Back

You can count back to subtract. You can count back by listing numbers. You can use a picture or your fingers to count back.

Example 1:

Use a number list to count back. Solve 7 – 3.

7 6 5 4 ← You are taking away 3. So, count back 3 times. The last number is the answer.

↑ Write 7. This is where you start.

7 – 3 = 4

Example 2:

Use pictures to count back. Solve 9 – 5.

9 8 7 6 5 4

9 – 5 = 4

Practice counting back a few times.

Example 3:

Use your fingers to count back. Solve 8 – 2.

7 6

8 – 2 = 6

You are taking away 2. So hold up 2 fingers. Count back.

1 Use fingers to count back.

9 8 7 6 5 4

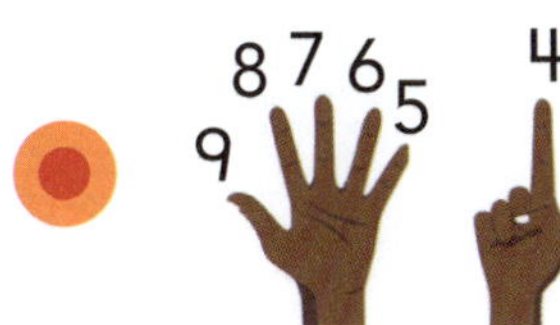

10 – 6 = 4

a

5 – 4 = ______

SELF CHECK	Mark how you feel	
Got it! ☐	Need help... ☐	I don't get it ☐

Practice

1 Make a number list to count back. Write the answer.

● 14 13 12 11 10 9 8 7 14 − 7 = 7

a 10 10 − 4 = ______

b 11 11 − 3 = ______

c 6 6 − 2 = ______

2 Use the pictures to count back. Write the equation with the answer.

●	9 ●●●	9 − 3 = 6
a	5 ▲▲	___ − ___ = ___
b	12 ♥♥♥♥♥♥♥	___ − ___ = ___
c	13 (10 flowers)	___ − ___ = ___

3 Use your fingers to count back. Write the answer.

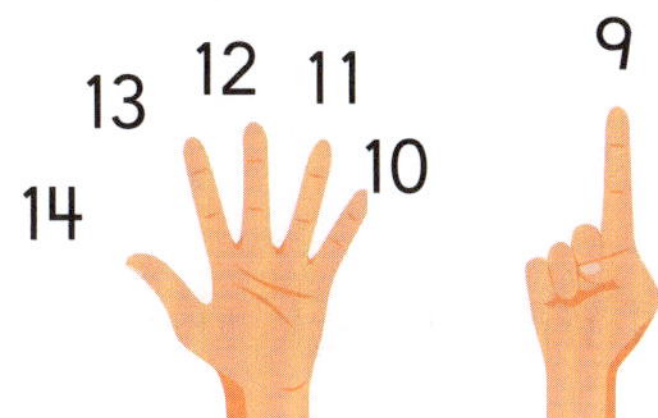

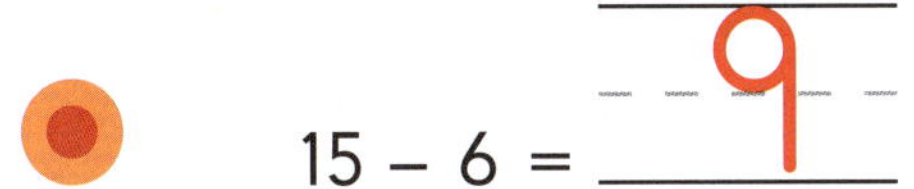

a 9 – 8 = ______

b 12 – 7 = ______

c 5 – 1 = ______

d 13 – 9 = ______

4 Subtract. Use any strategy.

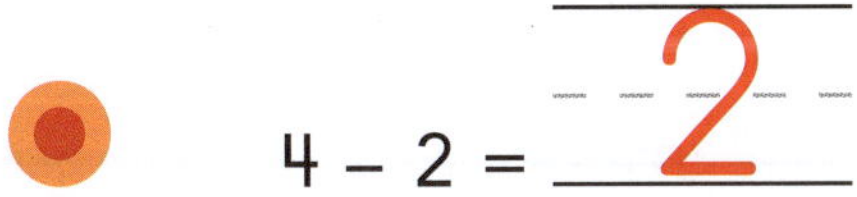

a 6 – 3 = ______

b 10 – 2 = ______

c 8 – 6 = ______

d 14 – 9 = ______

e 16 – 8 = ______

Use a Number Line

You can use a number line to subtract. You can jump back to take away.

Example 1:

Start at the larger number in the equation. Jump back the number of spaces you are taking away.

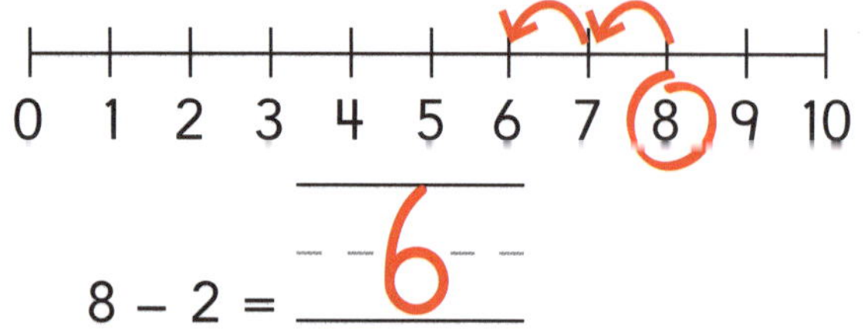

Subtracting is the opposite of adding. Go the opposite way on the number line.

Example 2:

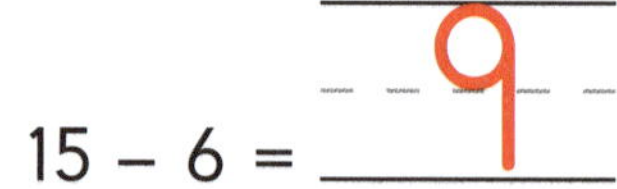

Your turn

1 Write the equation shown on each number line.

5 – 3 = 2

a

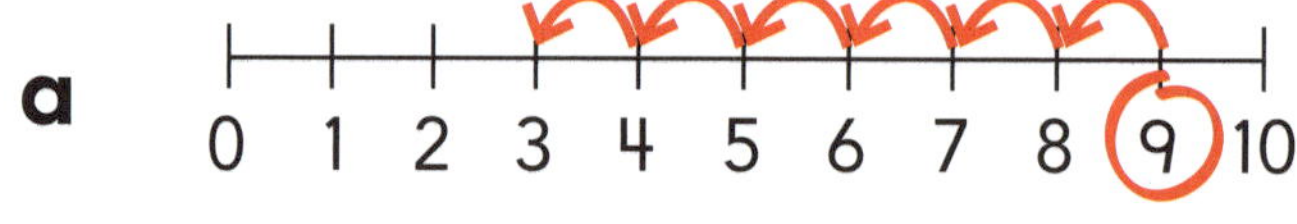

____ – ____ = ____

b

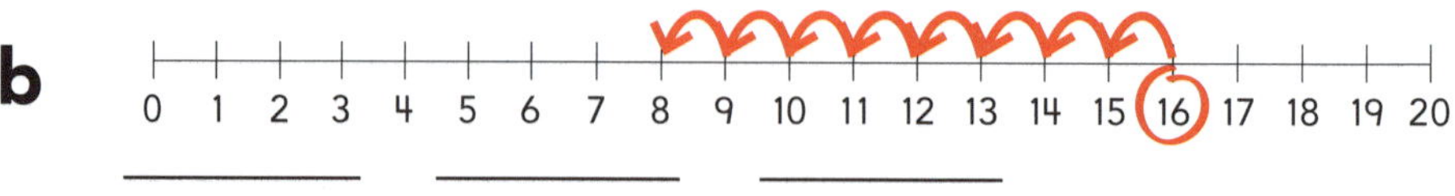

____ – ____ = ____

Practice

1. Use the number lines to subtract. Show your jumps.

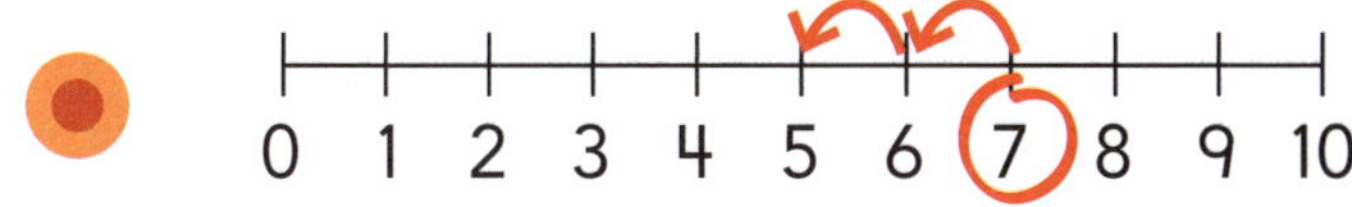

0 1 2 3 4 5 6 7 8 9 10

7 – 2 = 5

a 0 1 2 3 4 5 6 7 8 9 10

8 – 6 = ______

b 0 1 2 3 4 5 6 7 8 9 10

10 – 5 = ______

c 0 1 2 3 4 5 6 7 8 9 10

4 – 1 = ______

d 0 1 2 3 4 5 6 7 8 9 10

6 – 3 = ______

e

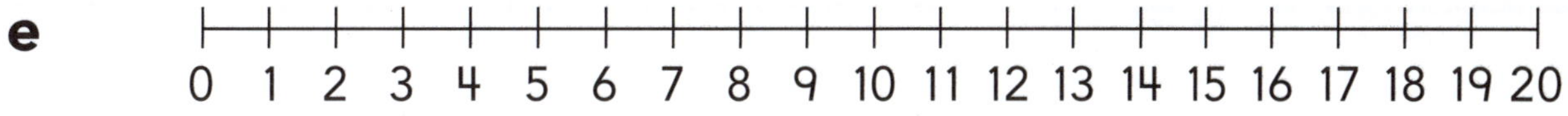

0 1 2 3 4 5 6 7 8 9 10 11 12 13 14 15 16 17 18 19 20

15 – 5 = ______

f 0 1 2 3 4 5 6 7 8 9 10 11 12 13 14 15 16 17 18 19 20

12 – 4 = ______

2 Write a number sentence to match each number line.

4 – 2 = 2

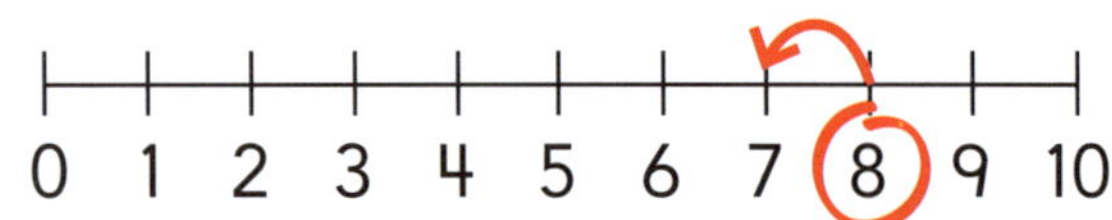

a ____ – ____ = ____

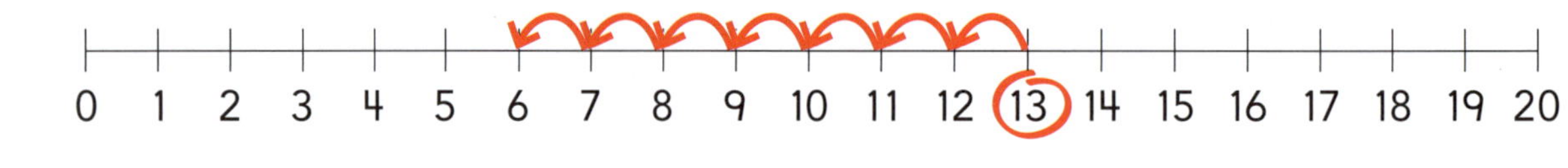

b ____ – ____ = ____

3 Subtract. Use any strategy.

13 – 3 = 10

a 9 – 6 = ____

b 18 – 9 = ____

c 5 – 1 = ____

Use Addition Facts

Knowing addition helps you learn subtraction. They are opposites.

Example 1:

Think about 4 + 2 = 6. Now, think about 6 – 2 = 4.

These equations use the same three numbers. They are related equations.

Example 2:

5 + 2 = 7

7 – 5 = ?

Both equations use a 5 and 7. They both must also use a 2. So, 7 – 5 = 2.

1 Use addition to subtract. Write the missing number in each equation.

- 9 + 2 = 11 11 – 9 = 2
- **a** 4 + 8 = 12 12 – 8 = ☐
- **b** 6 + 4 = 10 10 – 4 = ☐

You end with the biggest number in addition. You begin with it in subtraction. They are opposites!

SELF CHECK Mark how you feel

Got it! ☐	Need help... ☐	I don't get it ☐

Practice

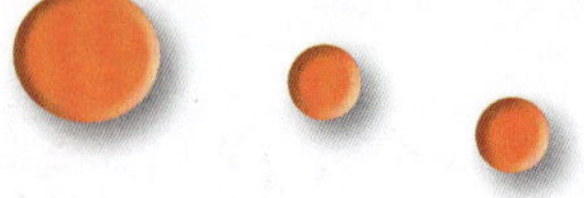

1 Write the missing number for each subtraction equation.

● $8 + 6 = 14$

$14 - 6 = $ [8]

b $2 + 3 = 5$

$5 - 3 = $ [ ]

a $1 + 8 = 9$

$9 - $ [ ] $= 1$

c $7 + 3 = 10$

$10 - $ [ ] $= 7$

2 Complete the related equations.

● [1] $+ 3 = 4$

$4 - 3 = $ [1]

c $6 + 3 = $ [ ]

[ ] $- 3 = 6$

a [ ] $+ 4 = 7$

$7 - 4 = $ [ ]

d $9 + $ [ ] $= 15$

$15 - $ [ ] $= 9$

b [ ] $+ 5 = 13$

$13 - 5 = $ [ ]

e $2 + 4 = $ [ ]

[ ] $- 4 = 2$

3 Match the related number sentences.

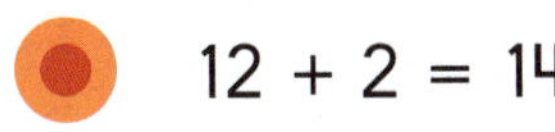

●	12 + 2 = 14	7 – 3 = 4
a	10 + 2 = 12	8 – 7 = 1
b	8 + 3 = 11	14 – 2 = 12
c	1 + 7 = 8	12 – 2 = 10
d	4 + 3 = 7	11 – 3 = 8

4 Write a related addition or subtraction equation.

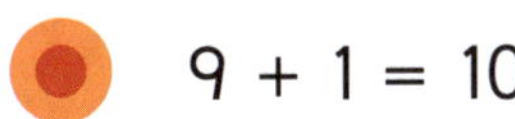

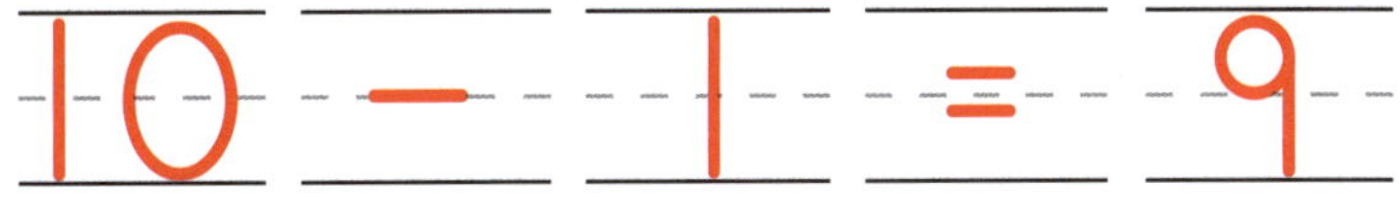

a 7 + 8 = 15 ______________

b 1 + 5 = 6 ______________

c 13 – 10 = 3 ______________

d 7 + 5 = 12 ______________

Fact Families

A fact family is a group of related equations. 2 are addition and 2 are subtraction. All of the equations use the same 3 numbers.

Example 1:

You can create a fact family house to show the number sentences.

These are the 3 related numbers.

The largest number goes at the top of the roof.

10
7 3

$7 + 3 = 10$
$3 + 7 = 10$
$10 - 7 = 3$
$10 - 3 = 7$

There are 2 addition equations.

There are 2 subtraction equations.

1 Write the missing number in each fact family.

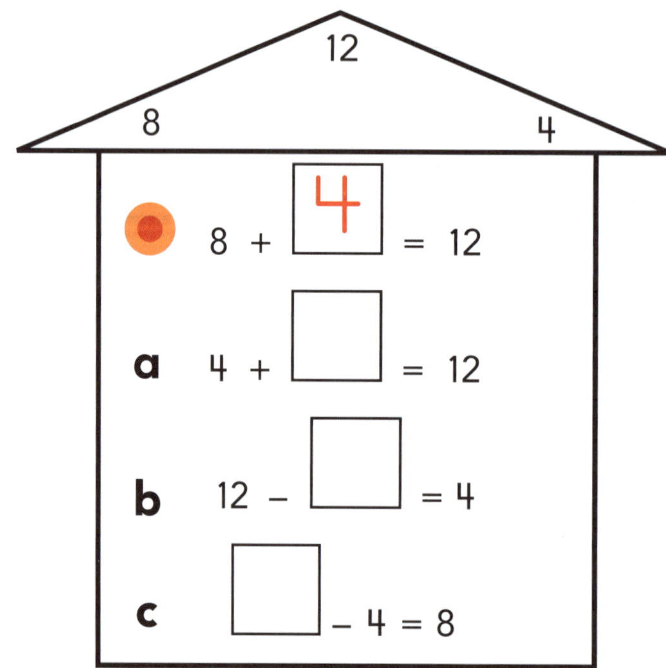

SELF CHECK Mark how you feel

Got it!	Need help...	I don't get it
☐	☐	☐

Practice

1 Write the missing numbers in each fact family.

a

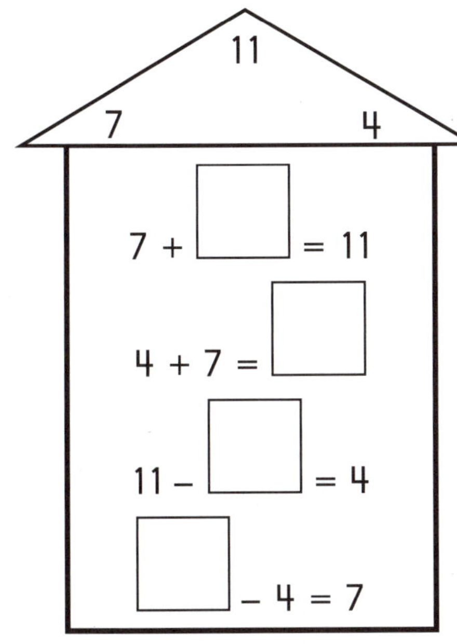

b

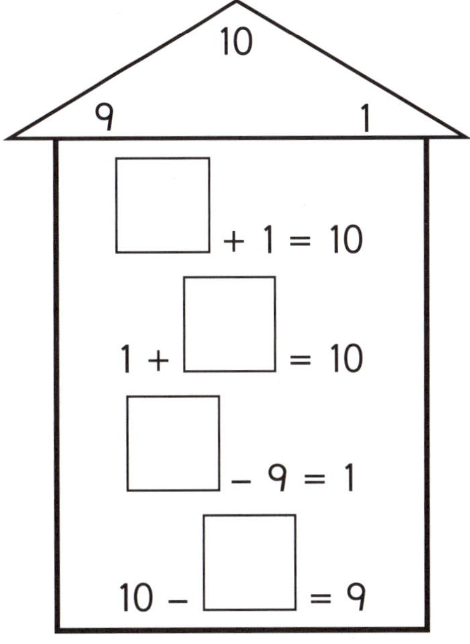

2 Write 4 number sentences for each fact family.

a

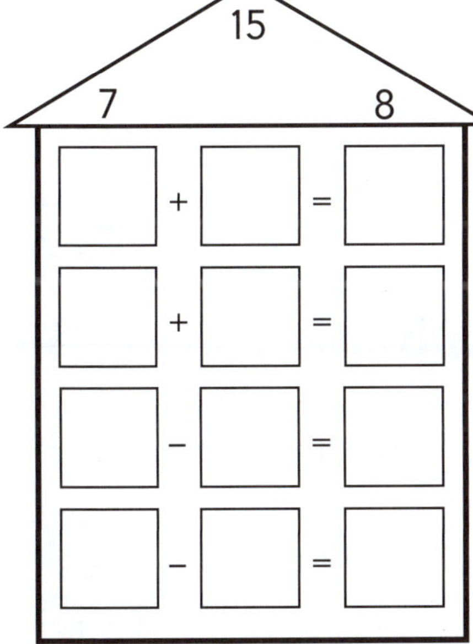

b

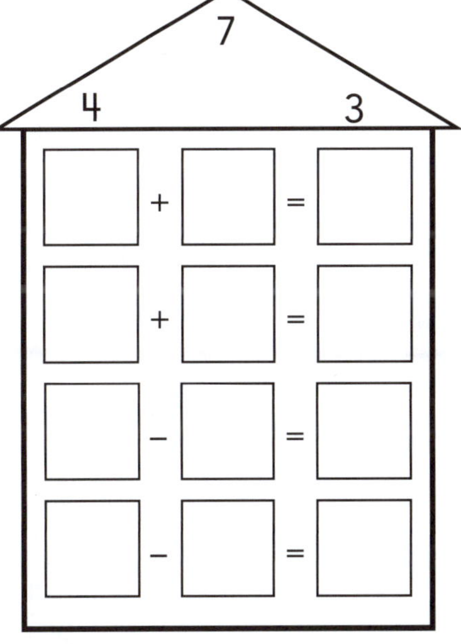

3 Write the missing number of the fact family. Then, write its 4 number sentences.

a

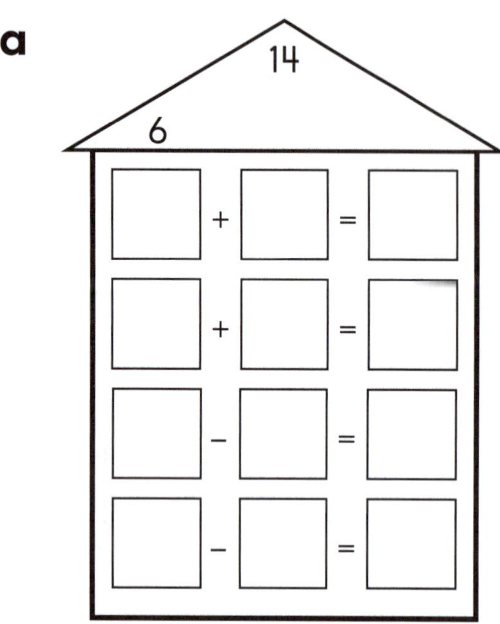

b

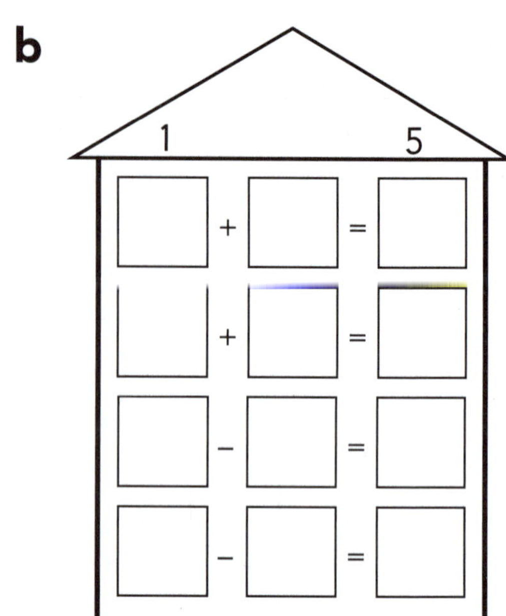

4 Write 2 numbers, or parts, for each fact family. There is more than one way to complete each one.

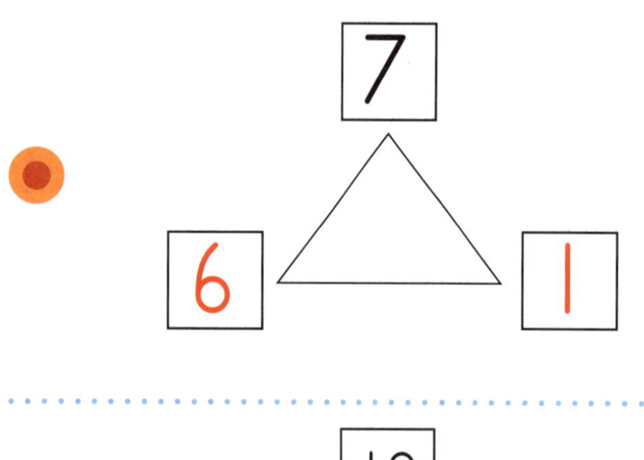

b

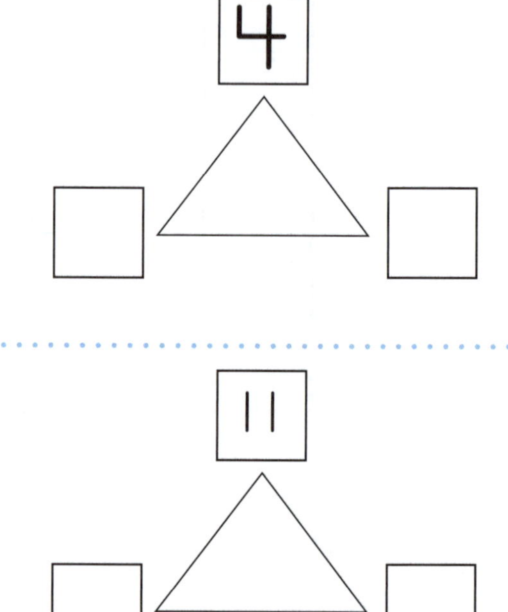

a

12

c

Subtraction: True or False?

You can find equal subtraction problems. Subtract on both sides of the equal sign. If the problems have the same value, they are equal.

Example 1:

Are these subtraction problems equal?  yes no

9 – 4 = 6 – 1

5 5

Both sides have the same value.

Example 2:

Are these subtraction problems equal? yes no 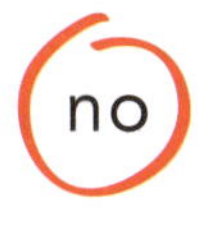

4 – 2 = 6 – 3

2 3

The sides have different values.

 **1** Circle the subtraction problem that has the same value.

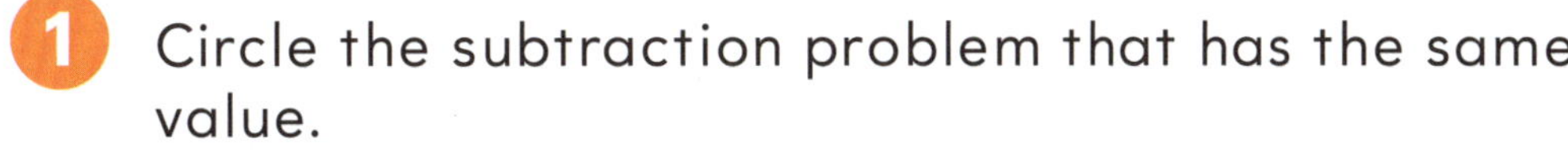

● 9 – 2 = ?

7

10 – 6	8 – 3	13 – 6
4	5	7

a 14 – 4 = ?

12 – 2	11 – 3	15 – 6

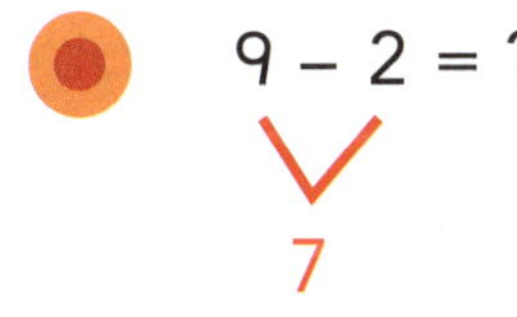

SELF CHECK	Mark how you feel	
Got it! ☐	Need help... ☐	I don't get it ☐

Practice

1 Are the subtraction problems equal? Circle ***yes*** or ***no***.

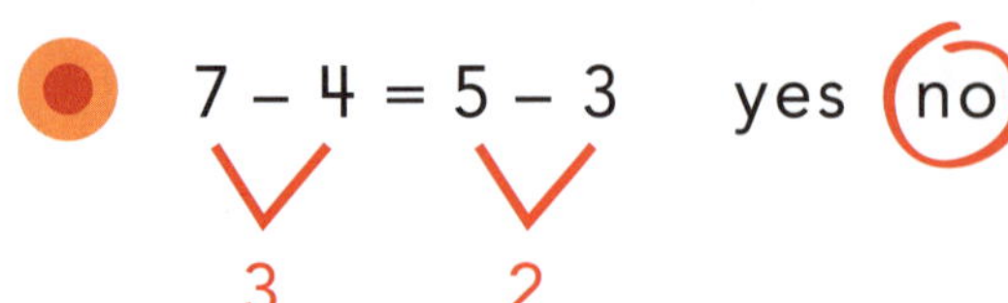

7 – 4 = 5 – 3 yes no

a 11 – 5 = 9 – 4 yes no

b 5 – 1 = 6 – 2 yes no

c 16 – 6 = 13 – 3 yes no

d 9 – 2 = 8 – 2 yes no

e 10 – 4 = 12 – 6 yes no

2 Circle all subtraction problems that have the same value as the given number.

9

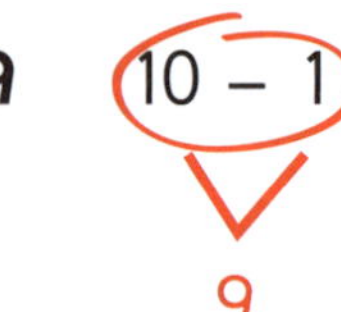

a	**4**	6 – 2	5 – 1	11 – 6	9 – 6
b	**6**	8 – 3	10 – 4	8 – 2	9 – 3
c	**3**	5 – 2	6 – 4	10 – 7	12 – 6

3 Write subtraction problems that are equal.

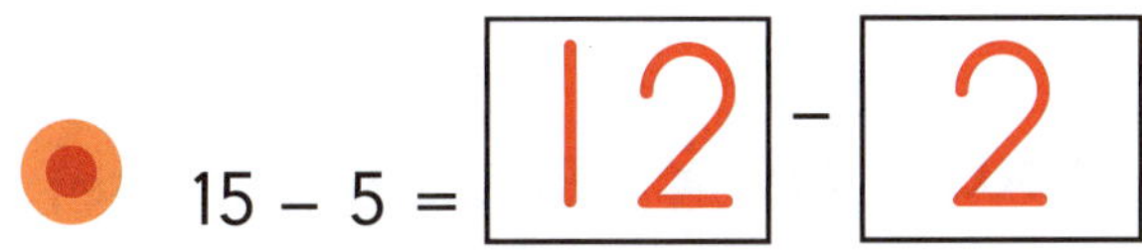

15 – 5 = 12 – 2

a 5 – 1 = ☐ – ☐

b 11 – 2 = ☐ – ☐

c 9 – 6 = ☐ – ☐

d 13 – 8 = ☐ – ☐

e 6 – 1 = ☐ – ☐

4 Write equal subtraction problems.

12 – 7 = 11 – 6

a ☐ – ☐ = ☐ – ☐

b ☐ – ☐ = ☐ – ☐

c ☐ – ☐ = ☐ – ☐

d ☐ – ☐ = ☐ – ☐

e ☐ – ☐ = ☐ – ☐

Subtraction Within 10

You can use many strategies to subtract when the large number is 10 or less.

Example 1: Use your fingers.

7 – 4 = 3

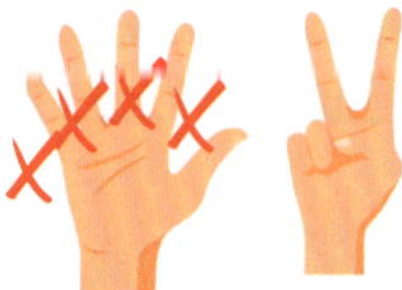

Example 2: Draw a picture.

6 – 4 = 2

Example 3: Count back.

10 – 3 = 7

10 ●●●
9 8 7

1 Subtract. Use any strategy.

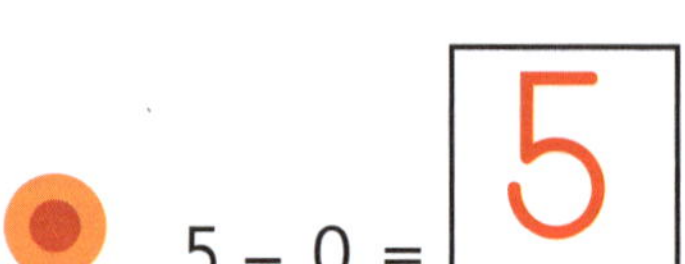

● 5 – 0 = 5

a 10 – 3 = ☐

b 6 – 1 = ☐

SELF CHECK Mark how you feel

Got it!	Need help...	I don't get it
 	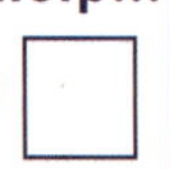 	

Practice

1 Subtract. Use any strategy.

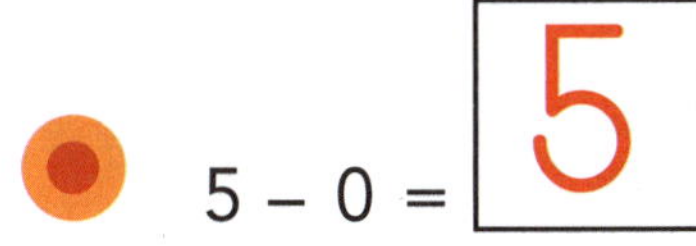

5 − 0 = 5

a 8 − 1 = ☐

b 7 − 3 = ☐

c 6 − 5 = ☐

d 4 − 2 = ☐

e 10 − 2 = ☐

f 5 − 1 = ☐

g 1 − 0 = ☐

h 5 − 4 = ☐

i 9 − 7 = ☐

j 9 − 5 = ☐

k 1 − 1 = ☐

l 7 − 0 = ☐

m 7 − 2 = ☐

Subtraction Within 20

When the large number is more than 10, these are helpful strategies to subtract.

Example 1: Use a number line.

12 – 4 = 8

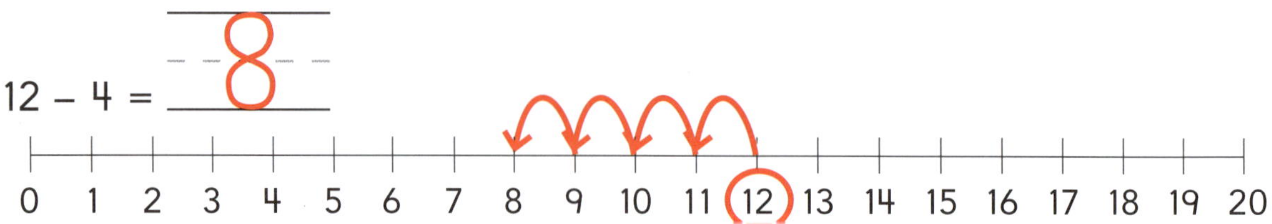

Example 2: Use addition facts.

16 – 9 = ?

9 + ? = 16

Since 9 + 7 = 16, we know that 16 – 9 = 7.

Example 3: Count back.

16 – 6 = 10

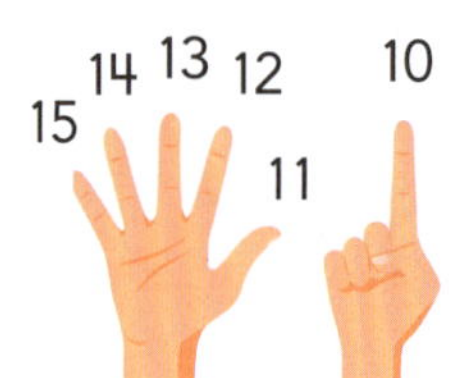

Which of these strategies do you like best? Do you know any others?

1 Subtract. Use any strategy.

15 – 6 = 9

a 17 – 8 = ☐

b 12 – 7 = ☐

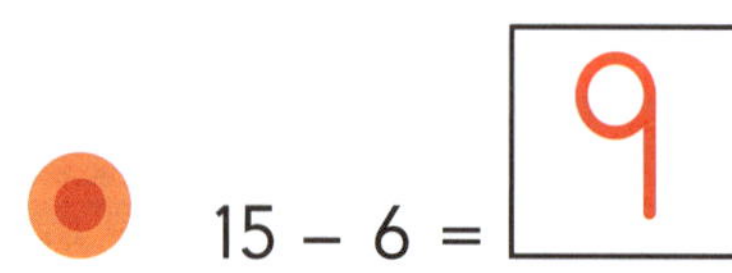

Practice

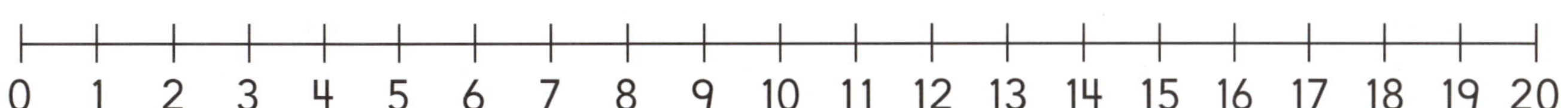

●	14 – 6 = 8	g	20 – 10 = ☐
a	16 – 4 = ☐	h	17 – 7 = ☐
b	14 – 7 = ☐	i	15 – 6 = ☐
c	20 – 5 = ☐	j	18 – 9 = ☐
d	15 – 6 = ☐	k	12 – 2 = ☐
e	11 – 2 = ☐	l	12 – 6 = ☐
f	16 – 7 = ☐	m	15 – 9 = ☐

Subtraction Word Problems

Subtraction can be written as a story. Look for the numbers. Look for a subtraction clue. Then, solve the problem.

Example 1: Circle the important numbers.

There are 10 pieces of candy. Then, 4 are eaten.

How many pieces are left?

The words *are left* are a subtraction clue.

Equation: 10 − 4 = 6 pieces of candy

1. Circle the numbers and clues. Write an equation for each word problem.

- There are 11 dogs at the shelter. Then, 4 of them are adopted. How many dogs are left?

Equation: 11 − 4 = 7 dogs

a There are 14 ladybugs. Then, 7 fly away. How many ladybugs are left?

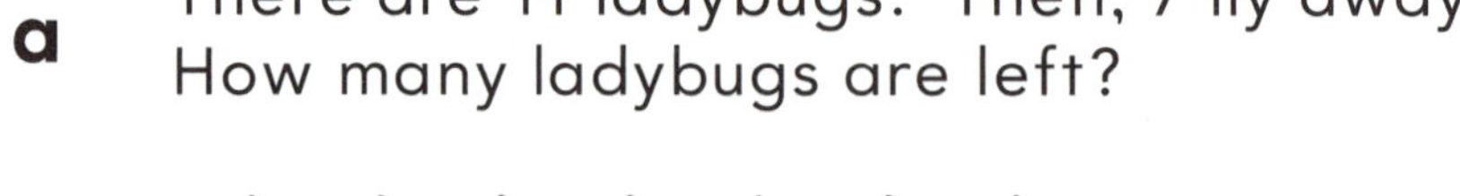

Equation: ____________ ladybugs

The words *how many more* are also a subtraction clue.

SELF CHECK Mark how you feel

Got it! ☐ Need help... ☐ I don't get it ☐

Practice

1 Circle the numbers and clues. Solve each word problem. You can draw pictures to help you.

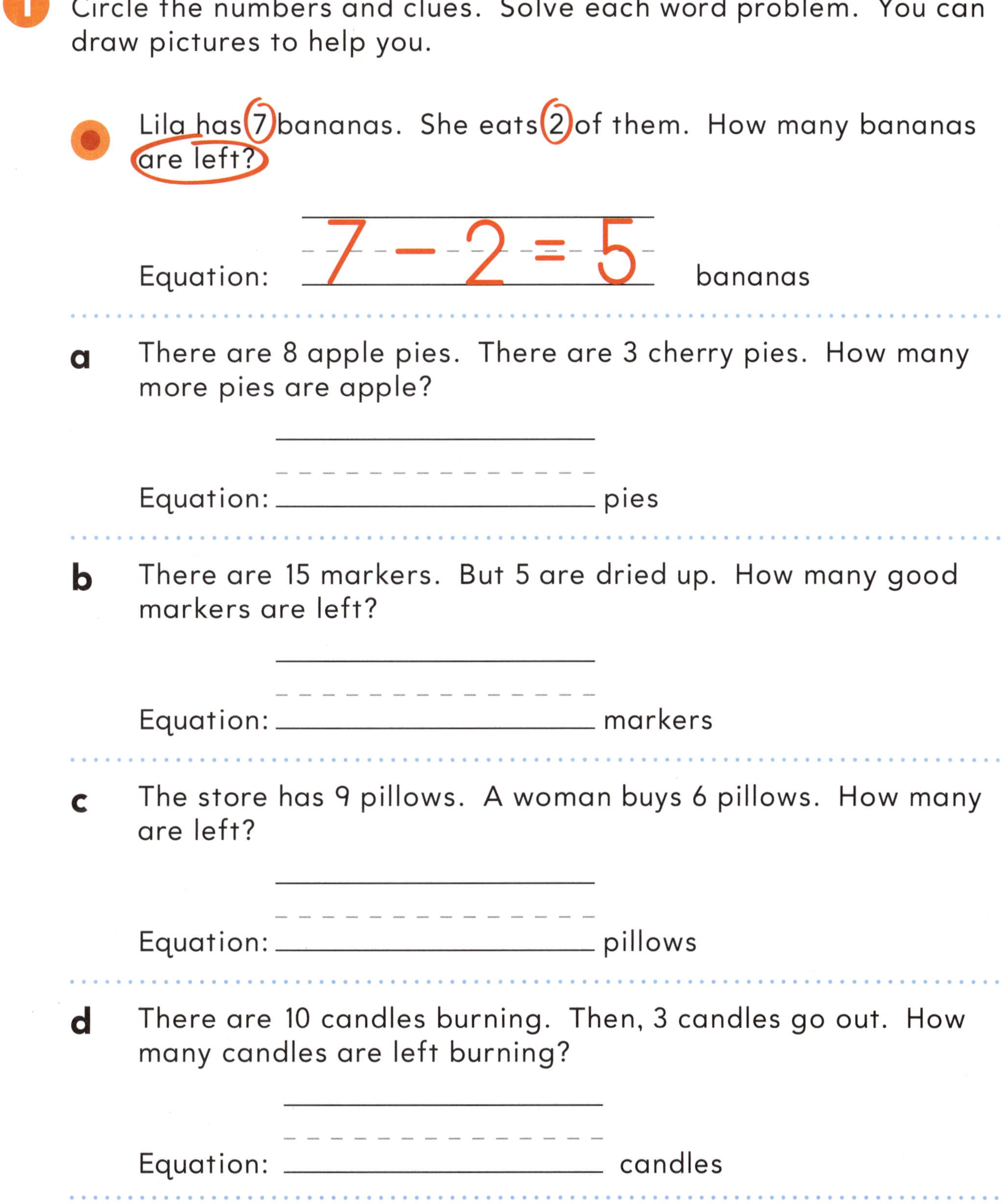

Lila has 7 bananas. She eats 2 of them. How many bananas are left?

Equation: 7 − 2 = 5 bananas

a There are 8 apple pies. There are 3 cherry pies. How many more pies are apple?

Equation: ____________________ pies

b There are 15 markers. But 5 are dried up. How many good markers are left?

Equation: ____________________ markers

c The store has 9 pillows. A woman buys 6 pillows. How many are left?

Equation: ____________________ pillows

d There are 10 candles burning. Then, 3 candles go out. How many candles are left burning?

Equation: ____________________ candles

e A toy has 6 batteries. Then, 1 battery falls out. How many batteries are left?

Equation: ____________________ batteries

Subtraction Review

1 Use the pictures to subtract. Write how many are left.

a 5 – 2 = ?

_______ squares are left.

b 17 – 8 = ?

_______ baseballs are left.

2 Use the numbers and symbols to write a subtraction equation.

a 7 12 5 – = _______________________

b – = 0 8 8 _______________________

c 15 6 9 – = _______________________

3 Circle the equation that is true for each set.

a 1 – 5 = 6 5 – 1 = 6 6 – 1 = 5

b 1 – 8 = 7 7 – 8 = 1 8 – 7 = 1

c 9 – 3 = 6 6 – 9 = 3 6 – 3 = 9

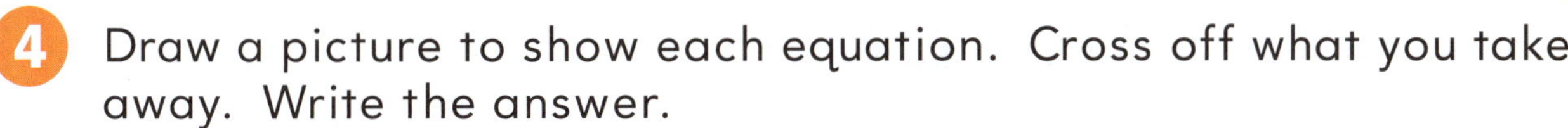

Review

4 Draw a picture to show each equation. Cross off what you take away. Write the answer.

a $5 - 2 =$ ______

b $14 - 6 =$ ______

c $9 - 6 =$ ______

5 Use the strategy listed to count back. Write each answer.

a Use a number list to count back.

15

$15 - 6 =$ ______

b Use pictures to count back.

7 

$7 - 2 =$ ______

c Use your fingers to count back.

$13 - 5 =$ ______

Review

6 Use the number lines to subtract

a

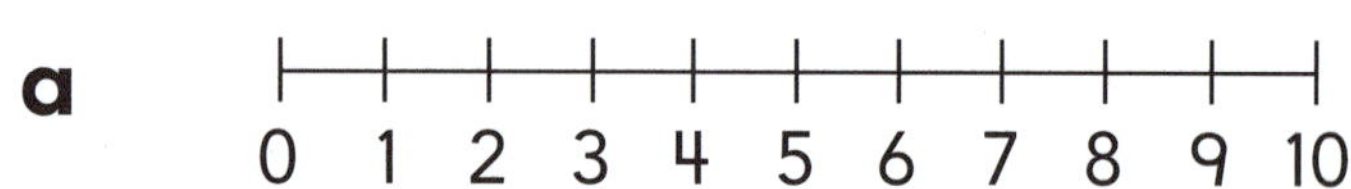

6 – 2 = ______

b

0 1 2 3 4 5 6 7 8 9 10 11 12 13 14 15 16 17 18 19 20

15 – 5 = ______

c

0 1 2 3 4 5 6 7 8 9 10

8 – 4 = ______

d

0 1 2 3 4 5 6 7 8 9 10 11 12 13 14 15 16 17 18 19 20

14 – 8 = ______

7 Complete the equations.

a

☐ + 8 = 12

12 – 8 = ☐

b

☐ + 5 = 11

11 – 5 = ☐

c

10 + 2 = ☐

☐ – 2 = 10

d

9 + ☐ = 17

17 – ☐ = 9

Review

8 Write the missing number in each fact family. Then, write its 4 number sentences.

a

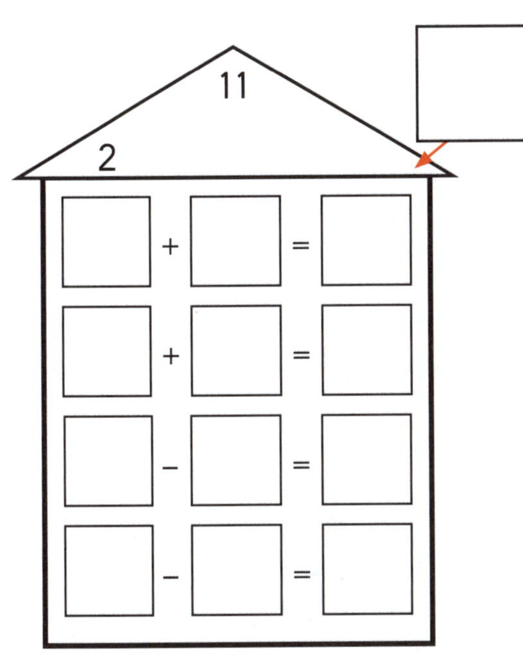

b

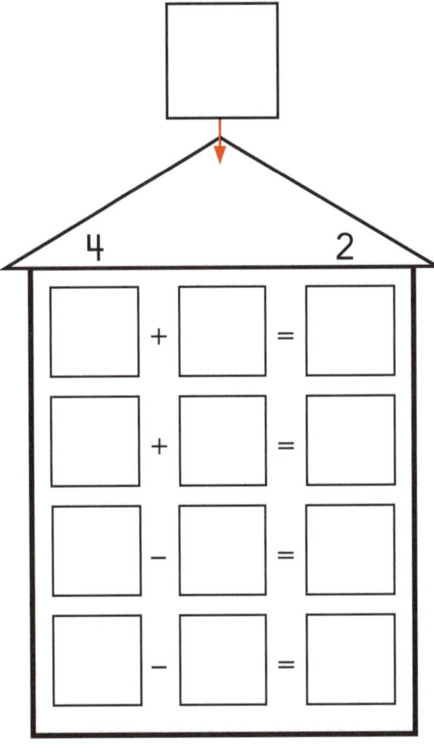

9 Write the 2 missing numbers in each fact family. There is more than one way to complete each one.

a

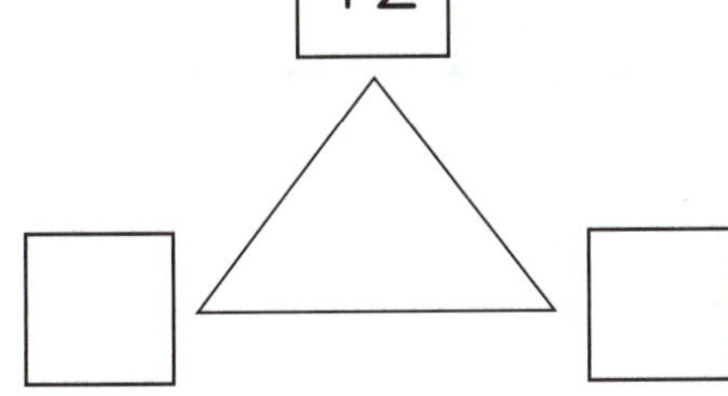

b

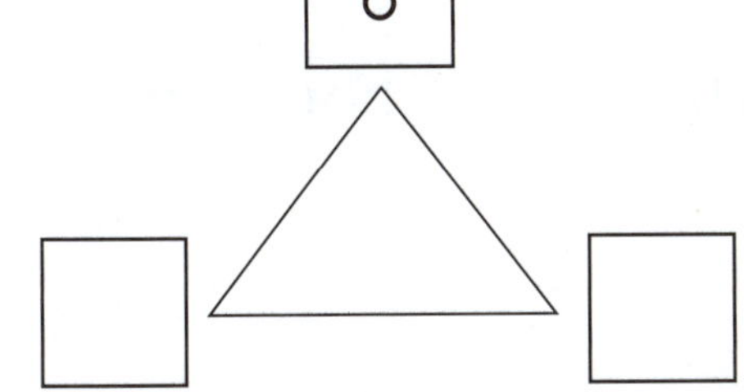

10 Write a different subtraction problem that has the same value.

a 8 – 1 = ______ – ______

b 11 – 5 = ______ – ______

c 12 – 3 = ______ – ______

d 6 – 3 = ______ – ______

11 Circle the numbers and clues. Write the equation for each problem with the answer.

a There are 10 green gumballs. There are 7 blue gumballs. How many more gumballs are green?

Equation: ______________ gumballs

b There are 12 cars. Then, 5 drive away. How many cars are left?

Equation: ______________ cars

c There are 8 bees flying. There are 4 bees at the hive. How many more bees are flying?

Equation: ______________ bees

d There are 8 hot dog buns. There are 6 hot dogs. How many more buns are there?

Equation: ______________ buns

Review

12 Subtract. Use any strategy.

a 17 − 9 = ☐

b 5 − 1 = ☐

c 4 − 2 = ☐

d 11 − 6 = ☐

e 16 − 8 = ☐

f 20 − 10 = ☐

g 18 − 10 = ☐

h 13 − 3 = ☐

i 10 − 7 = ☐

j 12 − 6 = ☐

k 2 − 0 = ☐

l 14 − 10 = ☐

m 8 − 4 = ☐

n 15 − 3 = ☐

Compare Length

Length is a type of measurement. It measures how long or short something is.

Example 1:

You can compare two lengths.
Put a check mark by the longer spoon.
Put an *X* by the shorter spoon.

Example 2:

You can compare three lengths.
Number the forks from the shortest to the longest.

Label the shortest fork 1. Label the next shortest fork 2. Label the longest fork 3.

Your turn

1 Circle the one that is shorter.

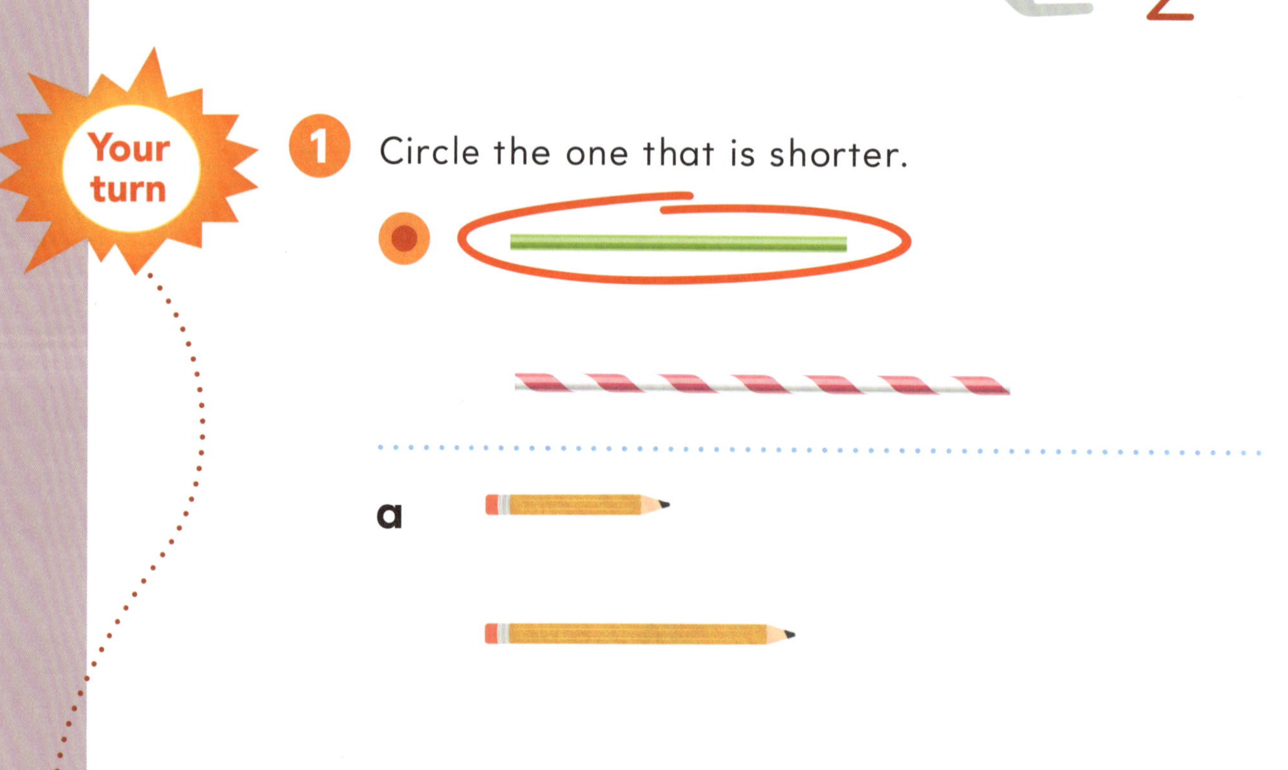

SELF CHECK Mark how you feel

Got it!	Need help...	I don't get it
☐	☐	☐

Practice

1. Circle the object that is longer.

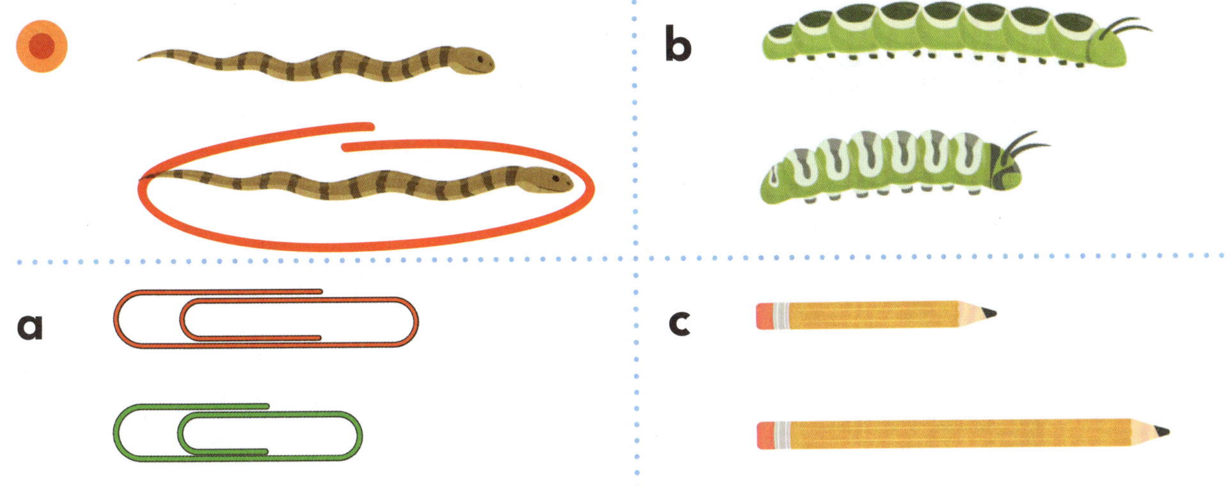

2. Circle the object that is shorter.

3. Circle the marker that is the same length as the first.

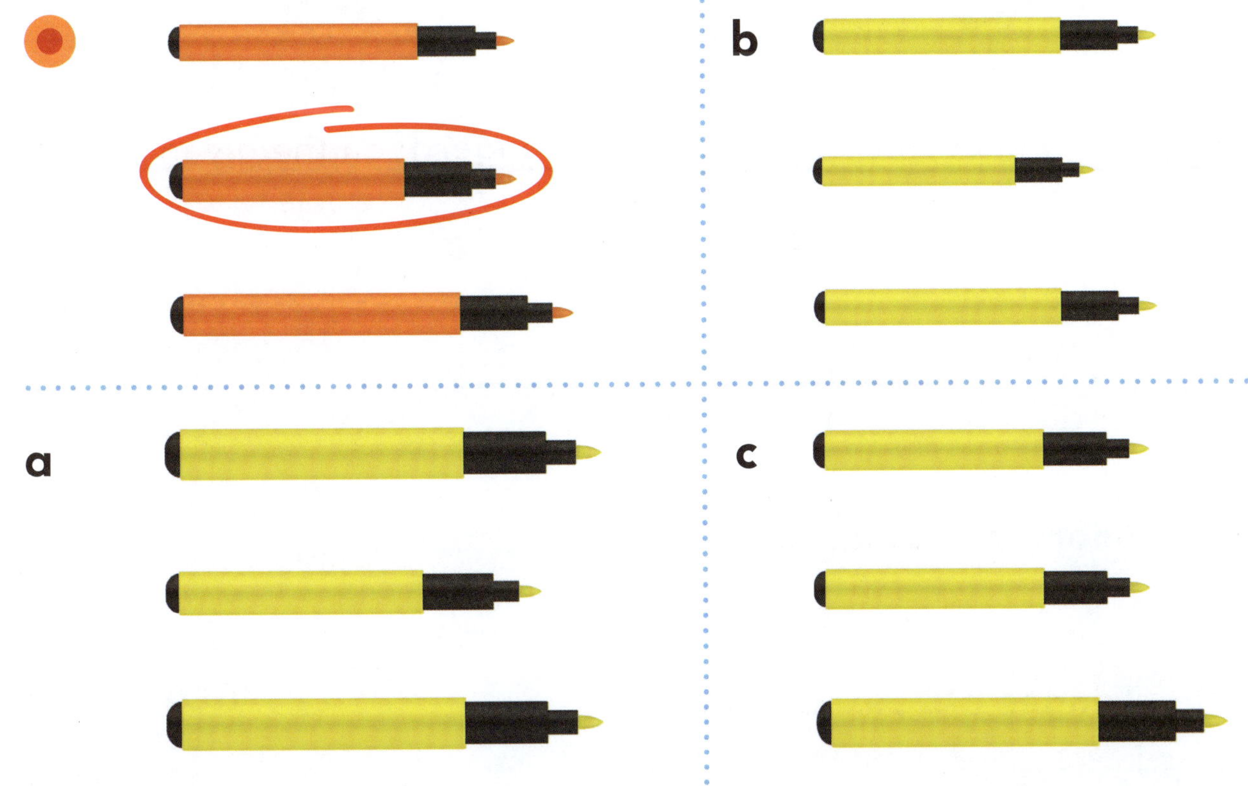

4 Number the objects in order from shortest (1) to longest (3).

● 2
3
1

b

a

c

5 Draw lines that are shorter and longer than the given line.

● a b

Shorter

Longer

Compare Weight

Weight is a type of measurement. It measures how light or heavy something is.

Example 1:

You can compare objects. If something is **heavier**, it weighs more. If it is **lighter**, it weighs less.

Circle the heavier object.

Name something heavier than you are. Name something lighter than you are.

Example 2:

Circle the object that is lighter.

1. Circle the object that is heavier.

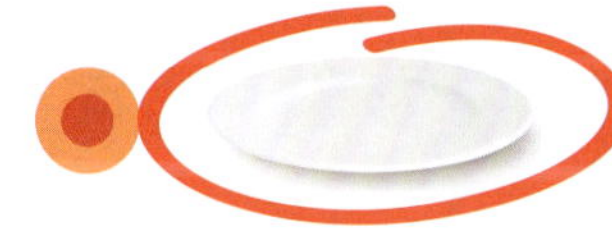 

a 

2. Circle the object that is lighter.

a  

SELF CHECK Mark how you feel		
Got it! ☐	Need help... ☐	I don't get it ☐

Practice

1 Write ***heavier*** or ***lighter*** to make each statement true.

● is heavier than

a is ______ than

b is ______ than

c is ______ than

d is ______ than

2 Is the first object heavier, lighter, or about the same as the second? Circle your answer.

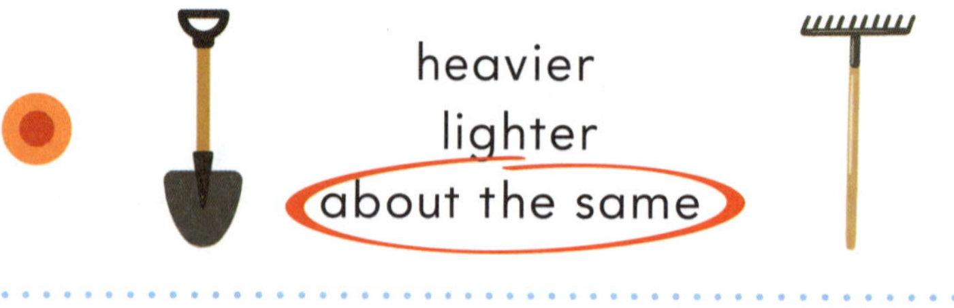

a  heavier / lighter / about the same 

b  heavier / lighter / about the same 

c  heavier / lighter / about the same 

Use a Unit of Length

Objects can be used to measure length.

Example 1:

Measure using paper clips. The paper clips must be lined up and touching.

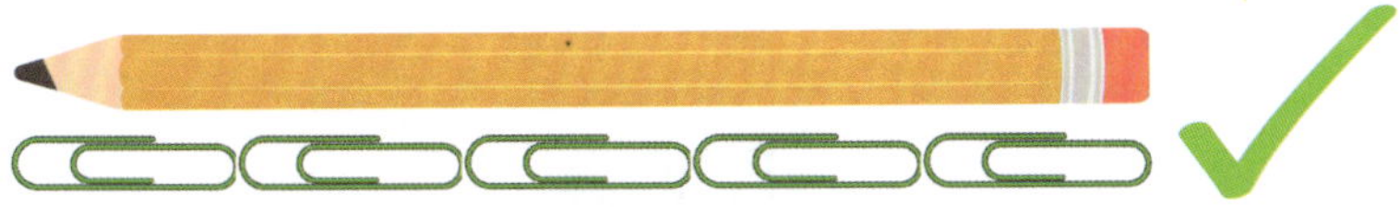

This pencil is 5 paper clips long.

Example 2:

The paper clips cannot have gaps between them.

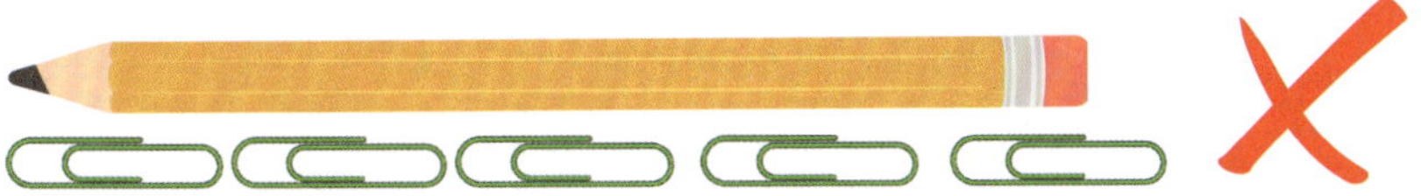

Example 3:

The paper clips cannot overlap.

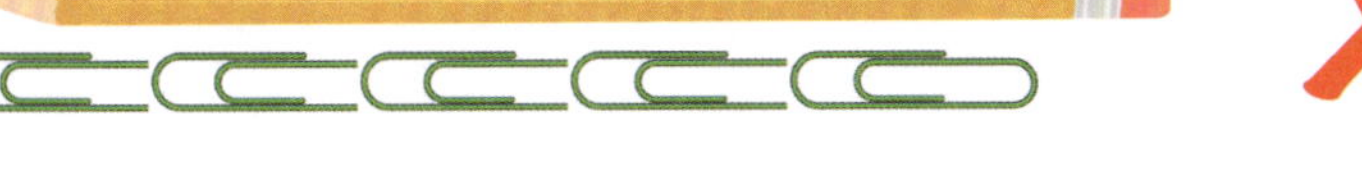

How many paper clips long is your pointer finger?

Example 4:

The paper clips must be going the same direction.

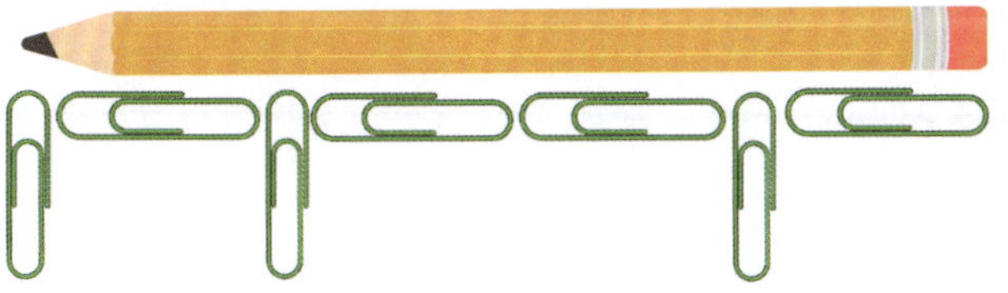

1 Are the lines being measured the right way? Circle yes or no.

yes no

a

yes no

Practice

1 Are the objects being measured the right way? Circle yes or no.

●  yes (no)

b  yes no

a  yes no

c  yes no

2 Write the length of each item.

●  3 paper clips long

a 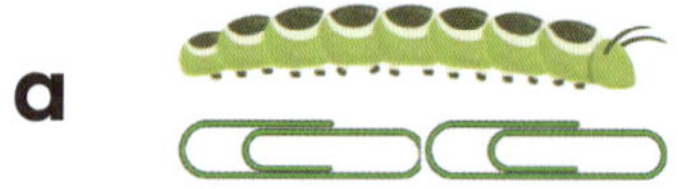 ____ paper clips long

b  ____ paper clips long

c 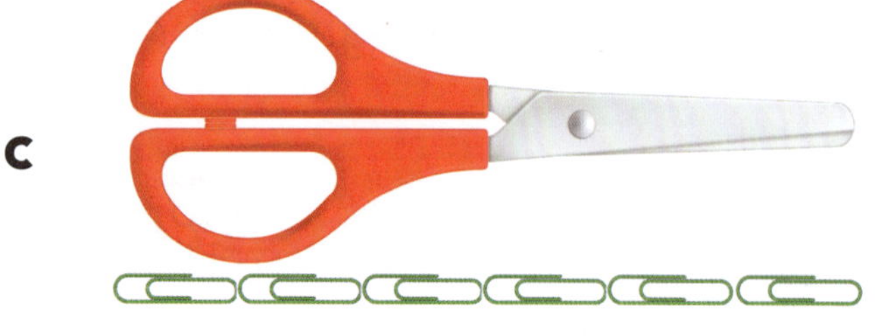 ____ paper clips long

d 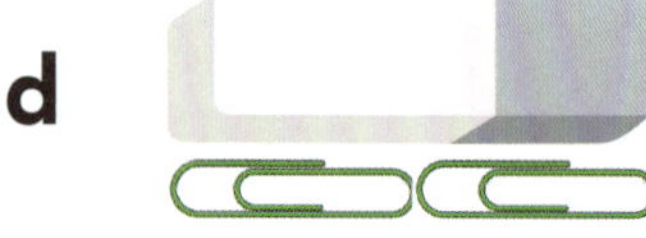 ____ paper clips long

Measure in Inches

Rulers are used for measuring. One unit of measurement is an inch.

Example 1:

Look at the ruler. One inch is between each number.

How many inches is the pencil?

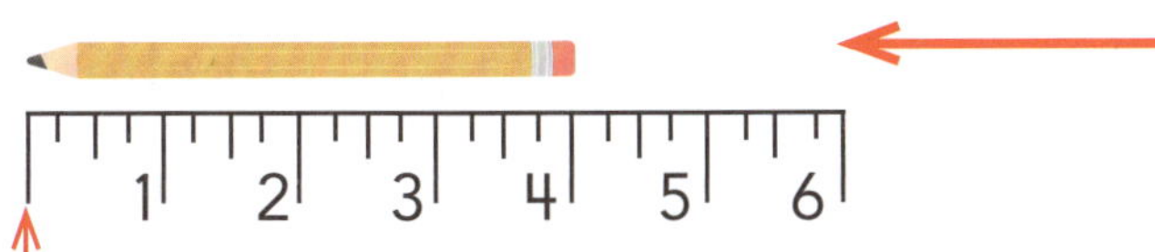

The pencil begins at the edge. It stops at 4.

Begin measuring here. From the edge to the 1 is 1 inch.

The pencil is 4 inches long.

1 Measure each pencil.

● 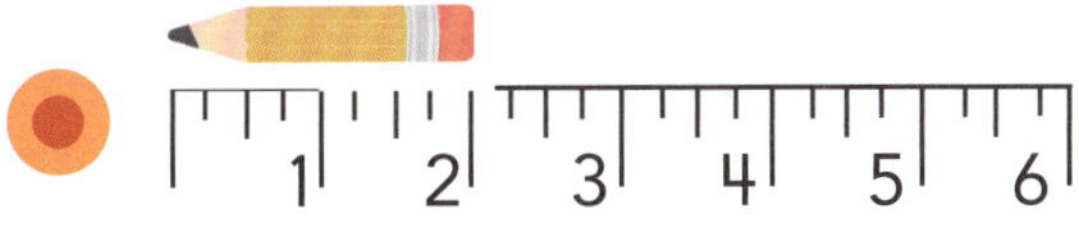 2 inches

a 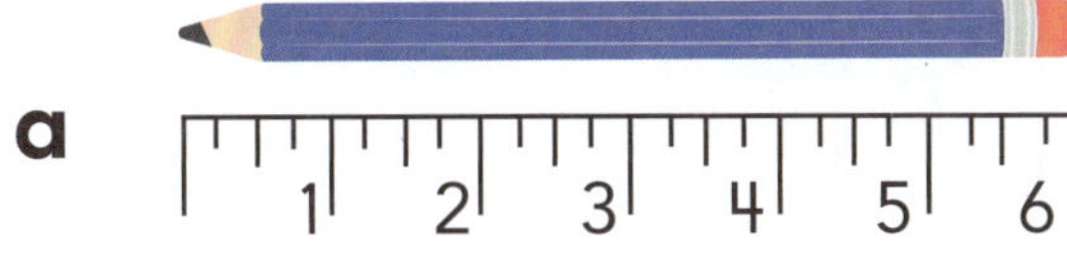 ____ inches

The short lines between the numbers measure parts of an inch.

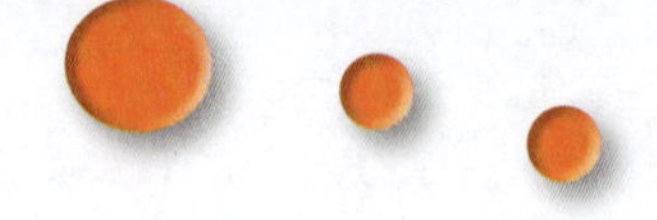

1 Measure each object in inches.

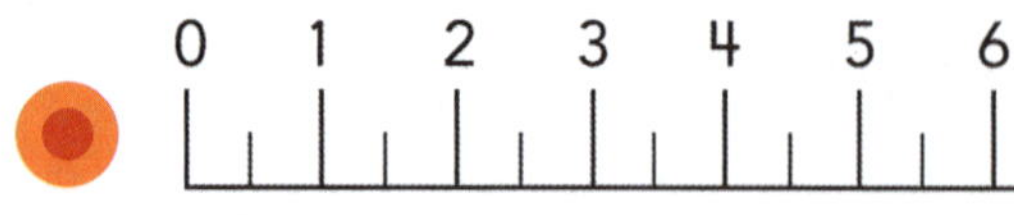

inch

a

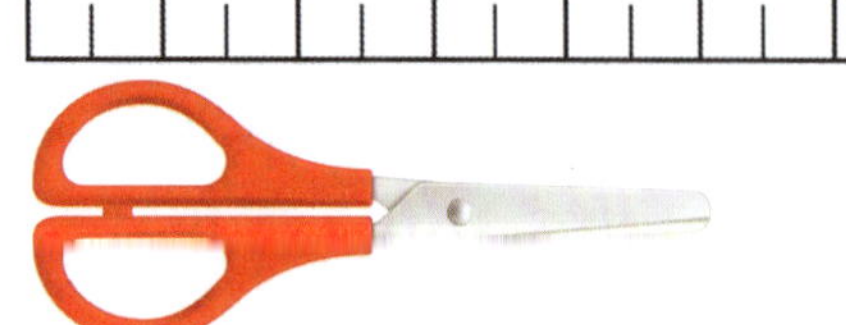

inches

b

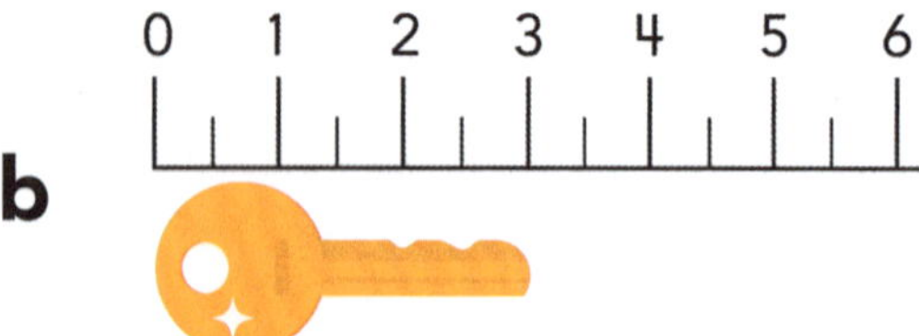

inches

c

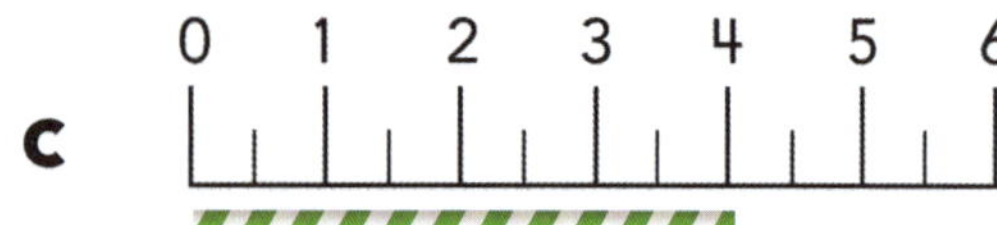

inches

2 Use the ruler to measure the shoelaces.

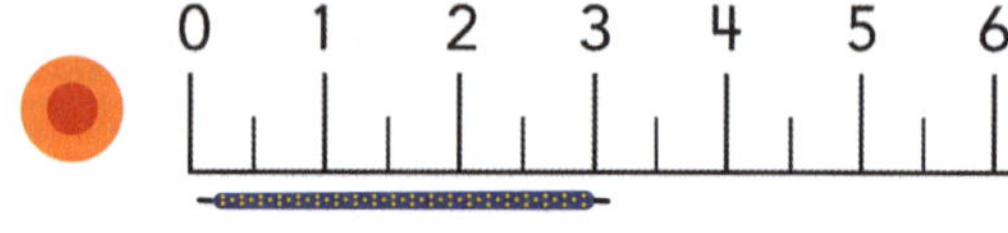

inches

a

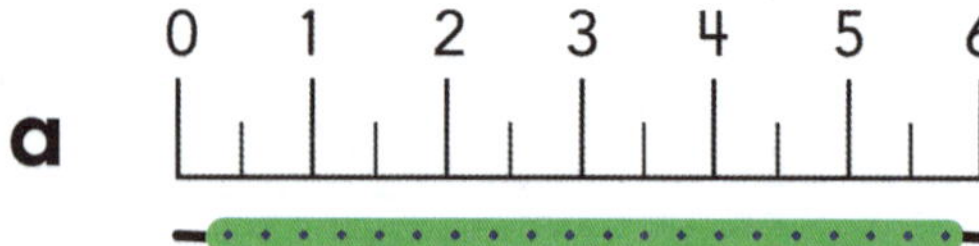

inches

b

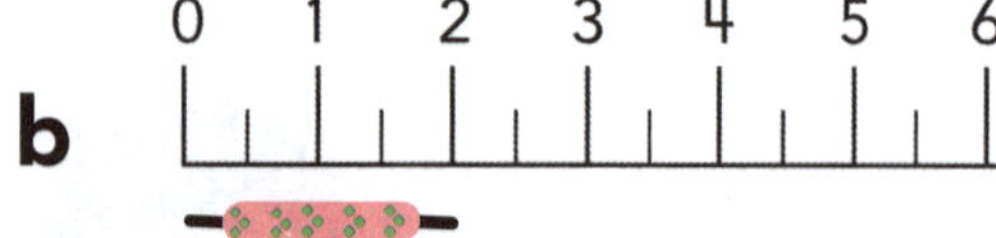

inches

c

______ inches

3 Draw lines in inches.

Draw a line that is 2 inches long.

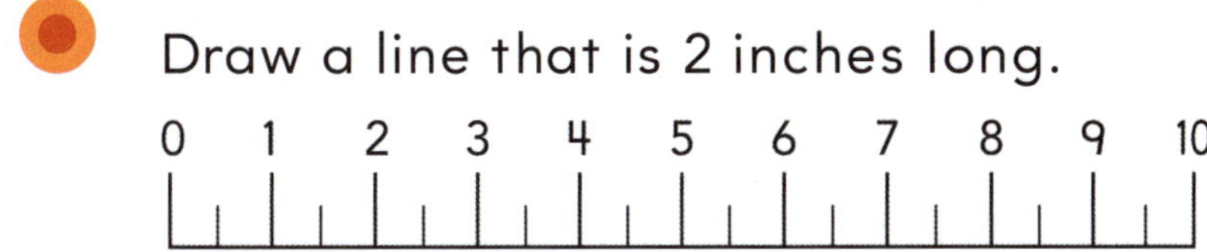

a Draw a line that is 3 inches long.

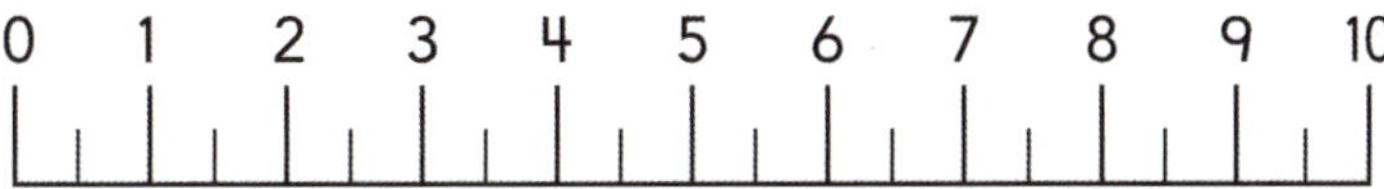

b Draw a line that is 1 inch long.

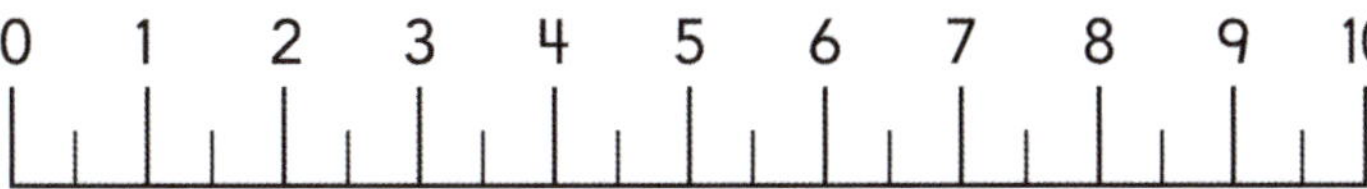

c Draw a line that is 5 inches long.

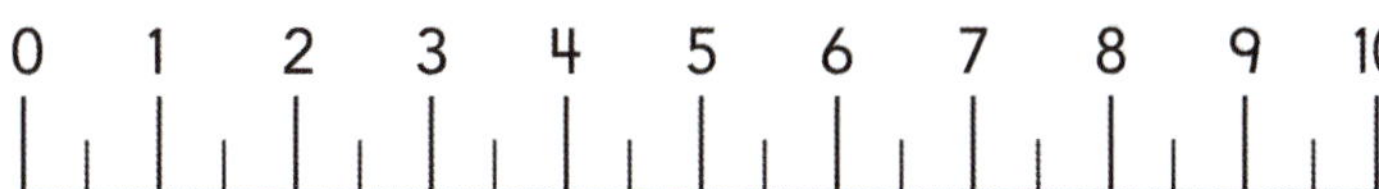

d Draw a line that is 6 inches long.

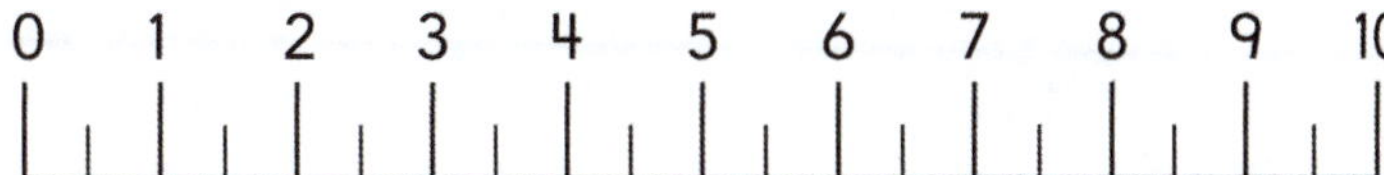

e Draw a line that is 4 inches long.

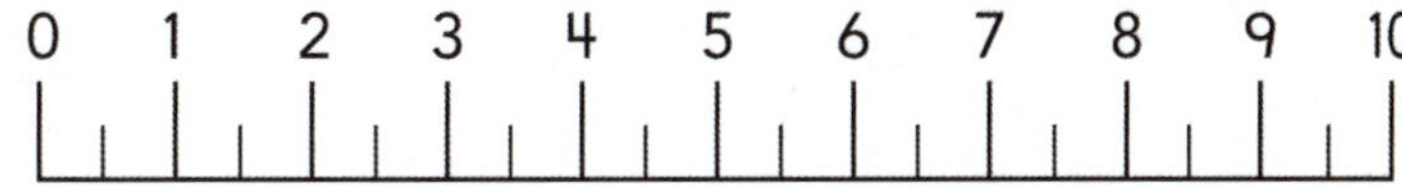

f Draw a line that is longer than 4 inches.

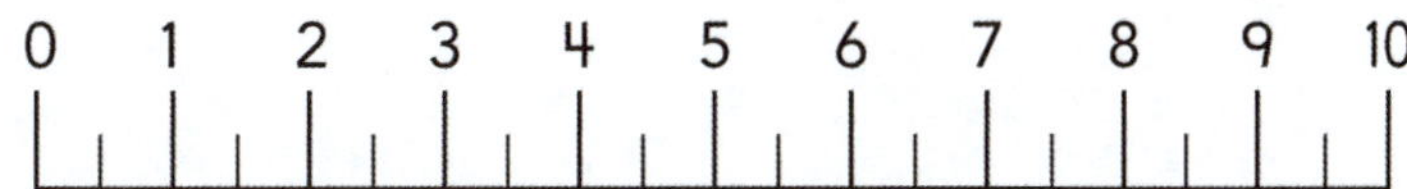

Measurement Review

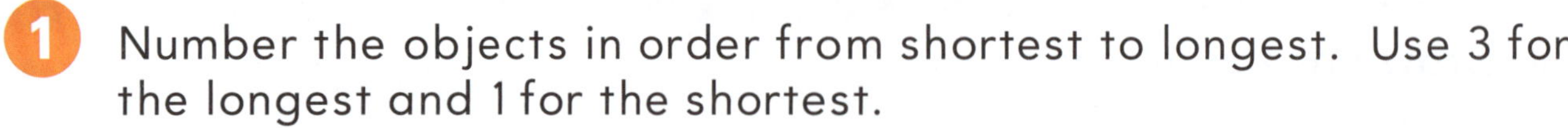

1 Number the objects in order from shortest to longest. Use 3 for the longest and 1 for the shortest.

2 Draw arrows that are shorter and longer than the given arrow.

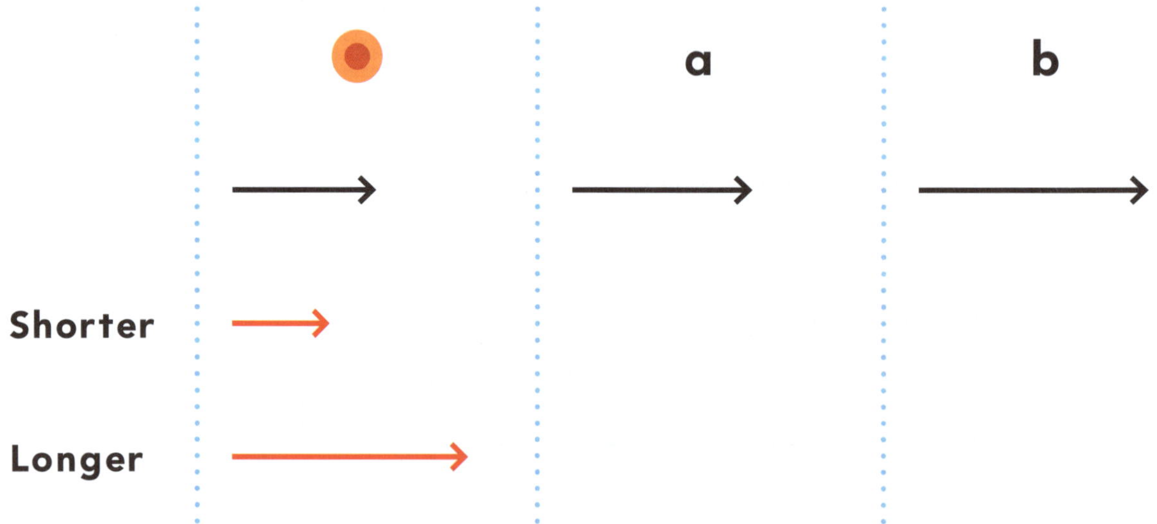

Review

3 Circle the heavier object.

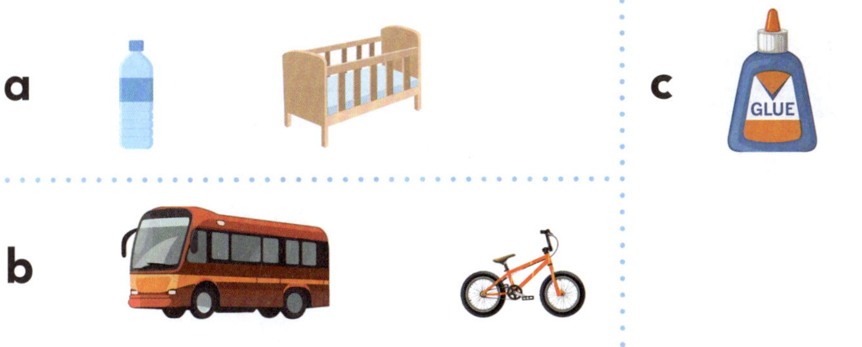

4 Circle the lighter object.

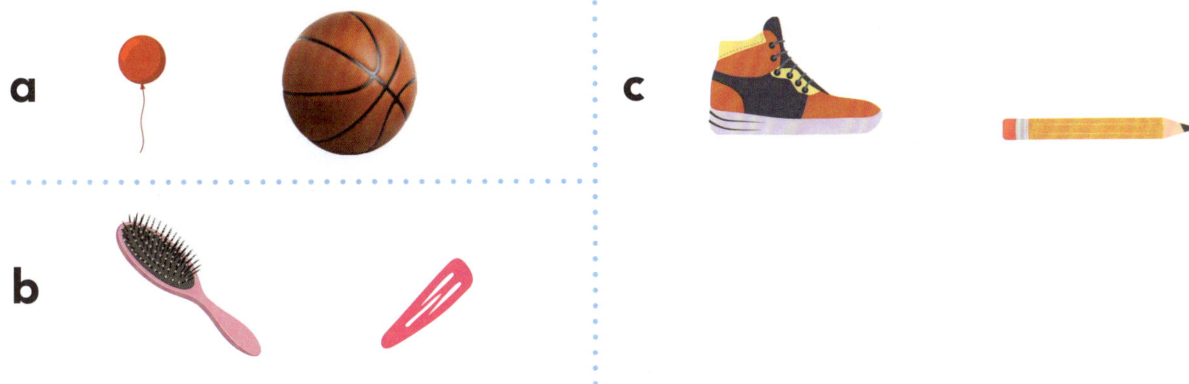

5 Are the objects being measured the right way? Circle yes or no.

Review

6 Write the length of each item.

a

_____ paper clips long

b

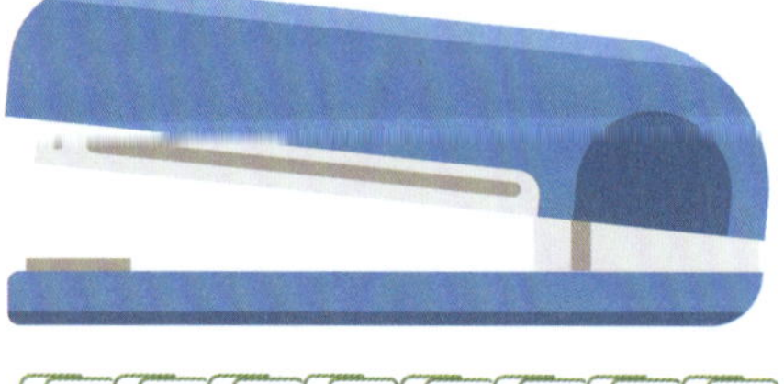

_____ paper clips long

c

_____ paper clips long

7 Measure each snake in inches.

a

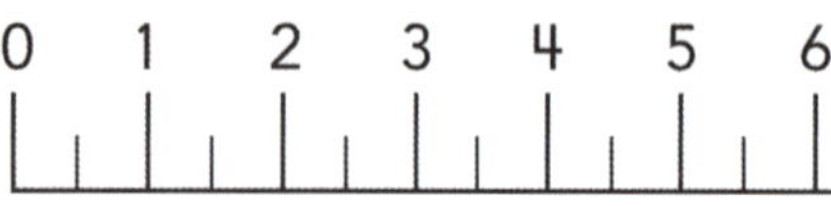

_____ inches

b

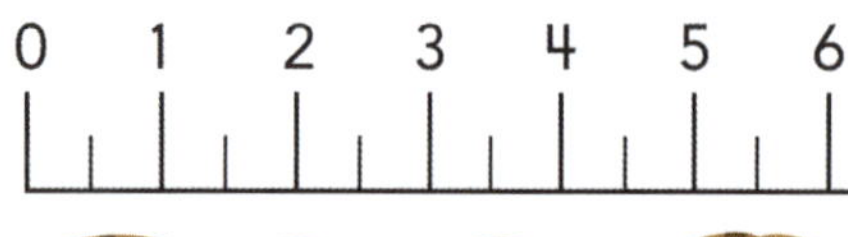

_____ inches

c

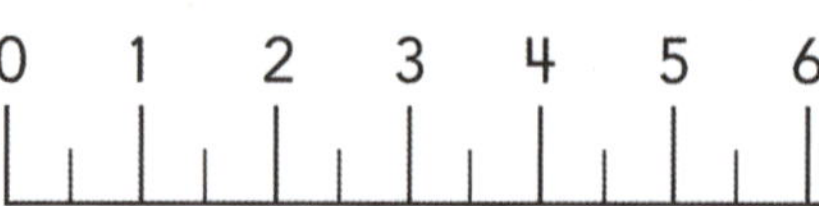

_____ inches

d

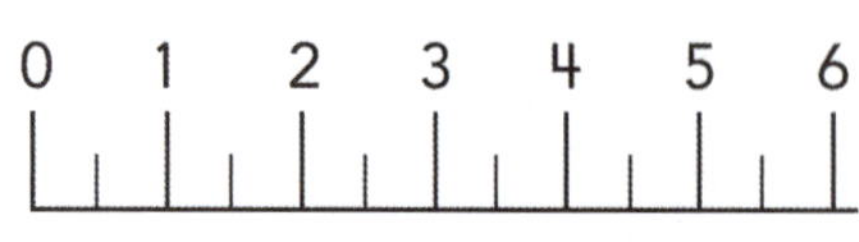

_____ inches

Classify Objects

Objects can be organized in many ways. You can put them into categories.

Think about a box of school supplies. How could you classify them?

Example 1:

You can classify by color. These are all purple.

Example 2:

You can classify by shape. These are all triangles.

Example 3:

You can classify by size. These are all small.

1 Complete each task.

9 A 7 ! 4 " " J R T ? ' 3

Circle the letters.

a Put *X*s on the numbers.

b Put boxes around the punctuation marks.

SELF CHECK Mark how you feel		
Got it! ☐	Need help... ☐	I don't get it ☐

Practice

1 Use the shapes to answer the questions.

● How many shapes are big?

6

a How many shapes are small?

b How many shapes are green?

c How many shapes are yellow?

d How many shapes are blue?

e How many shapes are squares?

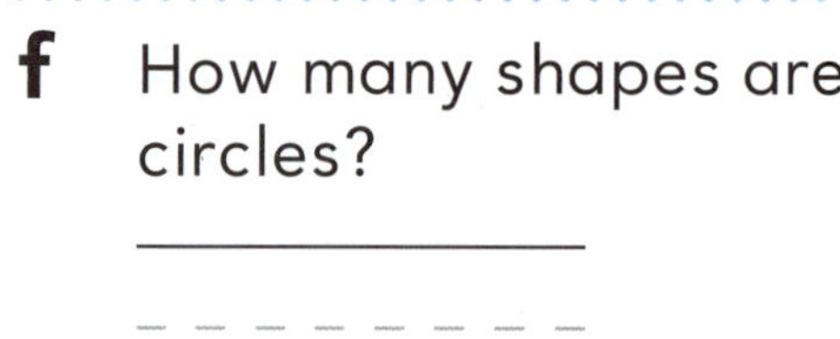

f How many shapes are circles?

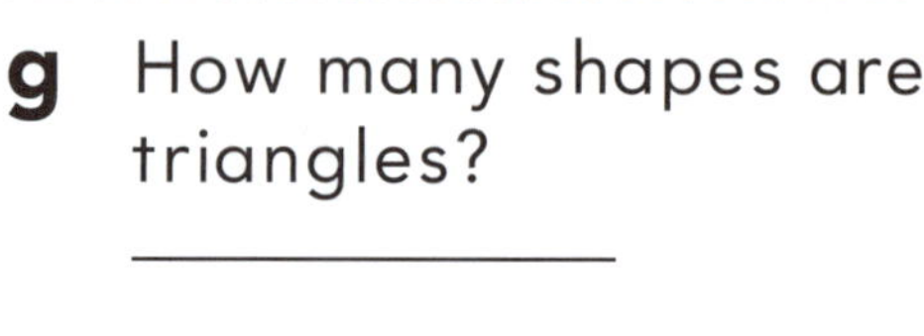

g How many shapes are triangles?

2 Complete each task.

● Circle the fruits.

a Put Xs on the vegetables.

b Put squares around the green foods.

c Put stars next to the yellow foods.

d Put check marks by the red foods.

Picture Graphs

Data is information. Graphs can help you understand data. Some graphs use pictures.

Example 1:

This is a picture graph.

The title says what the graph shows.

What We Eat for Lunch

pizza	🍕 🍕 🍕 🍕 🍕 🍕
sandwich	🥪 🥪 🥪 🥪 🥪 🥪 🥪 🥪
hamburger	🍔 🍔 🍔

The labels tell the choices. The data shows the numbers.

Count the pictures of food. They show how many people ate each kind of food.

Your turn

1 Answer the questions about the picture graph.

- What does this graph show?

  It shows what people ate for lunch.

a What are the three choices? ______________________

b How many people ate pizza? __________

c How many people ate sandwiches? __________

d How many people ate hamburgers? __________

SELF CHECK	Mark how you feel	
Got it! ☐	Need help... ☐	I don't get it ☐

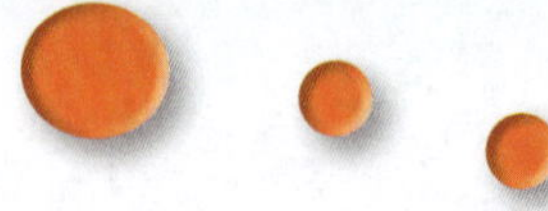

Practice

1 Answer the questions about the picture graph.

Our Pets

dog	🐶 🐶 🐶 🐶 🐶 🐶 🐶 🐶
cat	🐱 🐱 🐱 🐱 🐱
fish	🐟 🐟

What are the 3 choices?

dog cat fish

a What does this graph show?

____

b How many people have dogs?

____

c How many people have cats?

____

d How many people have fish?

____

e Which animal is the most popular pet?

____

2 Answer the questions about the picture graph.

Weekend Activities

park	
pool	
movies	

● How many people are going to the park?

5

a How many people are going to the pool?

b How many people are going to the movies?

c What is the title of the graph?

d Which activity would you choose?

e Which activity is the least popular?

Bar Graphs

You can show data on graphs with bars.

Example 1:

This is a bar graph.

The title says what the graph shows.

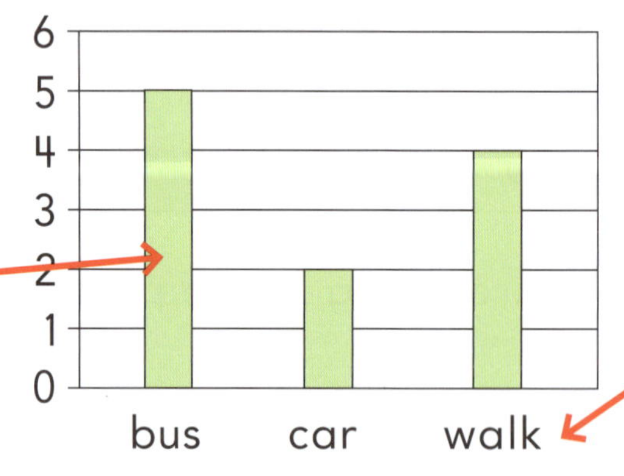

The data tells how many.

The labels tell the choices.

1 Answer the questions about the bar graph.

- What is the title of the graph?

How We Get to School

a What are the three labels?

______ ______ ______

b How many students walk?

______

c How many students ride the bus?

______

A bar graph uses numbers instead of pictures.

SELF CHECK Mark how you feel

Got it!	Need help...	I don't get it
 ☐	 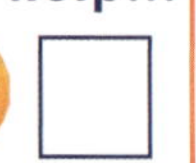 ☐	  ☐

Practice

1 Answer the questions about the bar graph.

Favorite Zoo Animals

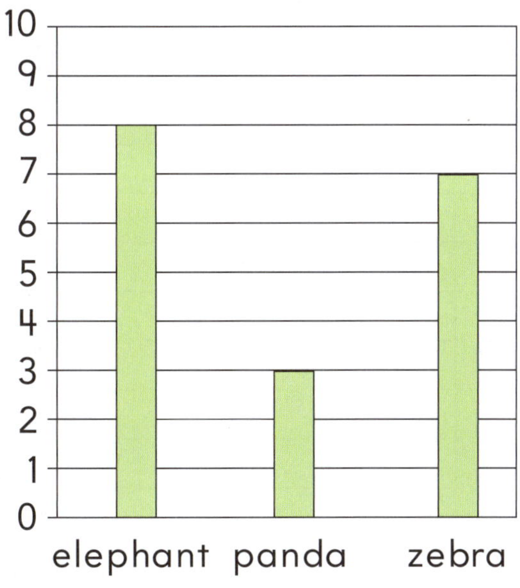

● How many people chose zebras?

7

a How many people chose elephants?

b How many people chose pandas?

c What is the title of the graph?

d Which animal got the most votes?

2 Answer the questions about the bar graph.

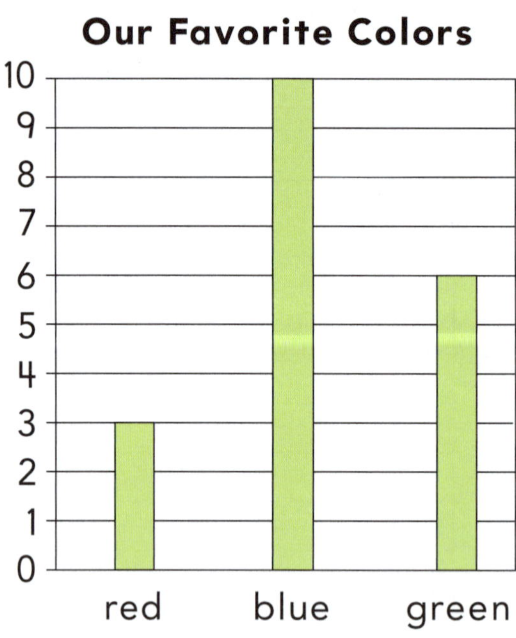

How many people chose red?

a How many people chose blue?

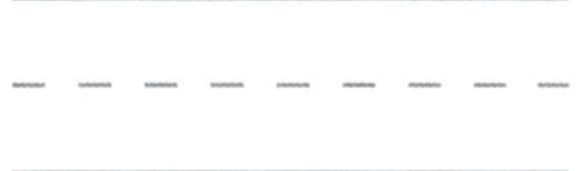

b How many people chose green?

c What data does this bar graph show?

d Which color got the fewest votes?

Questions About Graphs

Graphs share a lot of information. You can ask and answer questions to learn more.

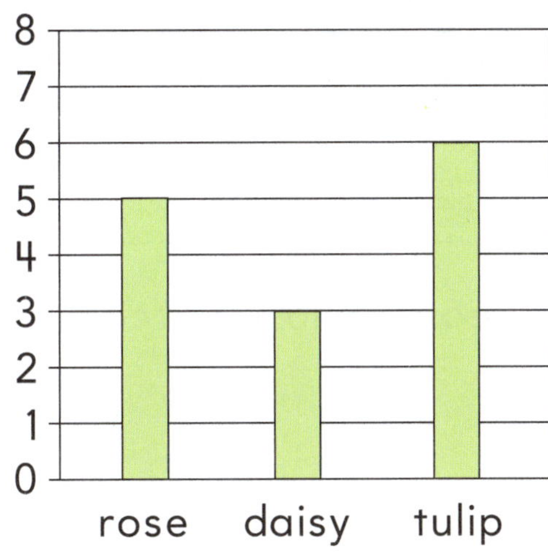

Example 1:

How many flowers in all? ← This is an addition clue!

5 roses + 3 daisies + 6 tulips = 14 flowers

1 Write equations to answer the questions.

- How many tulips and daisies are there in all?

  6 + 3 = 9

a How many daisies and roses are there in all?

____

What other questions could you ask about this graph?

SELF CHECK	Mark how you feel	
Got it!  ☐	Need help...  ☐	I don't get it  ☐

Practice

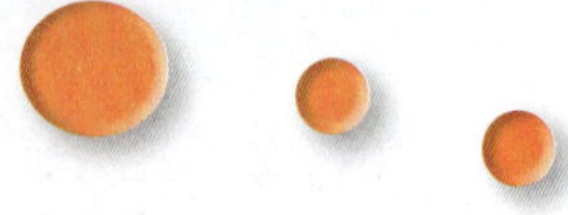

1 Write equations to answer the questions.

Our Favorite Sports

football	🏈 🏈 🏈
soccer	⚽ ⚽ ⚽ ⚽ ⚽ ⚽ ⚽
baseball	⚾ ⚾ ⚾

● How many more people chose soccer than baseball?

7 – 3 = 4

a How many people voted in all?

____

b Which two sports had the same number of votes?

____

c How many people chose baseball and football in all?

____

d Which sport did most people choose?

____

e Write your own question for the graph. Answer it.

Question: ______________________________

Answer: ______________________________

2 Write equations to answer the questions. Use information from the bar graph.

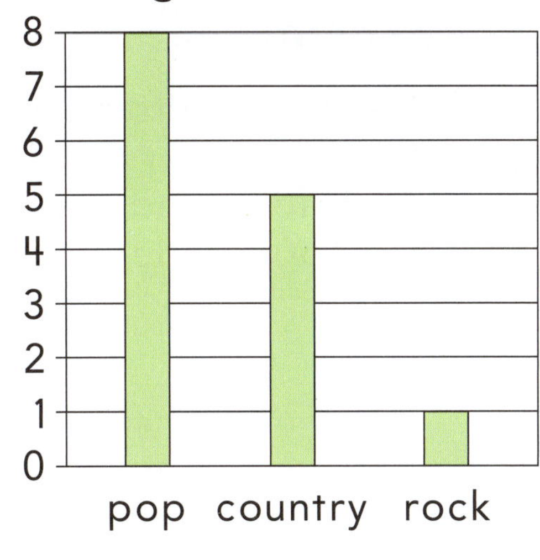

● How many songs were pop or rock in all?

$8 + 1 = 9$

a How many songs were played in all?

b How many more pop songs played than country songs?

c Which type of music was played the most?

d Which type of music was played the least?

e Write your own question for the graph. Answer it.

Question: ______________________

Answer: ______________________

Make Graphs

You can use data to create bar and picture graphs.

Example 1:

Use the data to make a bar graph.

People visited the ice cream store. 9 people ordered vanilla. 7 people ordered chocolate. 3 people ordered strawberry.

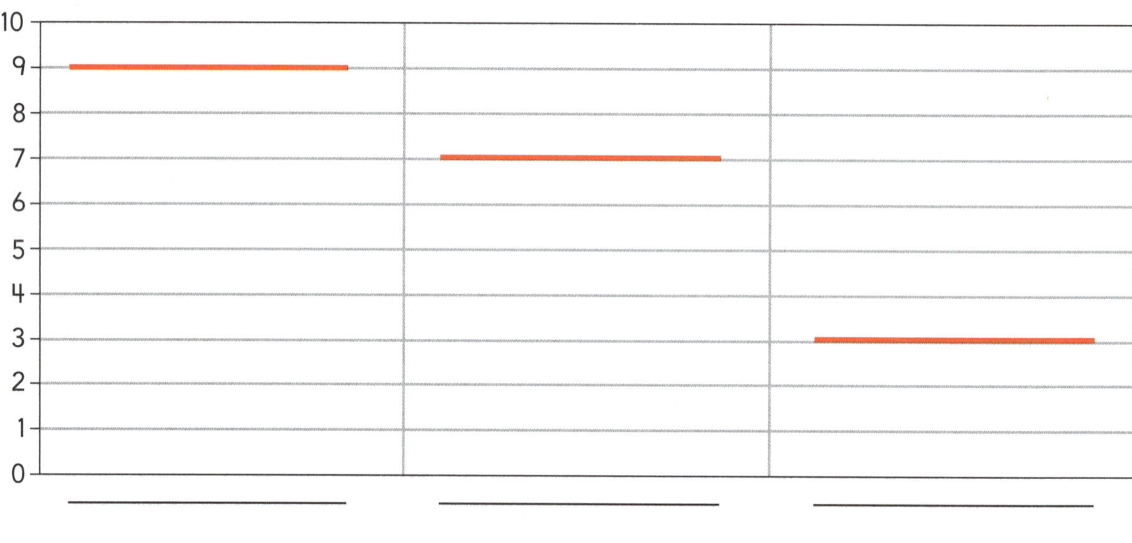

1 Follow the steps to finish the bar graph.

- Give the bar graph a title.

a Label the bars. Put vanilla first. Chocolate goes in the middle. Put strawberry last.

b Fill in the bars for the flavors. The top of each bar is marked.

Check the data when you make a graph. Make sure the numbers match.

SELF CHECK Mark how you feel

Got it!	Need help...	I don't get it
 ☐	 ☐	  ☐

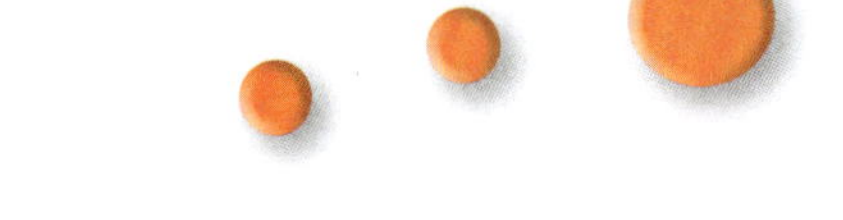

Practice

1 Use the data to make a picture graph.

Students found shapes in their classroom. They found 6 squares. They found 8 triangles. They found 5 circles.

squares	
triangles	
circles	

Write the label names.

a Write a title above the graph.

b Draw the squares.

c Draw the triangles.

d Draw the circles.

2 Use the data to make a bar graph.

Students voted on their favorite kind of movie. There were 3 votes for action. There were 7 votes for comedy. There were 8 votes for cartoon.

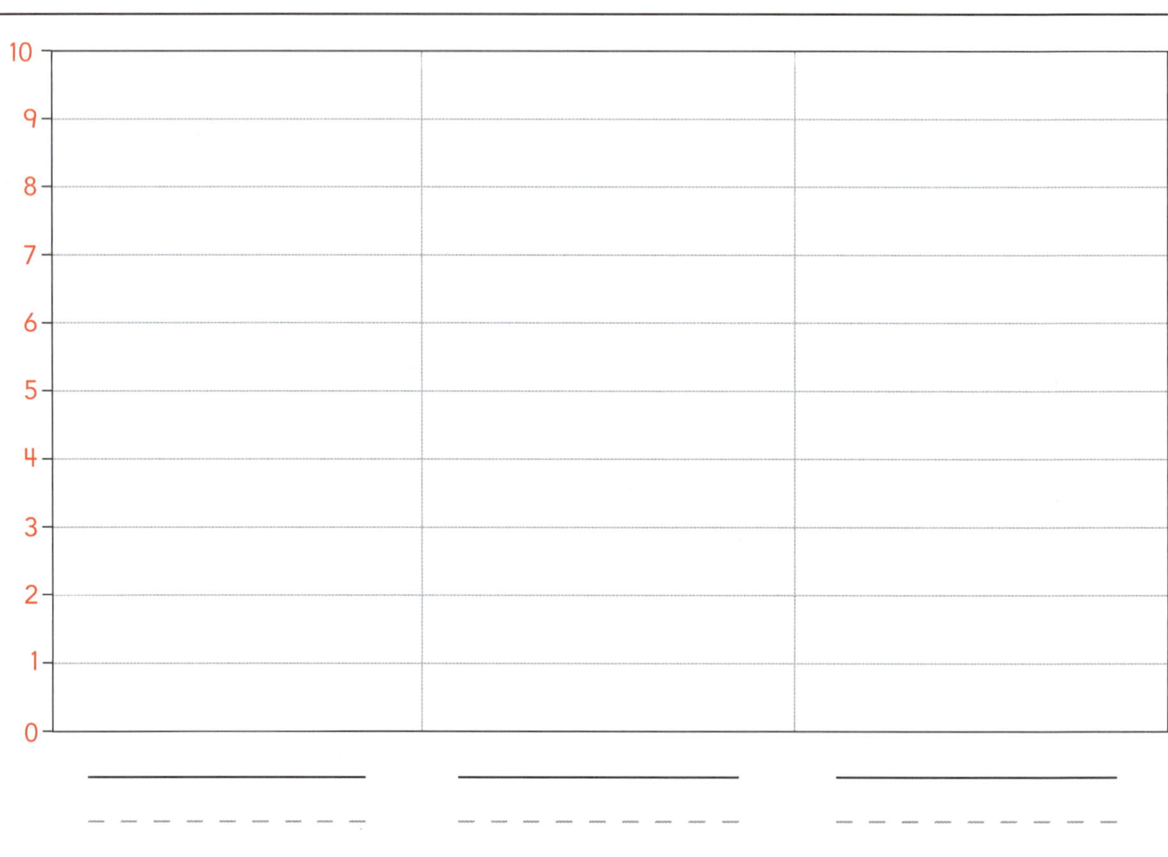

- Write the numbers for the data.

a Write a title for the graph.

b Write the labels beneath the graph.

c Shade the bar for action.

d Shade the bar for comedy.

e Shade the bar for cartoon.

Data and Graphs Review

1 Answer the questions.

a How many items are green?

b How many items are orange?

c How many items are markers?

d How many items are crayons?

e How many items are staplers?

f How many items are scissors?

g How many items are glue bottles?

h How many items are notebooks?

GLUE

Review

2 Answer the questions about the picture graph.

Drinks Sold

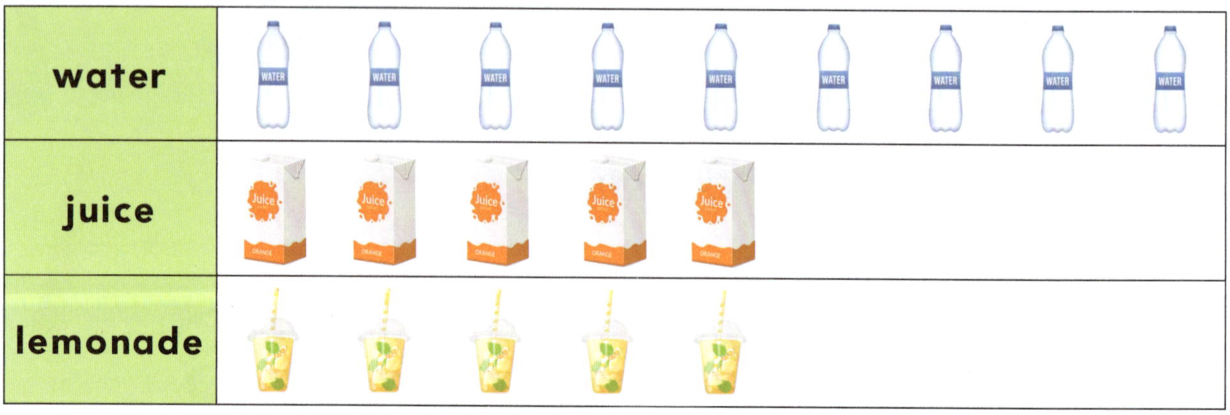

water	
juice	
lemonade	

a What are the categories for drinks?

b How many people bought juice?

c How many people bought lemonade?

d How many people bought water?

e Which drink would you buy?

Review

3 Answer the questions about the bar graph.

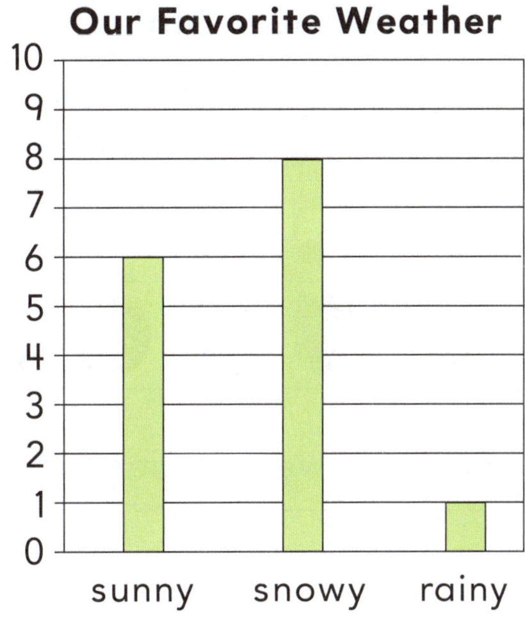

a How many people chose sunny?

b How many people chose snowy?

c How many people chose rainy?

d What data does this bar graph show?

e Which type of weather did the fewest people choose?

Review

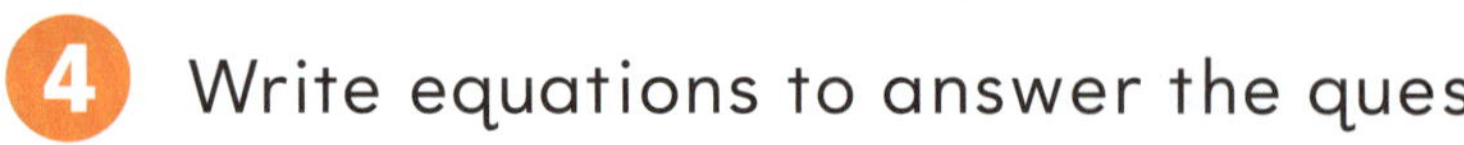

4 Write equations to answer the questions.

Our Favorite Subjects

Art	
Music	
P.E.	

a Which subject did the fewest students choose?

b How many students chose in all?

c How many more students chose art than music?

d How many students chose P.E. and music all together?

e Write your own question for the graph. Answer it.

Question: ______________________

Answer: ______________________

5 Use the data to make a bar graph.

Students voted on the snow day activity they like best. There were 5 votes for throwing snowballs. There were 7 votes for making a snowman. There were 9 votes for sledding.

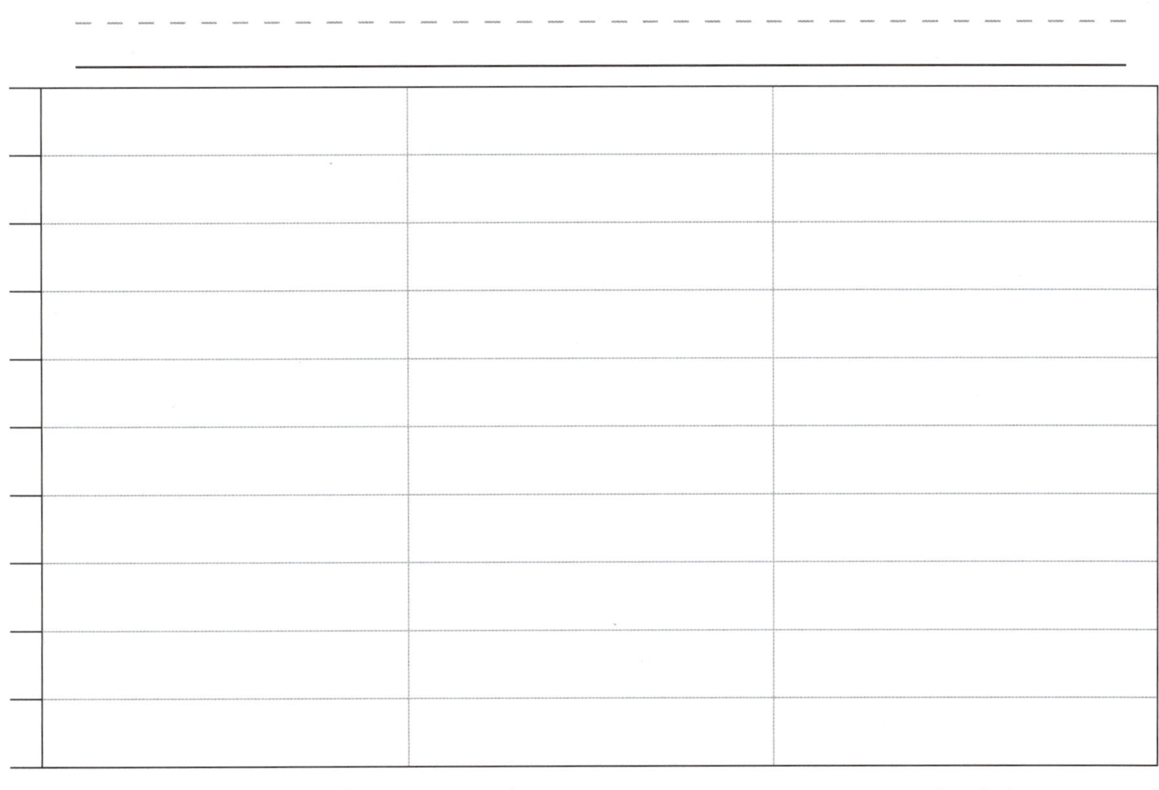

a Write a title for the graph.

b Number the rows from 1 to 10.

c Shade the bar for throwing snowballs.

d Shade the bar for making a snowman.

e Shade the bar for going sledding.

Time to the Hour: Analog Time

A clock tells you what time it is. It has an hour hand and a minute hand. This is also called an analog clock. Use these to tell time to the hour.

Example 1:

A clock can be a circle. It has the numbers 1 to 12. It has two hands. The hands move to show time is passing.

The short hand tells the hour. It takes one hour to move from one number to the next. This hour hand points to 10. That means it is the tenth hour.

The long hand tells the minutes. It moves a little bit every minute. This minute hand points to 12. That means it is a new hour.

hour minutes

This clock shows 10:00.

When the time is 10:00, you say, "ten o'clock."

1 Write the time shown on each clock.

● 3:00

a ______

Practice

1 Follow the directions to complete the clock.

- Add a 1 to the clock.

a Add 2 through 12 to the clock.

b Put the letter H by the hour hand.

c Put the letter M by the minute hand.

2 Circle the time shown on each clock.

- 6:00 / (12:00)

a

6:00

9:00

b

10:00

5:00

c

3:00

2:00

d

11:00

9:00

e

8:00

2:00

f

12:00

7:00

g

11:00

1:00

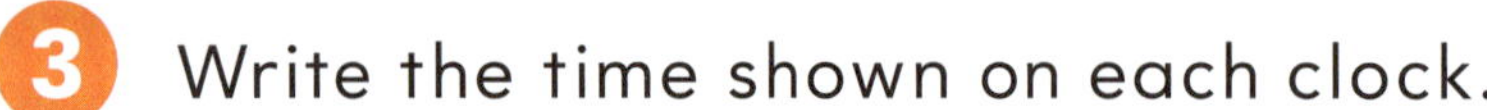

3 Write the time shown on each clock.

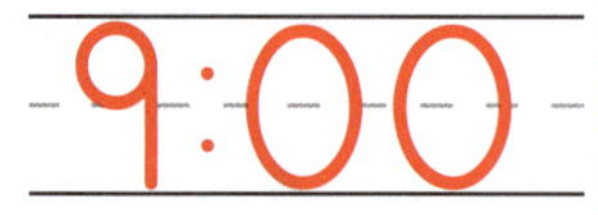

c 

a 

d

b 

e 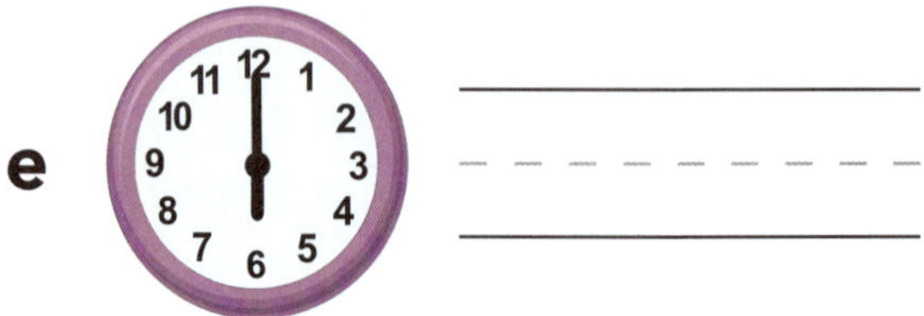

4 Draw the hour and minute hands to show each time.

7:00

c 

4:00

a 

2:00

d 

8:00

b

11:00

e

5:00

Time to the Hour: Digital Time

A digital clock tells you what time it is. It does not have hands. It only uses numbers.

Example 1:

A digital clock shows the hours and minutes as numbers. It changes every minute.

This side shows the hour. It is like the hour hand pointing to a number on the clock.

This side shows the minutes. The 00 shows it is a new hour. It is like the minute hand pointing to the 12 on the clock.

In words, we say it is "six o'clock."

Your turn

1 Circle the time shown on each clock.

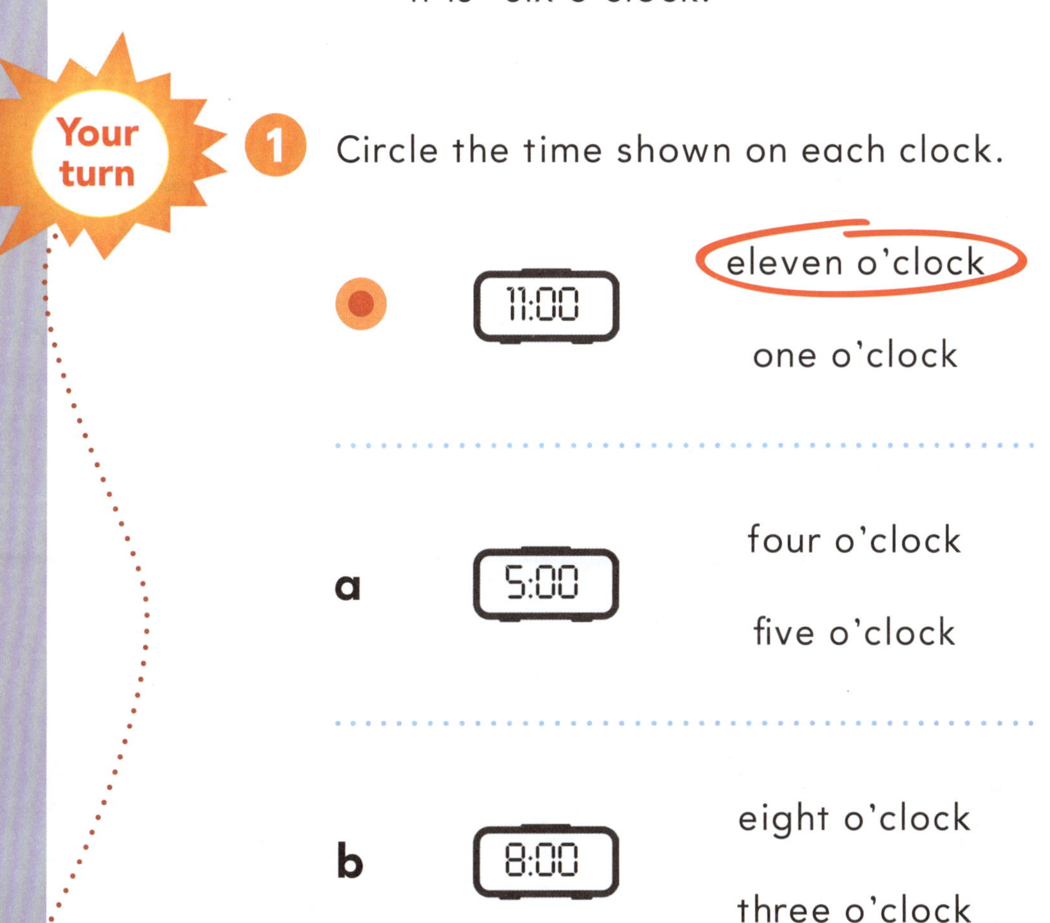

SELF CHECK Mark how you feel

Got it!	Need help...	I don't get it
☐	☐	☐

Practice

1 Circle the time shown on each clock.

● (example)	01:00	one o'clock (circled) / eight o'clock
a	04:00	three o'clock / four o'clock
b	07:00	two o'clock / seven o'clock
c	09:00	nine o'clock / six o'clock
d	12:00	twelve o'clock / three o'clock
e	03:00	two o'clock / three o'clock

2 Match the analog clocks to the digital clocks.

● 

a 

b 

c 

d 

11:00

02:00

06:00

10:00

05:00

Time to the Half-Hour: Analog Time

You can use an analog clock to tell time to the half-hour.

Example 1:

The hour hand is halfway between 9 and 10. This means it is halfway between 9:00 and 10:00.

The minute hand is at the 6. It is half way to the 12. This means 30 minutes have passed since it was at the 12.

This clock shows 9:30. It is halfway past 9:00.

Your turn

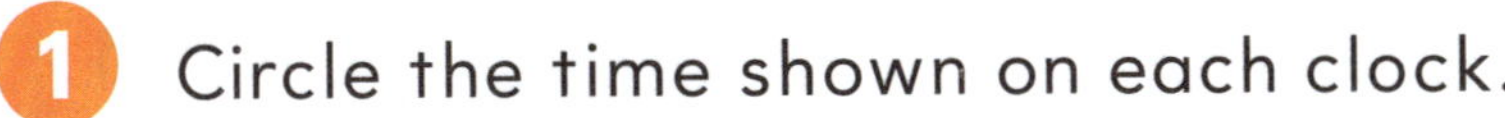

1 Circle the time shown on each clock.

4:30 (circled)

6:30

a

9:30

5:30

b

7:30

10:30

The hour hand slowly moves to the next hour. It does not always point directly at the hour.

SELF CHECK	Mark how you feel	
Got it! ☐	Need help... ☐	I don't get it ☐

Practice

1 Circle the time shown on each clock.

●	7:30	6:30 (circled)
a	5:30	3:30
b	7:30	8:30
c	11:30	12:30
d	4:30	6:30
e	10:30	11:30

2 Write the time shown on each clock.

● 12:30

a ______

b ______

c ______

d ______

e ______

3 Draw the hour and minute hands to show each time.

2:30

e 1:30

a 6:30

f 7:30

b 3:30

g 4:30

c 8:30

h 10:30

d 11:30

i  9:30

Time to the Half-Hour: Digital Time

A digital clock can also show the time to the half-hour.

Example 1:

Here is the hour. It is like the hour hand pointing to a number on the clock.

Here are the minutes. The 30 shows it is half-past, or 30 minutes past, the hour. It is like the minute hand pointing to the 6 on the clock.

In words, we say it is "eight-thirty."

1 Circle the time shown on each clock.

four-thirty

four o'clock

a

six-thirty

seven-thirty

b

ten-thirty

ten o'clock

Why do you think we have both types of clocks?

Practice

1. Circle the time shown on each clock.

	Clock	Choices		Clock	Choices
●	03:30	three-thirty / three o'clock	c	10:30	ten o'clock / ten-thirty
a	12:30	twelve-thirty / twelve o'clock	d	01:30	one-thirty / one-fifteen
b	04:30	four o'clock / four-thirty	e	08:30	nine-thirty / eight-thirty

2. Match the analog clocks to the digital clocks.

	Analog clock	Digital clock
●		02:30
a		09:30
b		05:30
c		06:30
d		11:30

Time Review

1 Write the time shown on each analog clock.

a 

d

b 

e 

c 

f 

2 Circle the time shown on each digital clock.

a 

nine o'clock

nine-thirty

c 04:30

four o'clock

four-thirty

b 

one o'clock

one-thirty

d 11:30

eleven o'clock

eleven-thirty

Review

3 Match the analog clocks to the digital clocks.

a 

01:30

b

05:30

c

02:00

d 

07:00

4 Draw the hands to show each time.

a 8:30

b 3:30

c 9:00

d 1:00

e 4:30

f 2:00

Pennies

A penny is a coin worth 1 cent.
The symbol for cent is ¢.

Example 1:

Pennies are a copper color.

President Lincoln is on the front.

This penny has the Lincoln Memorial on its back.

Pennies have smooth edges.

Example 2:

Find the value of a group of pennies by counting by 1s.

1 2 3 4 5 6

There are 6 pennies. These pennies are worth 6¢ altogether.

To make the cent sign, draw the letter *c*. Then, draw a line through it.

1 Write the value of each group of coins.

a

______

b

______

SELF CHECK Mark how you feel		
Got it!	Need help...	I don't get it

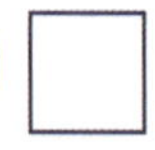

Practice

1 Circle the pennies.

●

a

b

2 Write the value of each group of coins.

●

9¢

a

____

b

____

3 Circle the coins to equal each amount.

● 5¢

a 10¢

b 8¢

Nickels

A nickel is a coin worth 5 cents.

Example 1:

Nickels are silver.

President Jefferson is on the front.

Jefferson's home is on the back.

Nickels have smooth edges.

Example 2:

Find the value of a group of nickels by counting by 5s.

5 10 15 20 25 30

There are 6 nickels. These nickels are worth 30¢.

Count by 5s! Only say the numbers that have a 5 or 0 in the ones place.

Your turn

1 Write the value of each group of coins.

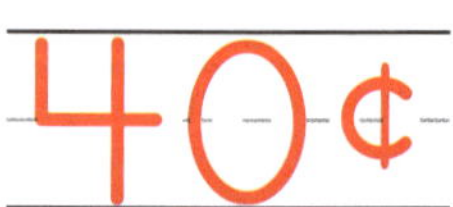

40¢

a

______

b

______

SELF CHECK Mark how you feel

Got it!	Need help...	I don't get it
 ☐	 ☐	  ☐

Practice

1 Circle the nickels.

a

b

2 Write the value of each group of coins.

a

b

c

3 Circle the coins to equal the amount.

40¢

a 25¢

b 35¢

Dimes

A dime is a coin worth 10 cents.

Example 1:

Dimes are silver.

President Roosevelt is on the front.

Symbols of liberty, strength, and peace are on the back.

Dimes have ridged edges.

Dimes are the smallest coins.

Example 2:

Find the value of a group of dimes by counting by 10s.

10	20	30	40	50	60

There are 6 dimes. These dimes are worth 60¢.

Your turn

1 Write the value of each group of coins.

●   

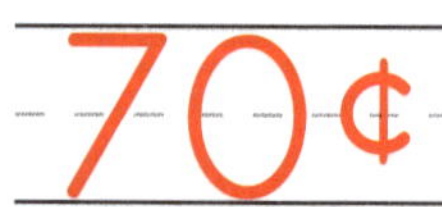

a   ______

b     ______

SELF CHECK	Mark how you feel	
Got it!  ☐	Need help...   ☐	I don't get it   ☐

Practice

1 Circle the dimes.

a

b

2 Write the value of each group of coins.

30¢

a ______

b ______

c ______

3 Circle the coins to equal the amount.

40¢

a 10¢

b 60¢

Quarters

A quarter is a coin worth 25 cents.

Example 1:

Quarters are silver.

George Washington is on the front.

The bald eagle is on the back of this quarter.

Quarters have ridged edges.

Example 2:

Find the value of a group of quarters by counting by 25s.

25 50 75

There are 3 quarters. These quarters are worth 75¢.

1 Write the value of each group of coins.

  25¢

a   ______

b    ______

SELF CHECK Mark how you feel		
Got it!  ☐	Need help... 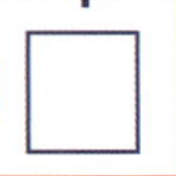 ☐	I don't get it  ☐

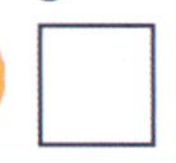

Practice

1 Circle the quarters.

a

b

c

2 Write the value of each group of coins.

50¢

a ____

b ____

3 Circle the coins to equal the amount.

50¢

a 25¢

b 75¢

Make a Dollar

There are 100 cents in a dollar. You can make a dollar using coins.

Example 1:

This table shows how many coins are needed to make a dollar.

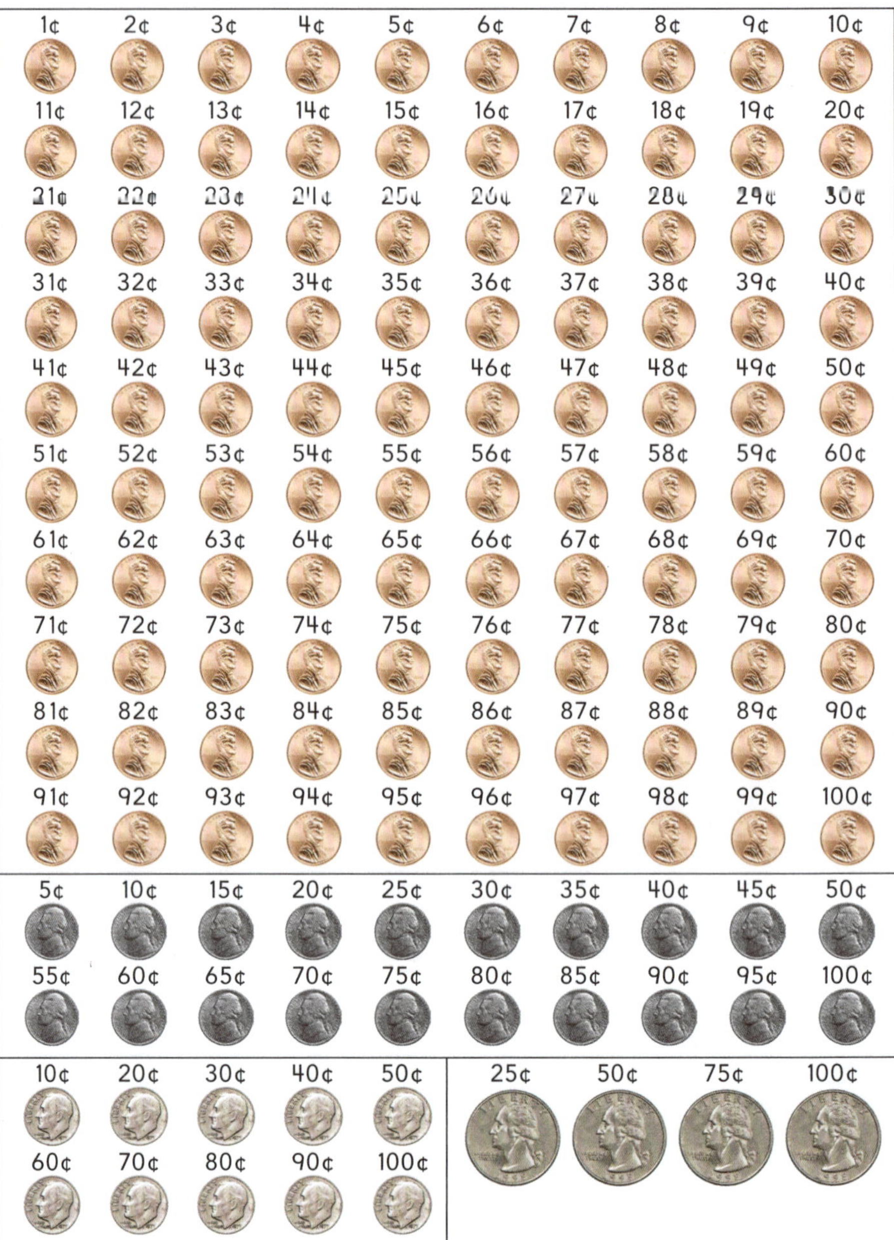

One dollar is written with a dollar sign and decimal point. It looks like this: $1.00.

1 Write the number of coins needed to make a dollar.

● How many nickels? 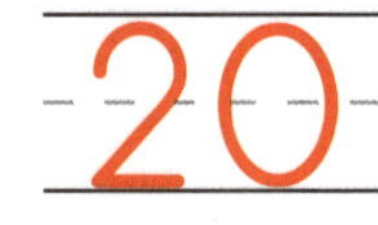

a How many pennies? ________

SELF CHECK Mark how you feel

Got it!	Need help...	I don't get it
 ☐	 ☐	 ☐

Practice

1 Complete the table.

	Picture of coin	Name of coin	Value	How many in a dollar?
●		penny	1¢	100
a				
b				
c				

2 Do the coins equal one dollar? Circle yes or no.

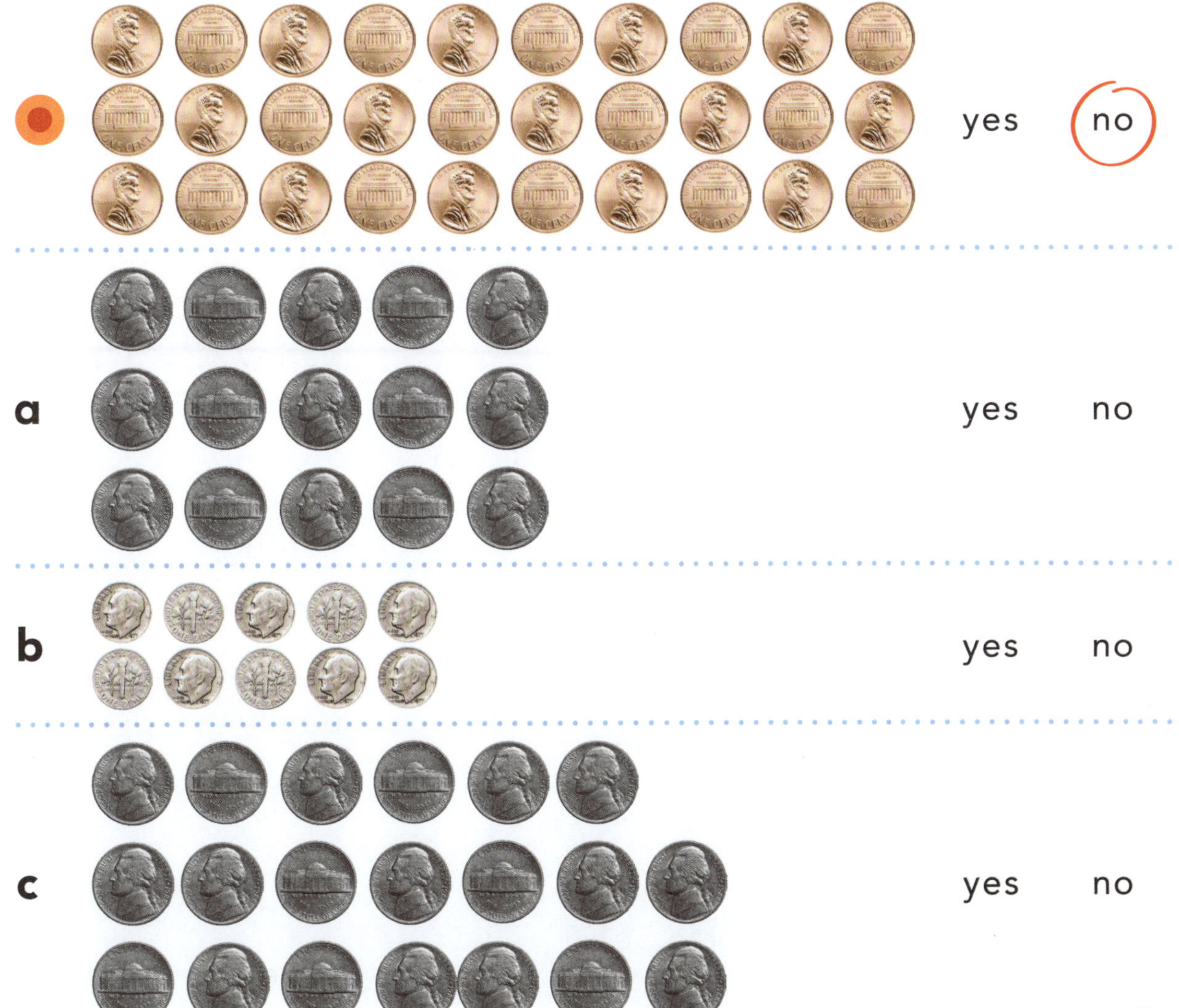

● yes (no)

a yes no

b yes no

c yes no

Money Review

1 Match the name of each coin to its picture.

a nickel 

b dime 

c penny 

d quarter 

2 Read each question. Circle the correct answer.

a Which coin is worth the least? penny nickel dime quarter

b Which coin is worth the most? penny nickel dime quarter

c Which coin is worth 10¢? penny nickel dime quarter

d Which coin is worth 1¢? penny nickel dime quarter

e Which coin is worth 25¢? penny nickel dime quarter

f Which coin is worth 5¢? penny nickel dime quarter

Review

3 Write the value of each set of coins.

a  ______

b  ______

c  ______

d  ______

e  ______

f  ______

g ______

h  ______

i  ______

j ______

k  ______

l  ______

Positions

There are many ways to say where something is. This is called its position.

Example 1:

Here are words used to describe positions.

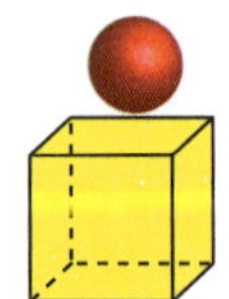

The ball is **above** the box.

The ball is **below** the box.

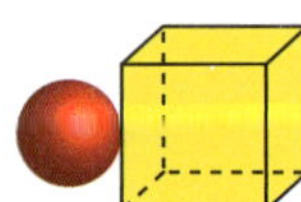

The ball is **beside** the box.

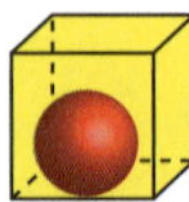

The ball is **inside** the box.

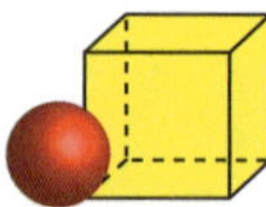

The ball is **in front of** the box.

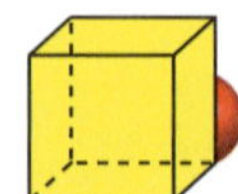

The ball is **behind** the box.

The ball is **between** the boxes.

1 Circle the position that describes the bird.

beside   inside   behind

a

above   in front of   below

Practice

1 Circle the position that best completes each sentence.

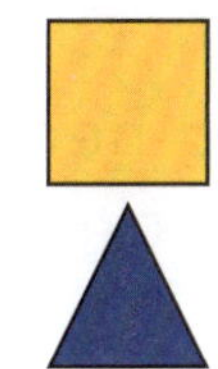

The triangle is ______ the square.

below beside behind

a 

The square is ______ the triangle.

in front of beside above

b   

The square is ______ the triangles.

in front of above between

c 

The triangle is ______ the square.

below in front of above

2 Match the position to the picture that describes the bee.

in front of

a inside

b behind

c above

d below

3 Follow the directions. Draw objects in positions.

- Draw an oval **behind** the basket.
- a Draw a circle **inside** the basket.
- b Draw a triangle **above** the basket.
- c Draw a square **beside** the basket.
- d Draw a heart **between** the square and the basket.
- e Draw a star **in front of** the basket.
- f Draw a rectangle **below** the basket.

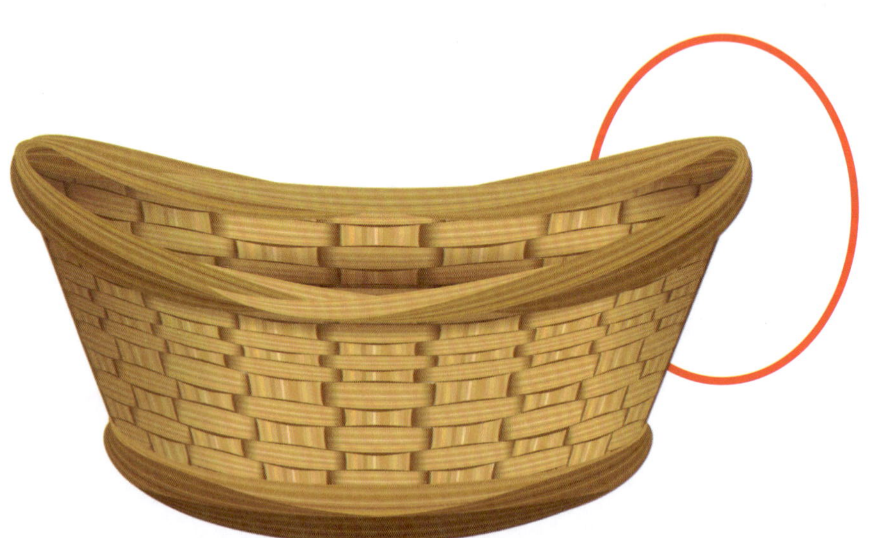

Sides and Vertices

Shapes have sides and vertices. Vertices are sometimes called corners.

A **side** is a straight edge.

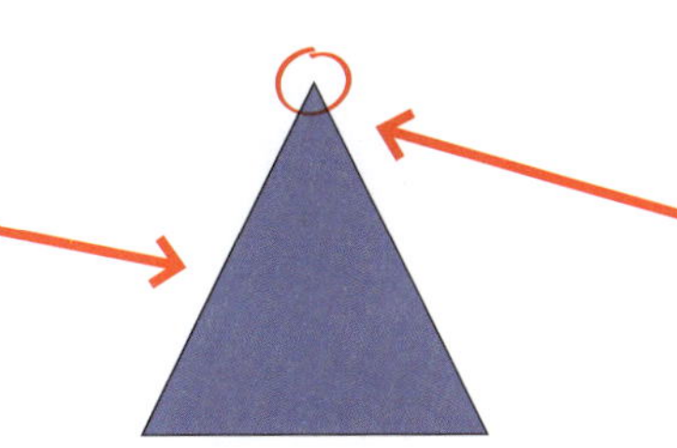

A **vertex** is where 2 sides come together.

A **square vertex** is a special vertex. A square will fit in it.

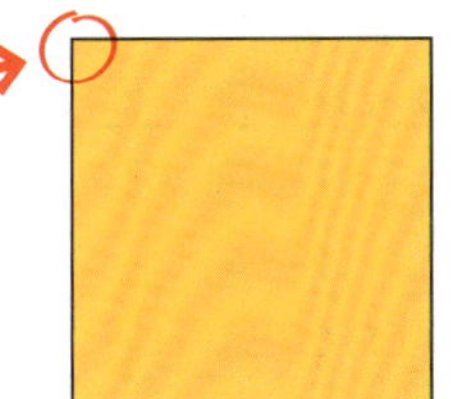

Example 1:

Circle each vertex.

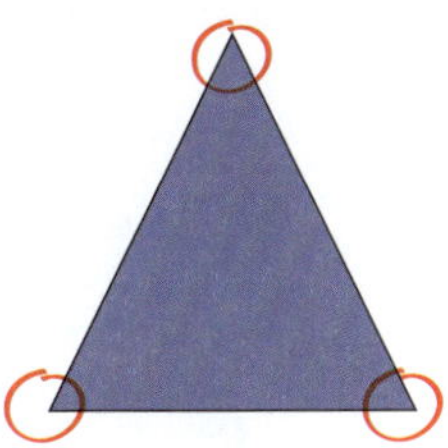

Example 2:

Put an *X* on each side.

One corner is called a vertex. More than one are vertices.

1 Write the number of sides and vertices for each shape.

 square:

4 sides

4 vertices

a trapezoid:

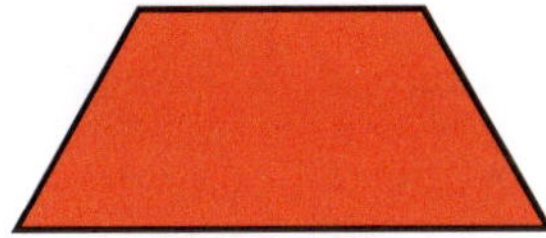

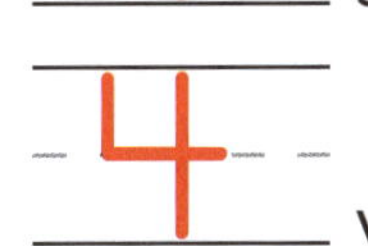

_____ sides

_____ vertices

SELF CHECK	Mark how you feel	
Got it! ☐	Need help... ☐	I don't get it ☐

1 Circle the vertices on each shape.

b 

a 

c 

2 Put an *X* on the sides of each shape.

b 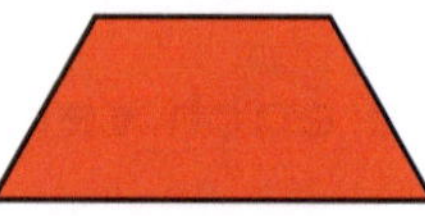

a 

c 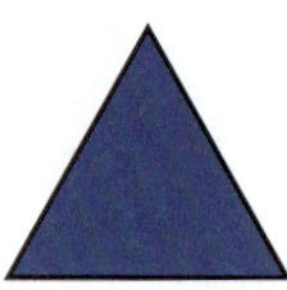

3 Write the number of square vertices for each shape.

 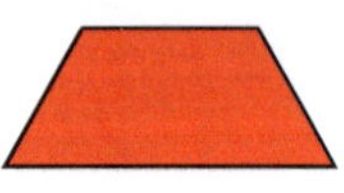 0 square vertices

a  ______ square vertices

b  ______ square vertices

c  ______ square vertices

Attributes

Attributes are traits of a shape. A shape's color, size, and the number of sides it has are attributes.

Example 1:

This shape has many attributes. 

It is red.

It has four sides.

It has four vertices.

It is small.

Example 2:

Some attributes must be true for a shape.

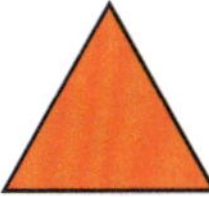

A triangle must have:
- 3 sides
- 3 vertices

A rectangle must have:
- 4 sides
- 4 square vertices

A square must have:
- 4 sides
- 4 square vertices
- equal sides

A trapezoid must have:
- 4 sides
- 4 vertices

1 Write the attributes of this shape. 

● It is tall.

a It is ______________.

b It has ______________ sides.

c It has ______________ vertices.

Practice

1 Write attributes for each shape.

● 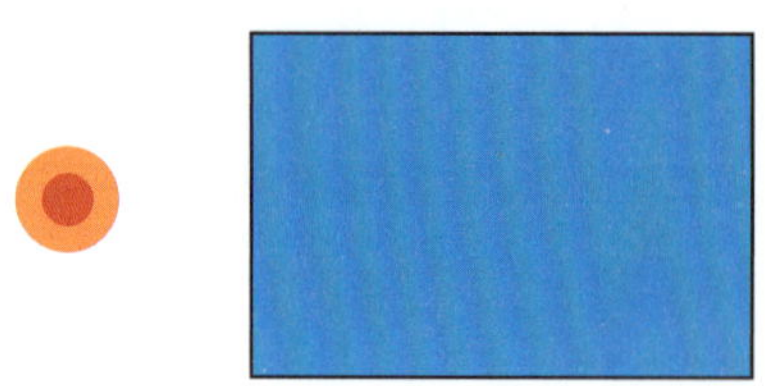

It has 4 vertices.
It has 4 sides.
It is blue.

a 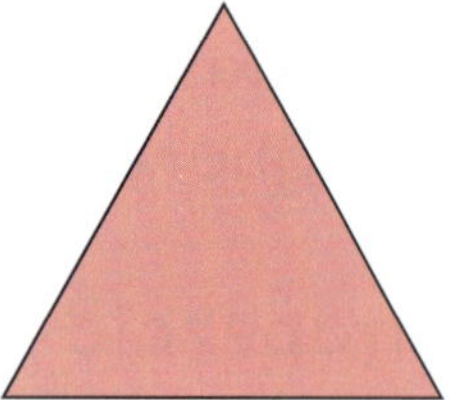

b 

2 Circle the attribute that must be true for each type of shape.

 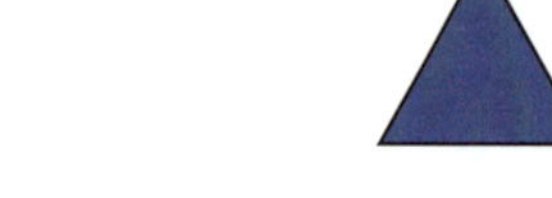

4 vertices small 3 sides

b 

yellow long 4 vertices

a 

4 sides green 3 sides

c 

purple 4 equal sides small

2D and 3D Shapes

Some shapes are two-dimensional (2D). They are flat. Others are three-dimensional (3D). They are solid.

This square is 2D.
It is a flat shape.

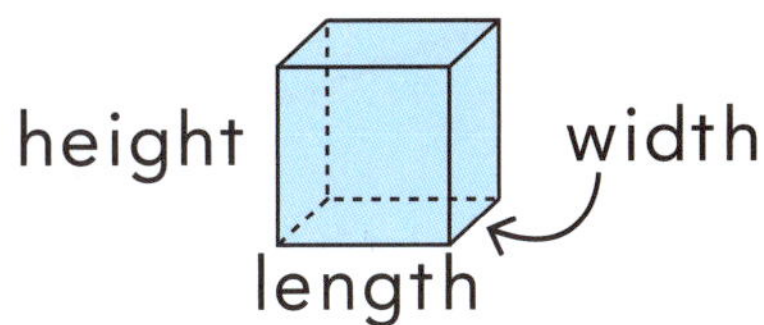

This cube is 3D.
It has thickness.

Example 1:

Two-Dimensional Shapes	Three-Dimensional Shapes
rectangle, square, triangle, circle, trapezoid	cube, rectangular prism, cone, cylinder, sphere

Your turn

1 Circle the 3D shapes.

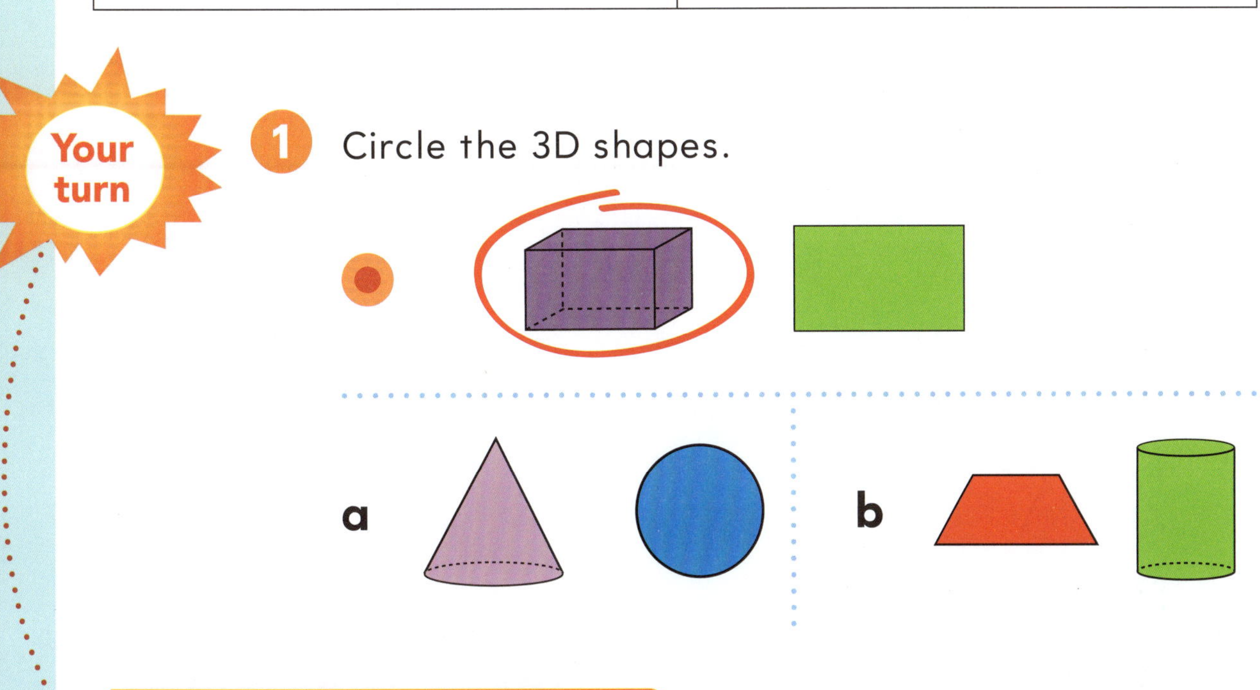

SELF CHECK Mark how you feel

Got it!	Need help…	I don't get it
☐	☐	☐

Practice

1 Match each 2D shape to its name.

- ● — trapezoid
- **a** — square
- **b** — triangle
- **c** — rectangle
- **d** — circle

2 Match each 3D shape to its name.

- ● 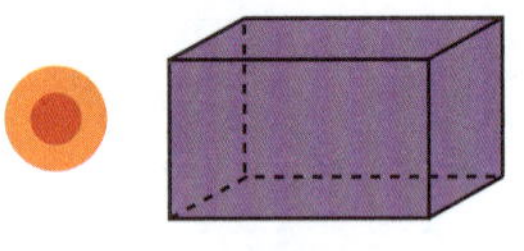 — cube
- **a** 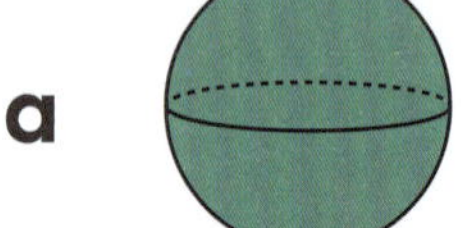 — rectangular prism
- **b** 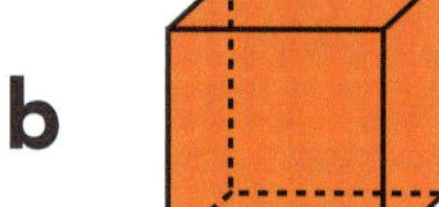 — cone
- **c**  — cylinder
- **d** 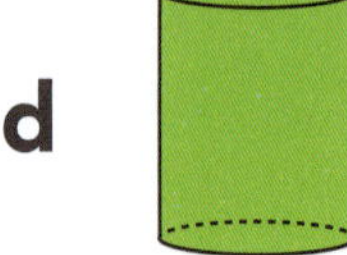 — sphere

3 Circle the 2D shapes. Put an *X* on 3D shapes.

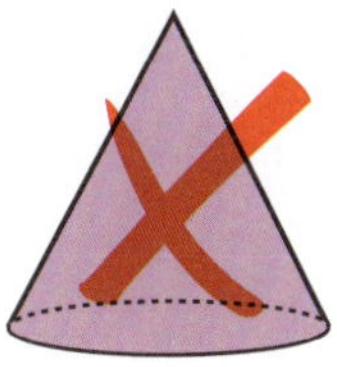

a

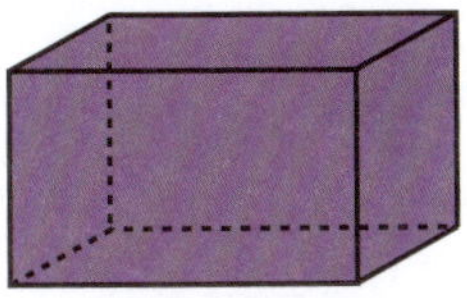

b

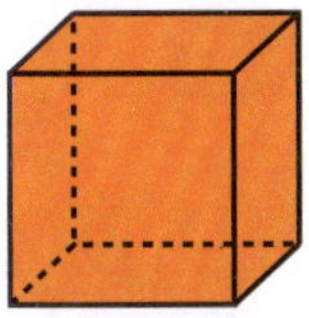

c

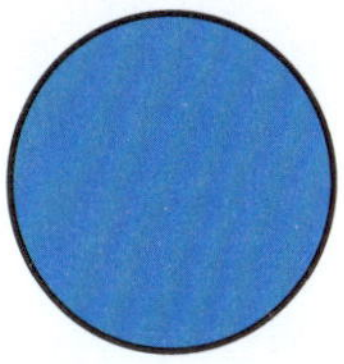

d

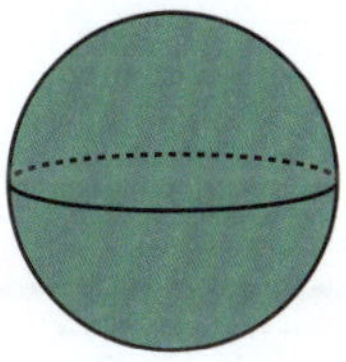

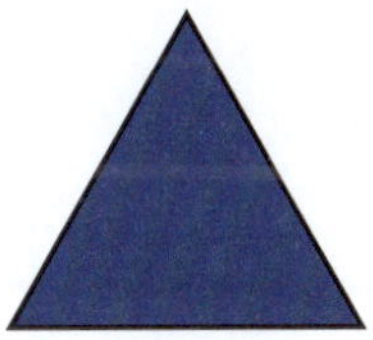

4 How are 2D and 3D shapes different?

Make Shapes

You can make, or compose, new shapes. This means putting 2D or 3D shapes together. The shapes can create something new.

Example 1:

Use a rectangle and triangle. Make a new shape.

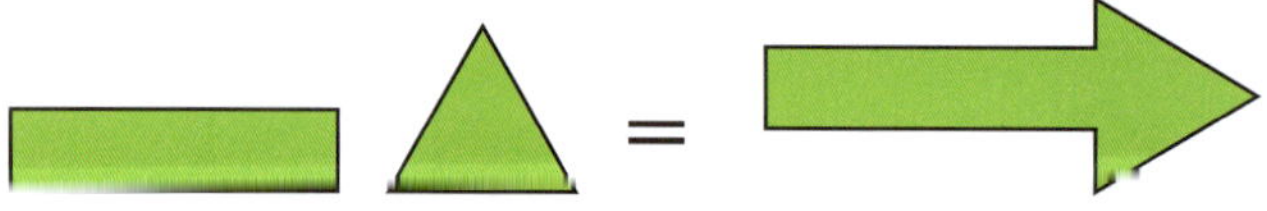

Example 2:

Use a cylinder and cone. Make a new shape.

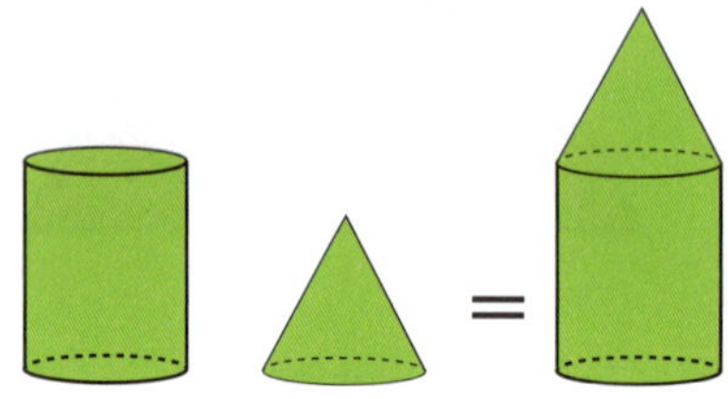

1. Look at the two shapes. Circle the shape they could make together.

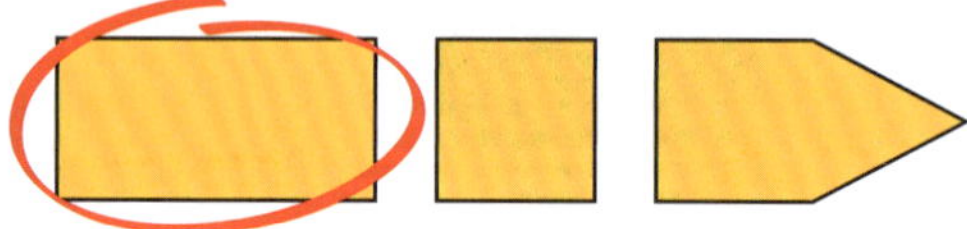

a

b

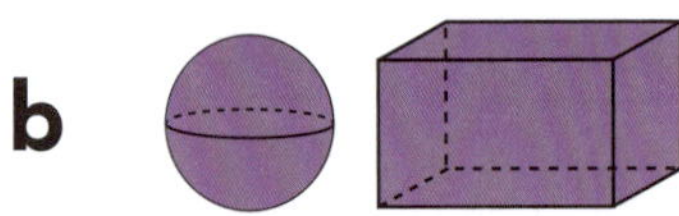

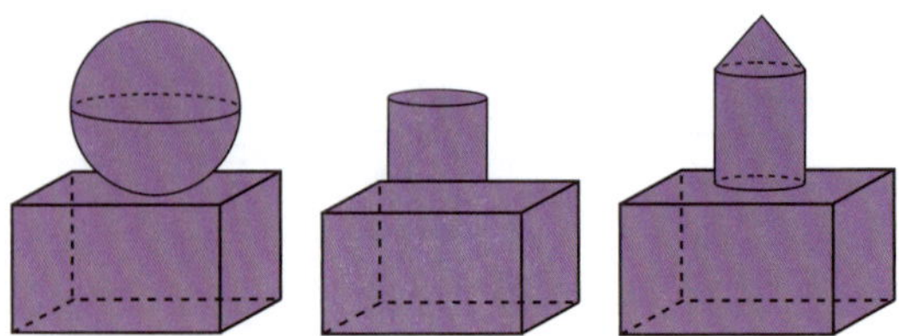

SELF CHECK	Mark how you feel	
Got it! ☐	Need help... ☐	I don't get it ☐

Practice

1 Match the shapes to the composed shape.

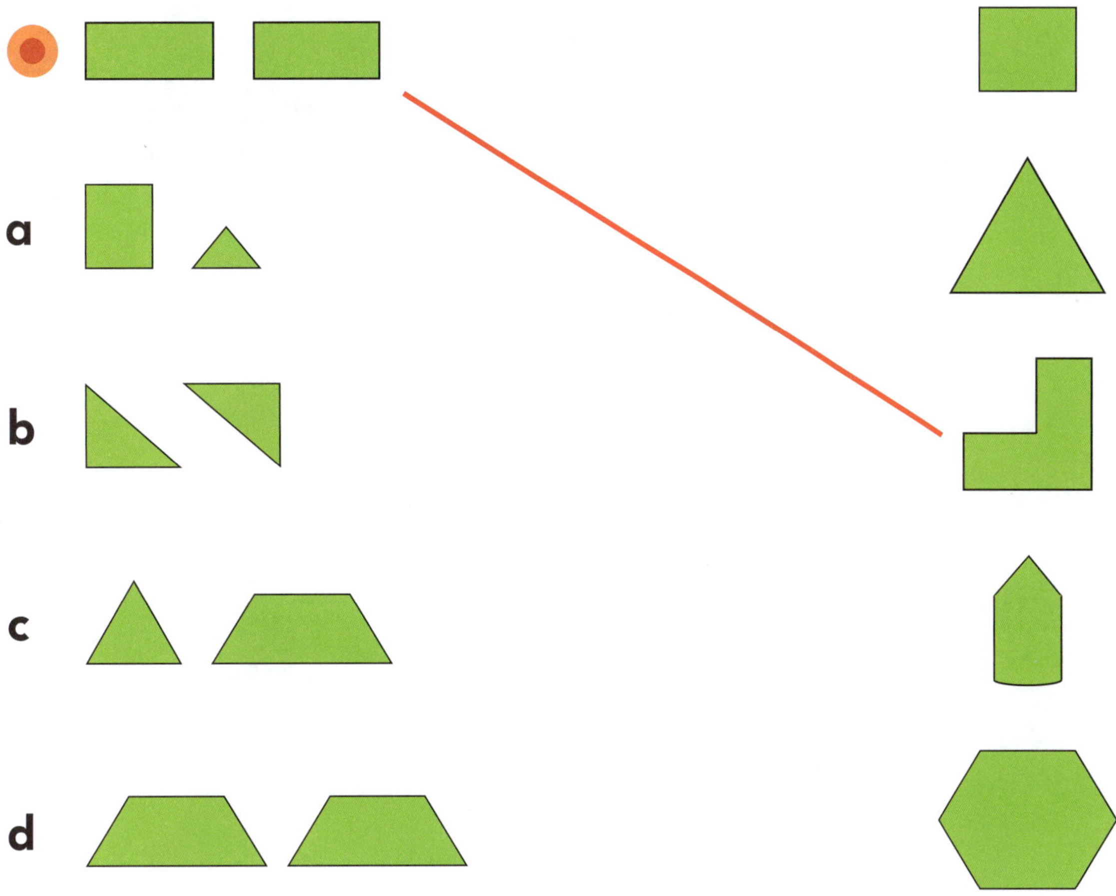

2 Look at the composed shapes. Trace the lines to show how they were made.

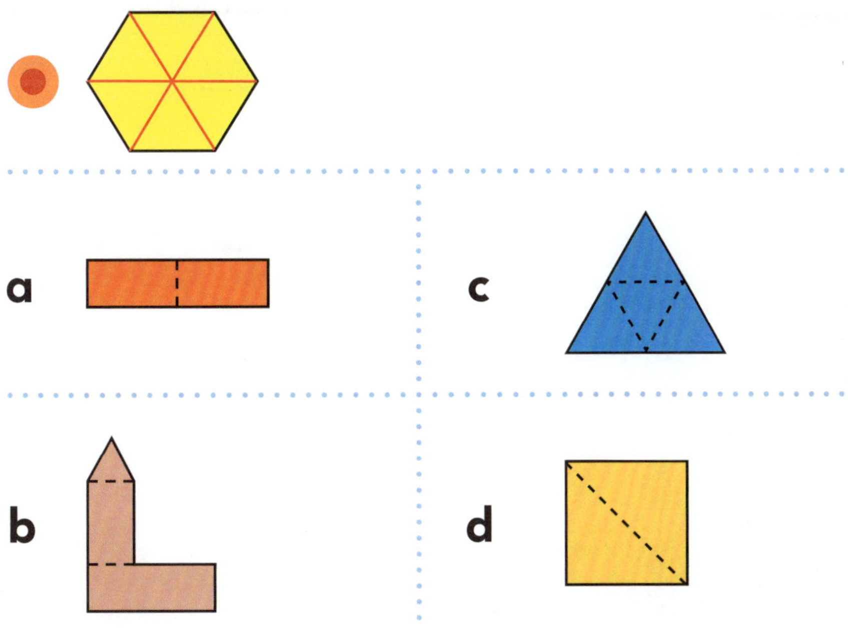

3 Match the 3D shapes to the composed shapes.

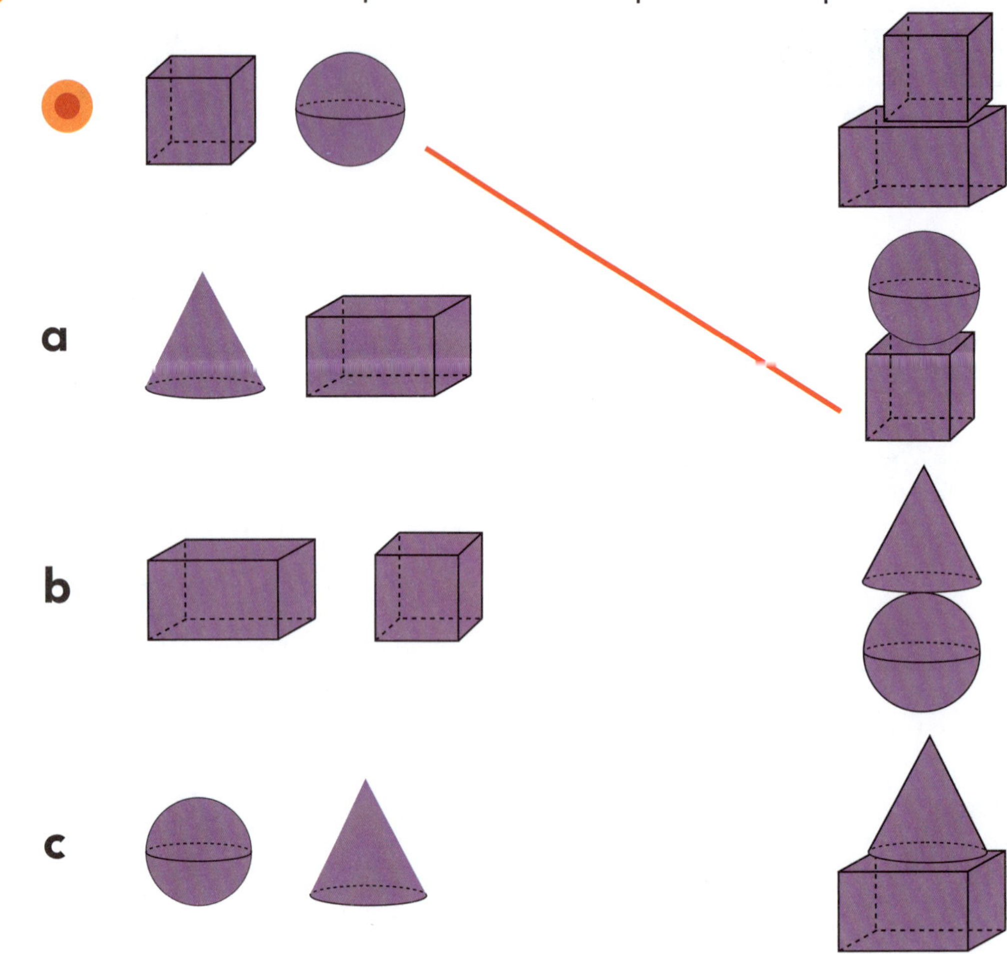

4 Match each 3D shape to a real object.

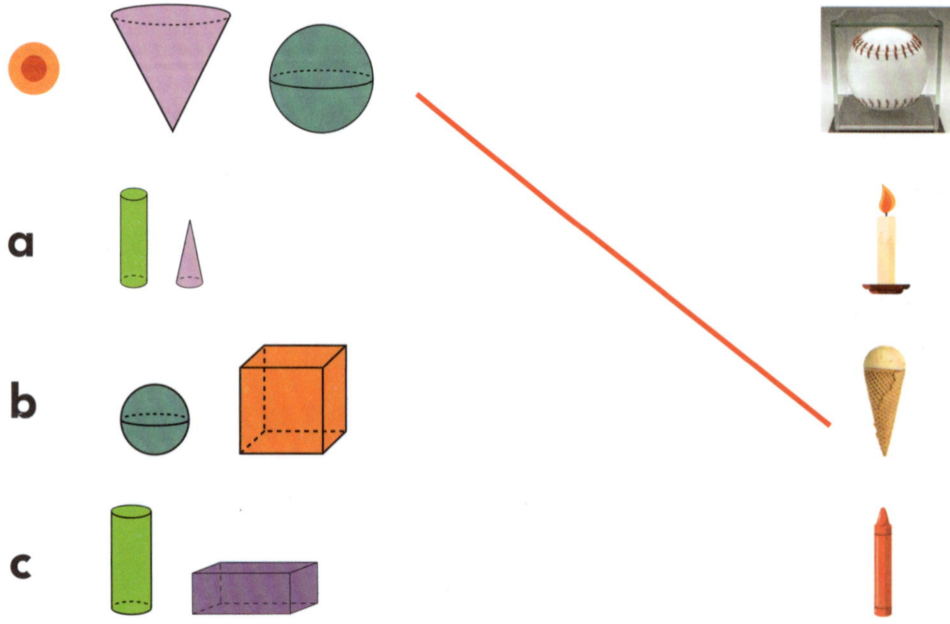

Shapes Review

1 Use the word bank to complete the sentences. Words may be used more than once.

above	beside	
between	in front of	inside

a The sidewalk is ______________________ the house.

b The house is ______________________ the bushes.

c The bird is ______________________ the house.

d The door is ______________________ the windows.

e The cat is ______________________ the house.

f The tree is ______________________ the house.

g The cloud is ______________________ the bird.

Review

2 Circle each vertex. Put an ***X*** on each side.

a 

c 

b 

d 

3 Circle the attribute that must be true for each type of shape.

a 

4 square vertices   green   small

b 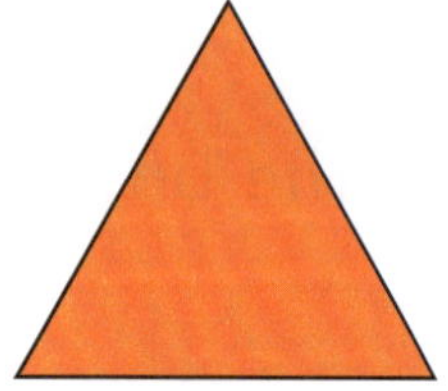

black   3 sides   3 square vertices

c 

4 sides   blue   5 corners

d 

yellow   tall   4 square vertices

Review

4 Match each shape to its name.

a cone 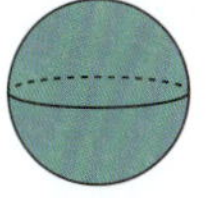

b rectangular prism 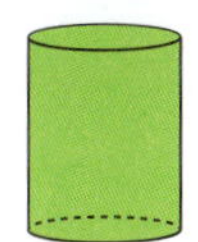

c sphere 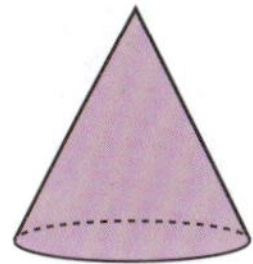

d cylinder 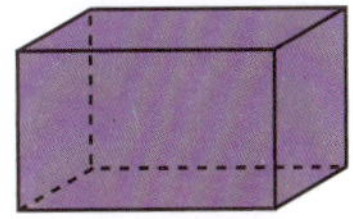

e cube 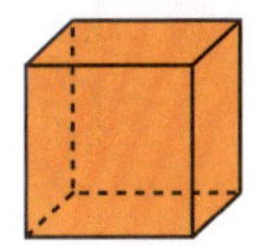

5 Match each set of shapes to their composed shape.

a   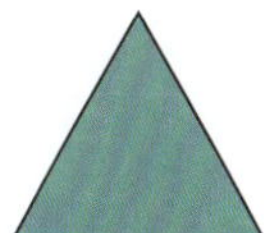

b 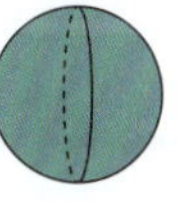  

c 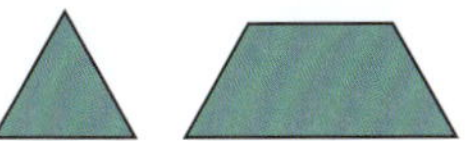 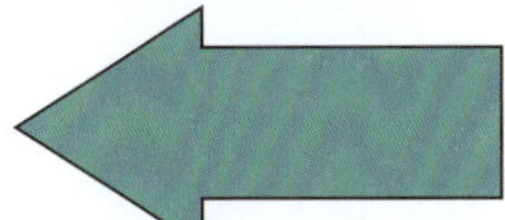

d 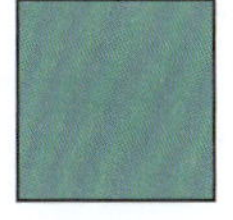 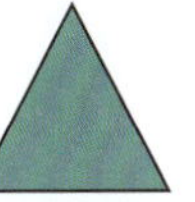 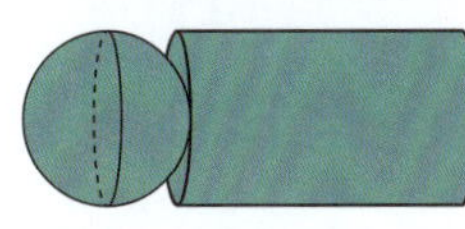

e  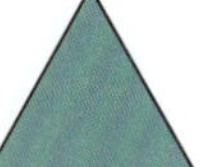 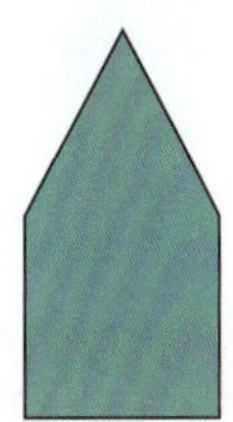

Equal Parts

Shapes can be divided into parts. Sometimes the parts are equal. Sometimes they are not.

Example 1:

Which shape shows equal parts?

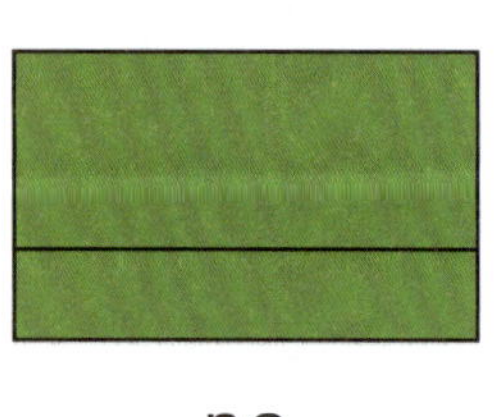

no

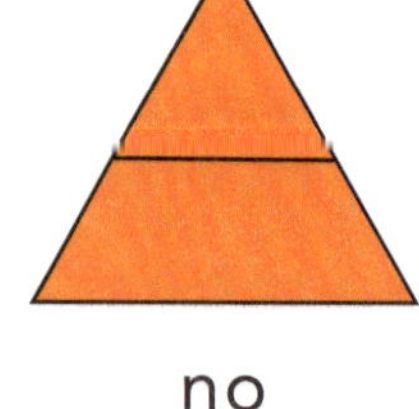

no

yes

Do the shapes show equal parts?
Circle your answers.

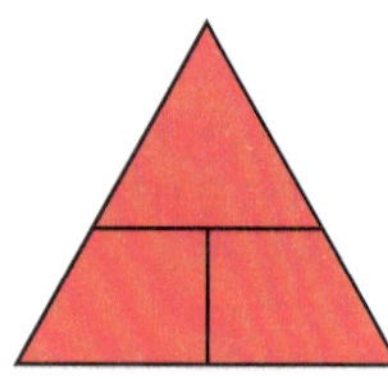

yes no

a

yes no

b

yes no

You need equal parts to make fractions.

SELF CHECK Mark how you feel

Got it!	Need help...	I don't get it
 	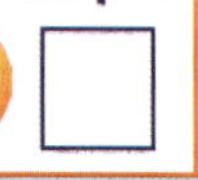 	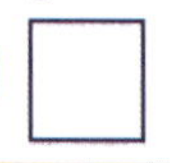

Practice

1 Circle the shapes that have equal parts.

●

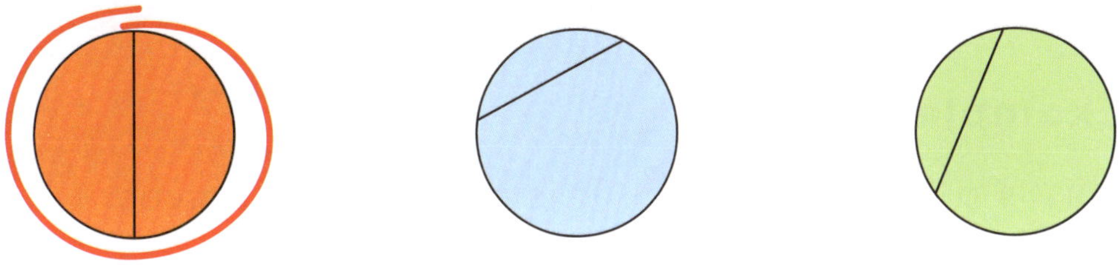

a

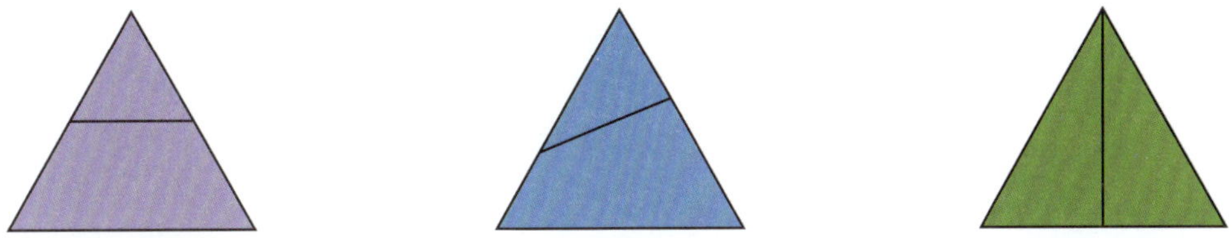

b

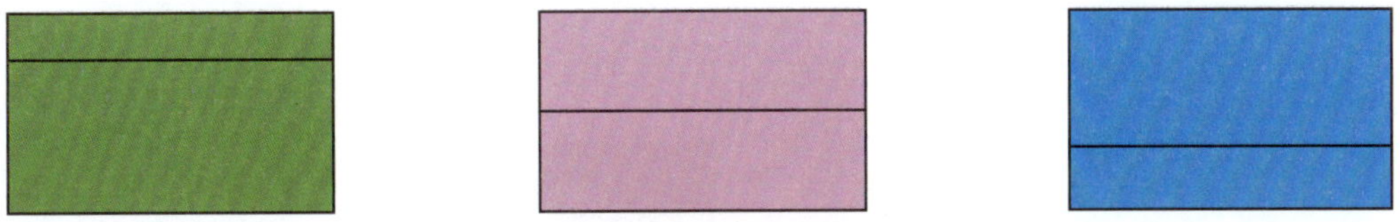

c

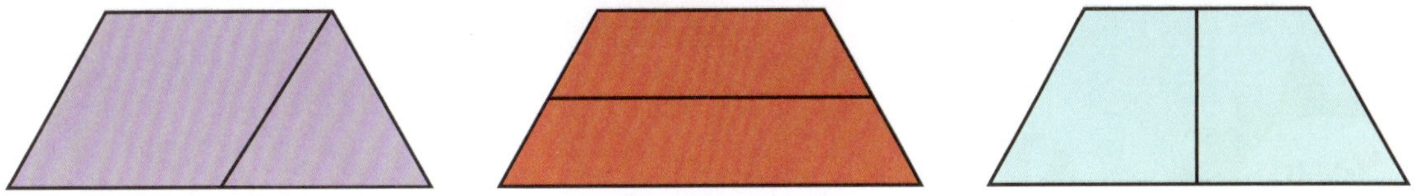

d

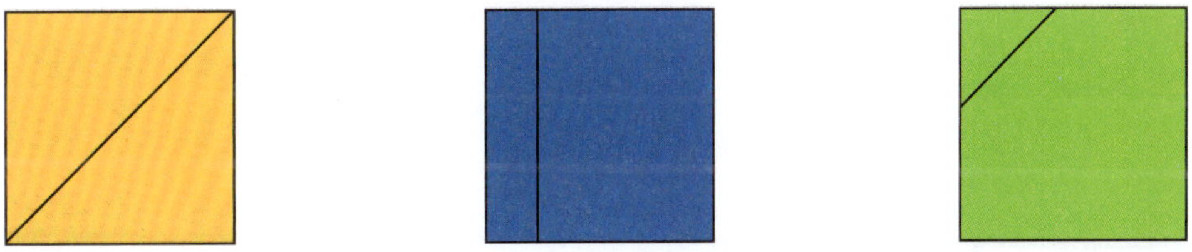

2 Do the shapes have equal parts? Circle your answer.

●

yes no

b

yes no

d

yes no

a

yes no

c

yes no

e

yes no

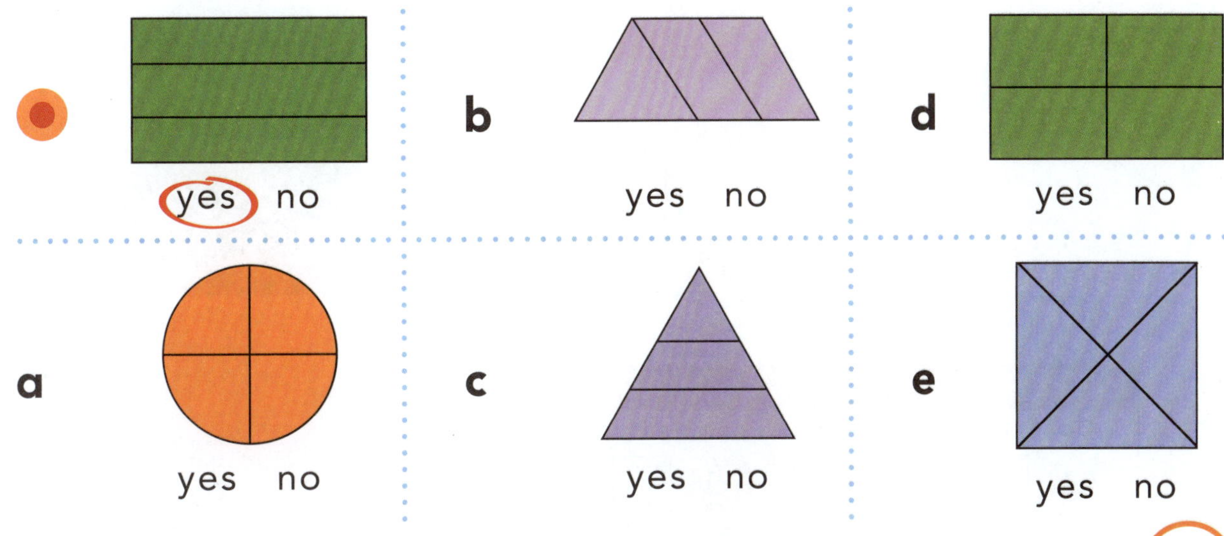

Halves

A shape can be divided into 2 equal parts. Each part is called a *half*. The whole is made of the two parts.

Example 1:

This is one whole circle. It is divided into halves.

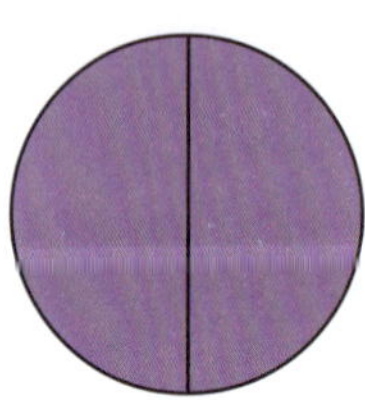

Example 2:

This rectangle is divided into halves.

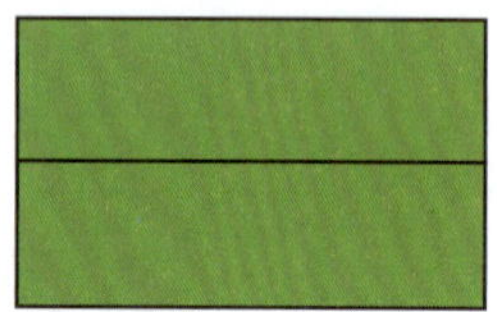

1 Circle the shapes that are divided into halves.

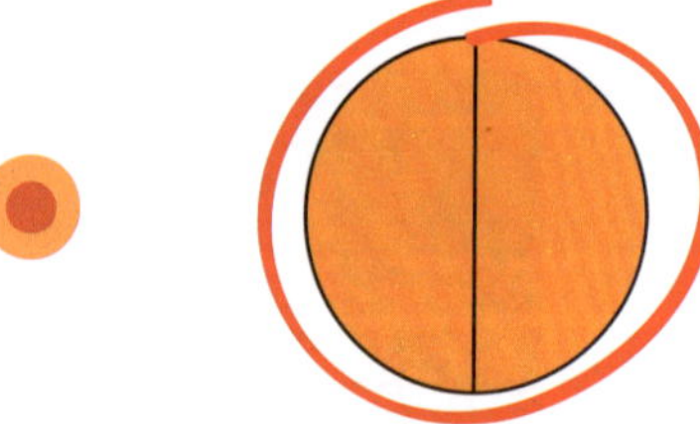

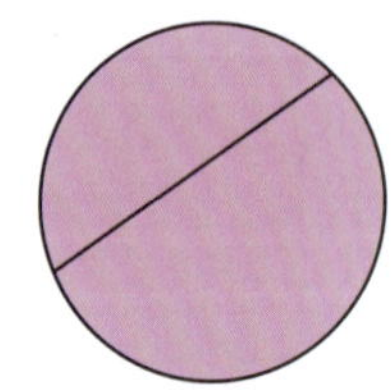

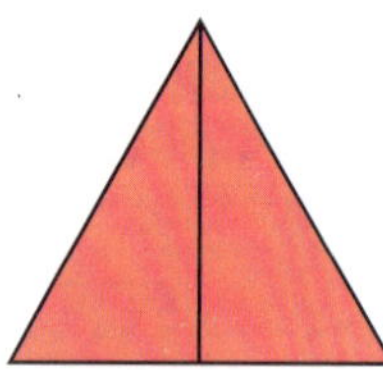

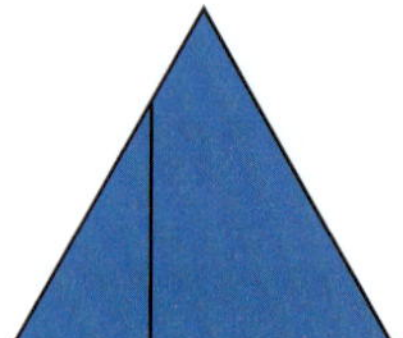

a

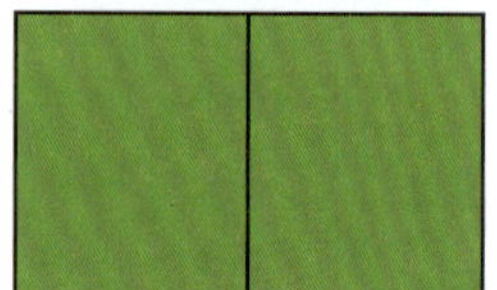

b

SELF CHECK	Mark how you feel	
Got it! ☐	Need help... ☐	I don't get it ☐

Practice

1 Circle the shape that is divided into halves.

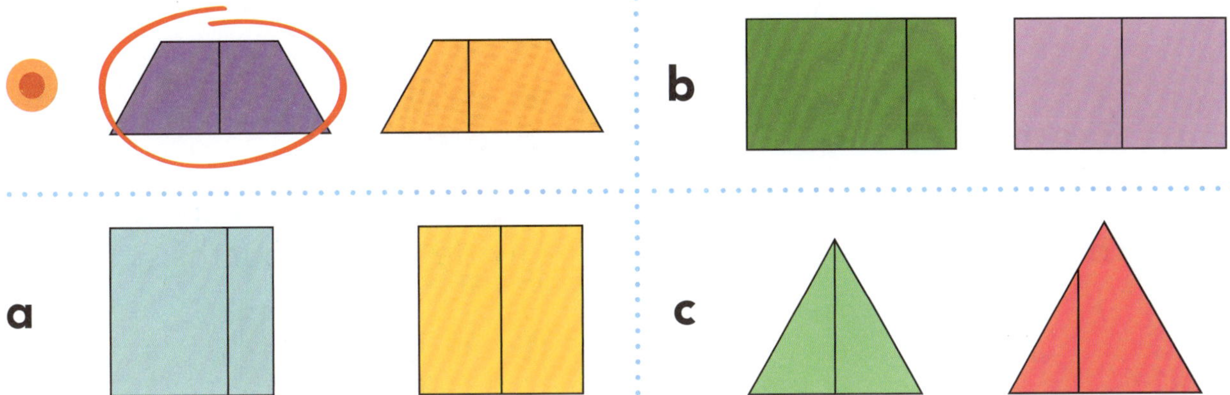

2 Draw a line on each shape to divide it into halves.

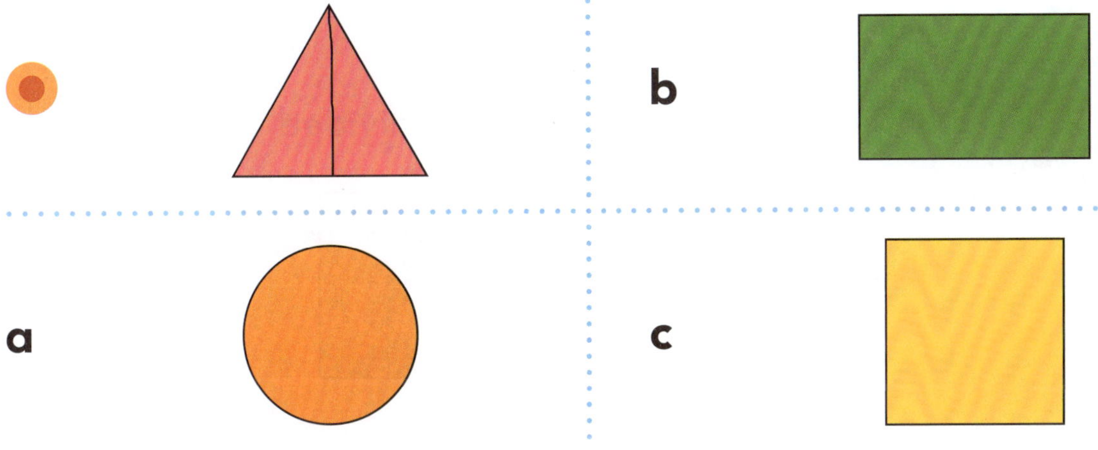

3 Draw a line on each object to divide it into halves.

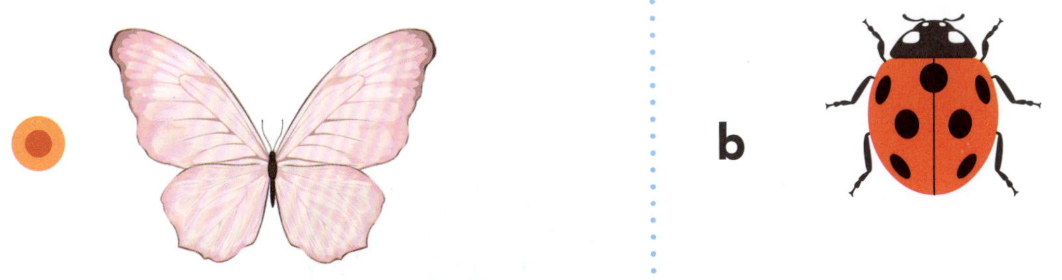

Fourths

A shape can be divided into 4 equal parts. Each part is called a fourth. The whole is made of the four parts.

Example 1:

This square is divided into fourths.

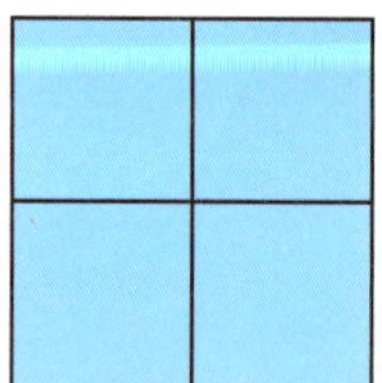

Example 2:

Here is another way to divide it into fourths.

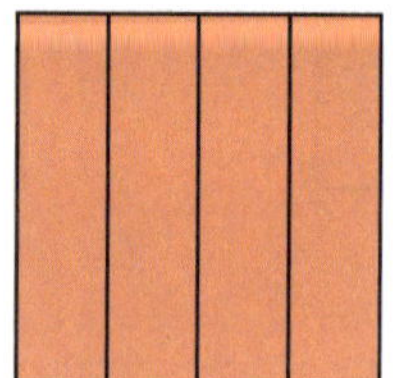

1 Circle the shapes that are divided into fourths.

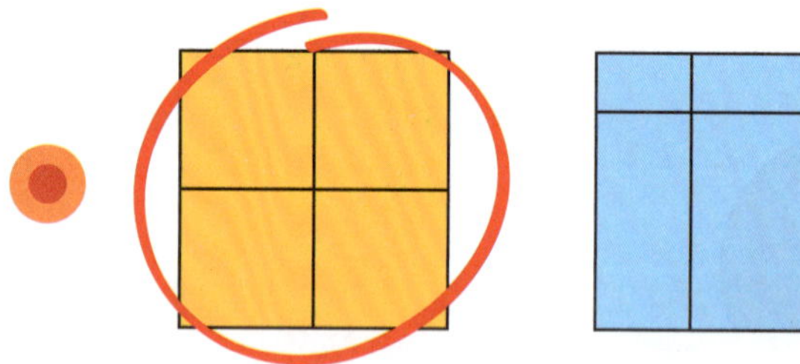

a

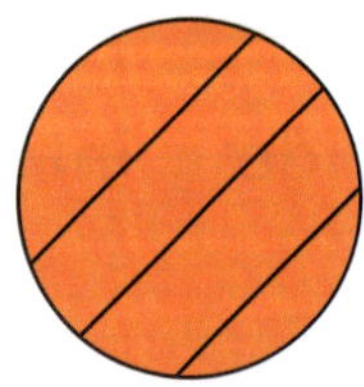

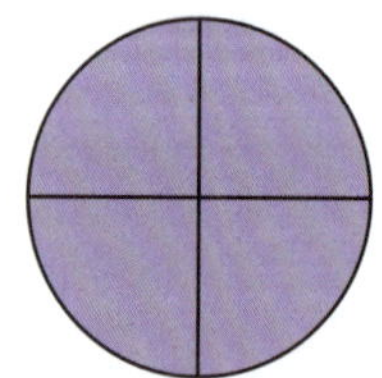

b

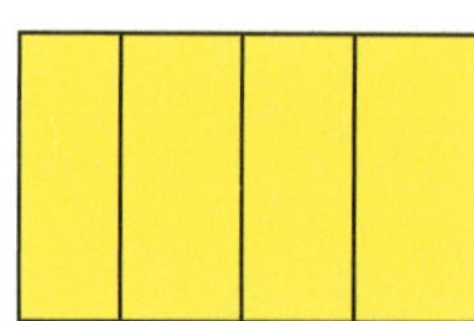

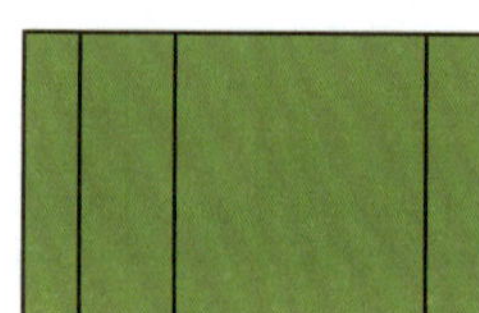

Practice

1 
Circle the shapes that are divided into fourths.

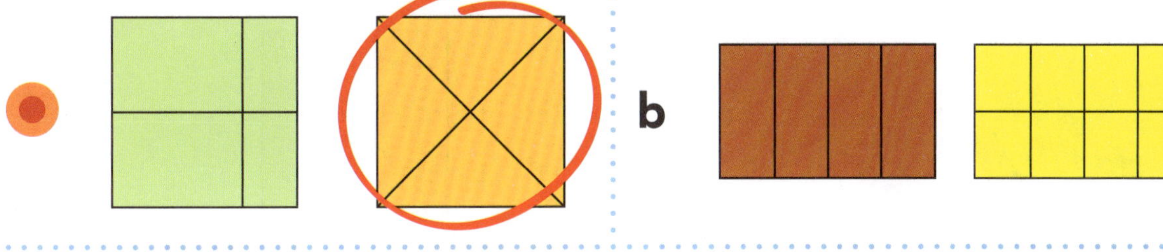

a 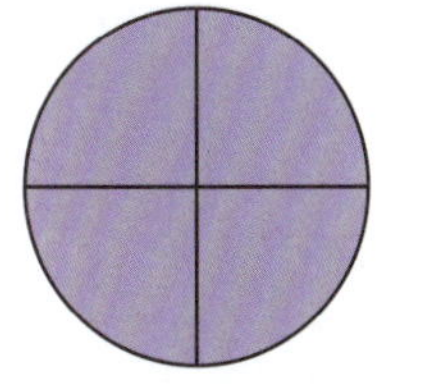 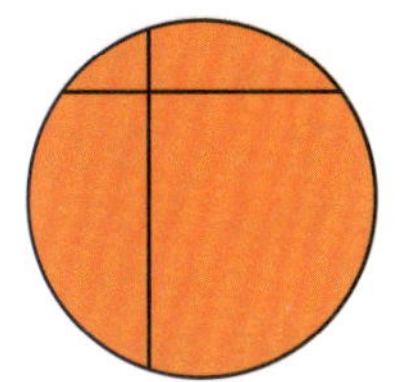

c 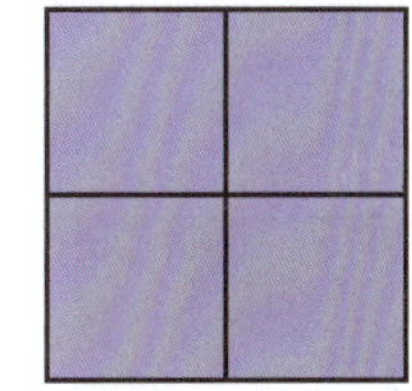 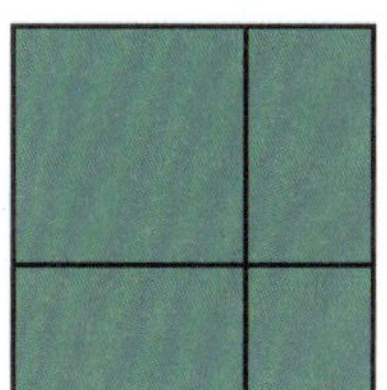

2 Divide each shape into fourths a different way.

 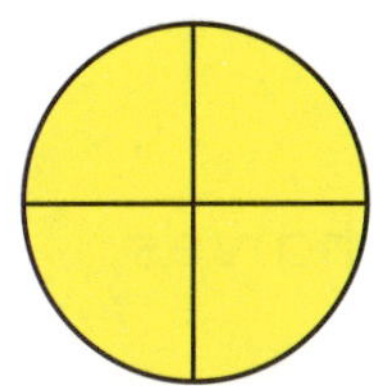 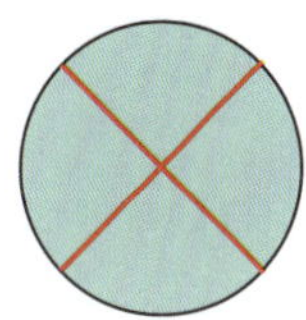

a   

b   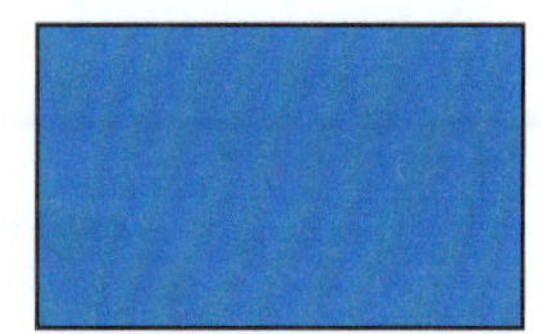

3 Color each whole shape. Write how many fourths you colored.

 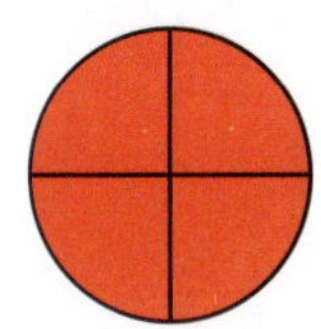

I filled in 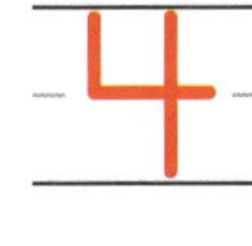 fourths to color the whole.

a 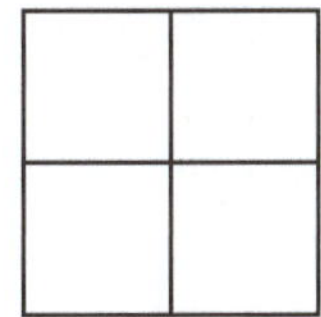

I filled in ______ fourths to color the whole.

Fractions Review

1 Do the shapes show equal parts? Circle your answer.

a

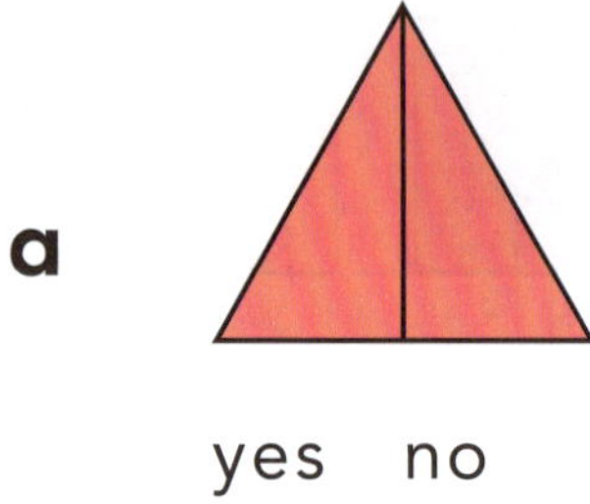

yes no

b

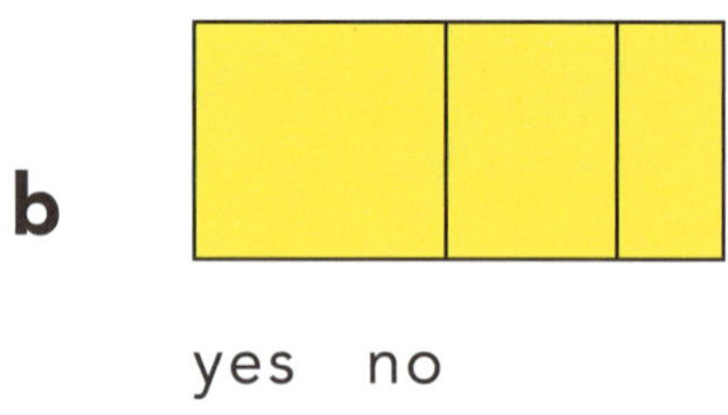

yes no

c

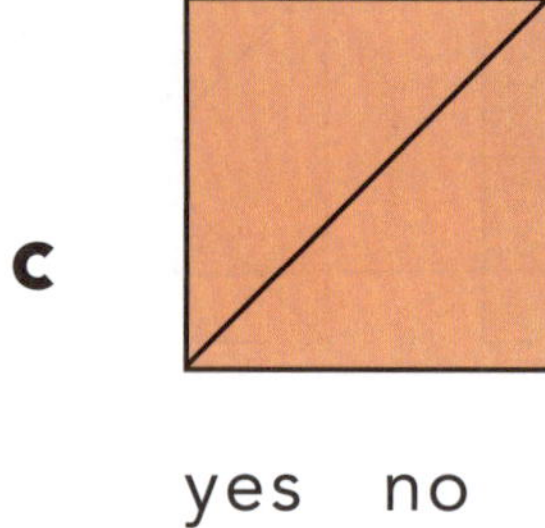

yes no

d

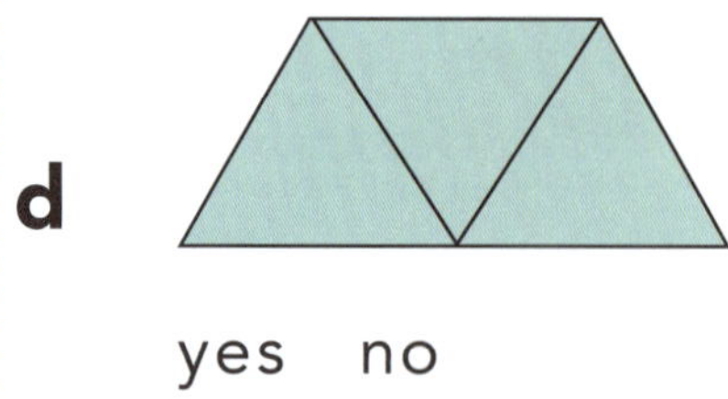

yes no

2 Draw a line on each shape to make equal halves.

a

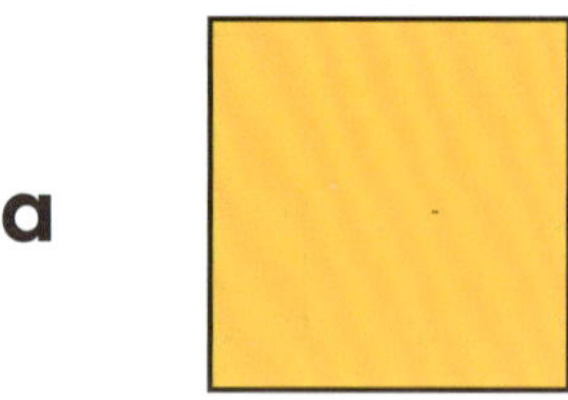

b

c

d

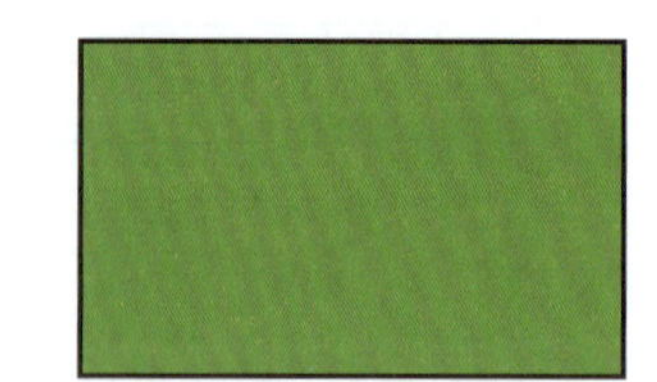

Review

3 Draw lines on each shape to make quarters.

a

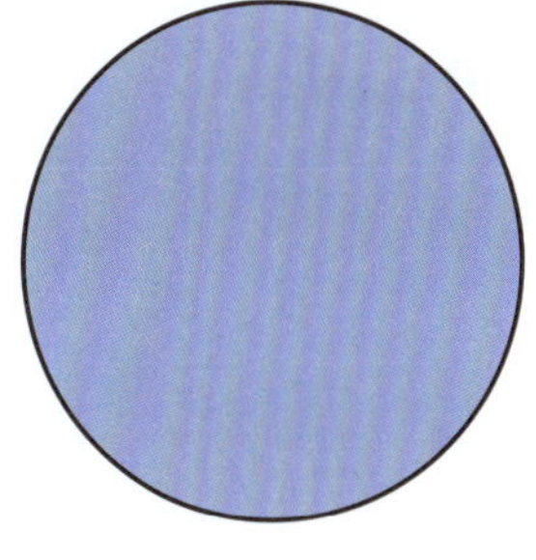

c

b

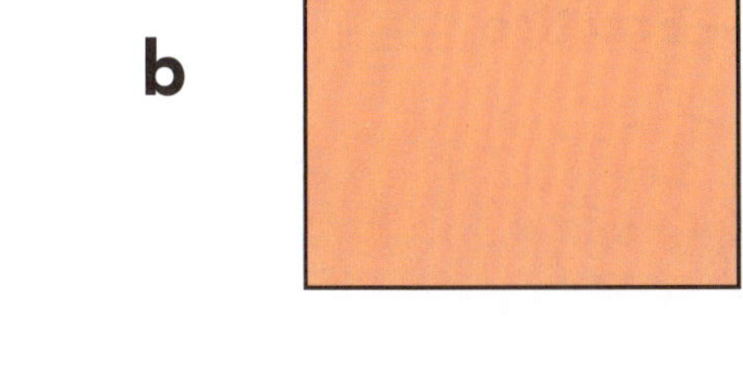

4 Color each whole shape. Write how many parts you colored.

a

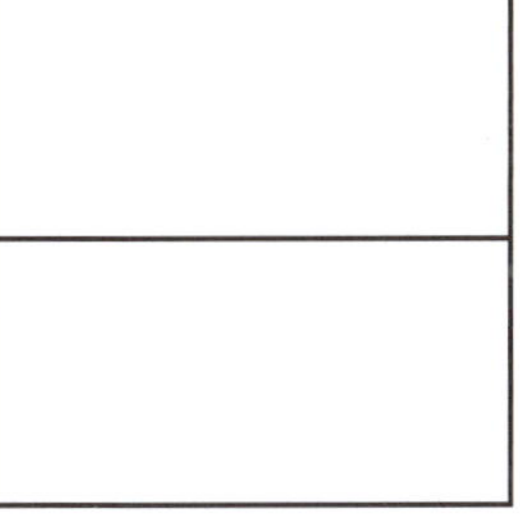

I filled in ______ halves to color the whole.

b

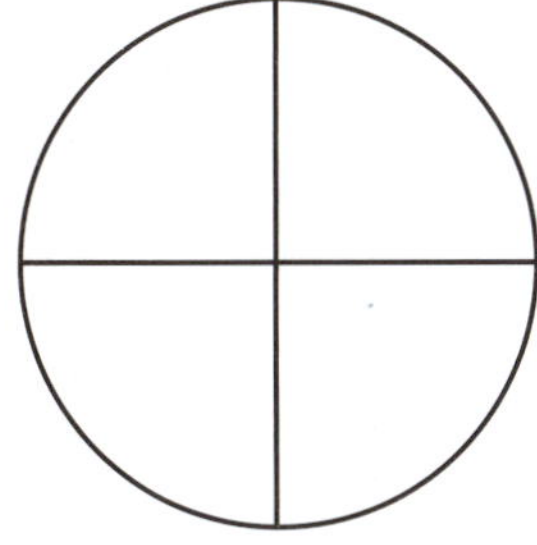

I filled in ______ fourths to color the whole.

Answers

1. COUNTING

Write Numbers 0–20

Page 9 — Your Turn

8

Page 10 — Practice

1. a 2 c 4 e 6
   b 3 d 5 f 7

2. a 9 c 11 e 13
   b 10 d 12 f 14

3. a 
   b
   c 
   d
   e 

16
17
18
19
20

Count Forward to 120

Page 13 — Your Turn

1. a 102 c 58; 60
   b 33 d 84; 85

Page 14 — Practice

1. a 110 e 55; 56; 57
   b 93 f 79; 80; 81
   c 49 g 118; 119; 120
   d 70 h 41; 42; 43

Count Objects

Page 15 — Your Turn

1. a 10

Page 16 — Practice

1. a 4 c 8 e 15
   b 2 d 10 f 11

More or Less?

Page 17 — Your Turn

1. a 
   b 12

Page 18 — Practice

1. a 
   b
   c 
   d 

2. a 11 c 18 e 6
   b 7 d 17

3. a 
   b 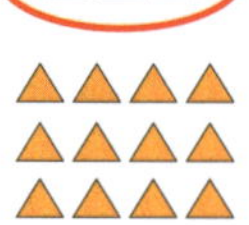
   c

4. a 9 c 3 e 19
   b 7 d 14

Answers

Use a Hundred Chart

Page 20 — Your Turn

1.

11	12	13	14	15	16	17	18	19	20
21	22	23	24	25	26	27	28	29	30
31	32	33	34	35	36	37	38	39	40

Page 21 — Practice

1.

1	2	3	4	5	6	7	8	9	10
11	12	13	14	15	16	17	18	19	20
21	22	23	24	25	26	27	28	29	30
31	32	33	34	35	36	37	38	39	40
41	42	43	44	45	46	47	48	49	50
51	52	53	54	55	56	57	58	59	60
61	62	63	64	65	66	67	68	69	70
71	72	73	74	75	76	77	78	79	80
81	82	83	84	85	86	87	88	89	90
91	92	93	94	95	96	97	98	99	100

Count by 10s

Page 22 — Your Turn

1. **a** 70 **b** 90

Page 23 — Practice

1. **a** 40 **c** 10; 40
   b 70 **d** 50; 60; 70

2.

1	2	3	4	5	6	7	8	9	10
11	12	13	14	15	16	17	18	19	20
21	22	23	24	25	26	27	28	29	30
31	32	33	34	35	36	37	38	39	40
41	42	43	44	45	46	47	48	49	50
51	52	53	54	55	56	57	58	59	60
61	62	63	64	65	66	67	68	69	70
71	72	73	74	75	76	77	78	79	80
81	82	83	84	85	86	87	88	89	90
91	92	93	94	95	96	97	98	99	100

Counting Review — Page 24

1.

1	2	3	4	5	6	7	8	9	10
11	12	13	14	15	16	17	18	19	20
21	22	23	24	25	26	27	28	29	30
31	32	33	34	35	36	37	38	39	40
41	42	43	44	45	46	47	48	49	50
51	52	53	54	55	56	57	58	59	60
61	62	63	64	65	66	67	68	69	70
71	72	73	74	75	76	77	78	79	80
81	82	83	84	85	86	87	88	89	90
91	92	93	94	95	96	97	98	99	100

2. **a** 3 **c** 5
   b 9 **d** 18

3. **a**

b

4. **a**

b

5. **a** 4 **c** 8
   b 12 **d** 9

6. **a** 14 **c** 7
   b 2 **d** 5

7. **a** 70
   b 80; 100
   c 50; 60
   d 20; 50; 60

Answers

2. PLACE VALUE

Digits

Page 27 — Your Turn

1. a 3 0 76
   b 97 1 44
   c 8 4 19

Page 28 — Practice

1. a 88 ~~4~~ ~~1~~ c ~~9~~ 46 ~~6~~
   b ~~0~~ 80 40

2.

One-Digit Numbers	Two-Digit Numbers
3 7 6 5 0 8 1	19 65 88 35 17 20 44 96

3. a 16; 61 b 28; 82 c 45; 54

Ones Place

Page 29 — Your Turn

1. a 6 b 2

Page 30 — Practice

1. a 7 c 2
   b 8

2.

a	9	●●●●●●●●●
b	5	●●●●●
c	1	●

Tens Place

Page 31 — Your Turn

1. a 2 b 4

Page 32 — Practice

1. a 15 87 36 c 72 19 50
   b 90 44 58

2. a 2 tens c 4 tens
   b 9 tens

3.

a	1	|
b	5	|||||
c	8	||||||||

Multiples of 10

Page 33 — Your Turn

1. a 3 tens 0 ones = 30
   b 7 tens 0 ones = 70

Page 34 — Practice

1. a

Tens	Ones
1	0

= 10

b

Tens	Ones
7	0

= 70

2. a 20 = || b 40 = ||||

Tens and Ones to 99

Page 35 — Your Turn

1. a 82

Page 36 — Practice

1. a 45 29 55
   b 35 62 46
   c 67 75 87

2. a 16 d 21
   b 27 e 53
   c 38

Answers

3.

<table>
<tr><th></th><th>Tens</th><th>Ones</th><th>Number</th></tr>
<tr><td>a</td><td>|||</td><td>•••••••</td><td>37</td></tr>
<tr><td>b</td><td>||||||||</td><td>•••</td><td>83</td></tr>
<tr><td>c</td><td>||</td><td>•••••••</td><td>27</td></tr>
<tr><td>d</td><td>||||||</td><td></td><td>60</td></tr>
<tr><td>e</td><td>|||||</td><td>•••••••••</td><td>59</td></tr>
<tr><td>f</td><td>||||</td><td>•</td><td>41</td></tr>
<tr><td>g</td><td>|||||||||</td><td>•••••••••</td><td>99</td></tr>
</table>

4.

Tens Place Underlined	Ones Place Underlined
11 45 28 13 86 29 78	71 99 59 10 38 32 30

5. a 42 = 4 tens and 2 ones
   b 39 = 3 tens and 9 ones
   c 18 = 1 ten and 8 ones
   d 56 = 5 tens and 6 ones
   e 71 = 7 tens and 1 one
   f 69 = 6 tens and 9 ones

Greater Than, Less Than, Equal To

Page 39 — Your Turn

1. a > b = c <

Page 40 — Practice

1. a < b > c =
2. a greater than
   b less than
   c equal to
3. a = c < e >
   b > d <

Compare Numbers to 19

Page 41 — Your Turn

1. a < b <

Page 42 — Practice

1. a <
   b =
   c >
   d >
2. a =
   b >
   c <
   d =
3. a 5 d 12 g 13
   b 19 e 2 h 13
   c 11 f 15 i 14

Compare Numbers to 99

Page 44 — Your Turn

1. a < b >

Page 45 — Practice

1. a 29 > 17 c 76 < 92
   b 34 < 55 d 61 > 23
2. a 89 > 85 c 76 < 79
   b 35 < 38 d 54 > 51
3. a = c >
   b > d <
4. a is greater than c is less than
   b is equal to
5. a 80 b 46 c 90
6. a Check that the number is greater than 35.
   b Check that the number is greater than 54.
   c 90 = 90

Answers

10 More

Page 47 — Your Turn

1. a 83

Page 48 — Practice

1.

	Number	10 More
a	89	99
b	37	47
c	70	80
d	22	32
e	69	79
f	43	53

1	2	3	4	5	6	7	8	9	10
11	12	13	14	15	16	17	18	19	20
21	22	23	24	25	26	27	28	29	30
31	32	33	34	35	36	37	38	39	40
41	42	43	44	45	46	47	48	49	50
51	52	53	54	55	56	57	58	59	60
61	62	63	64	65	66	67	68	69	70
71	72	73	74	75	76	77	78	79	80
81	82	83	84	85	86	87	88	89	90
91	92	93	94	95	96	97	89	99	100

2. a 42; 52
   b 74; 84
   c 33; 43
   d 82; 92
   e 55; 65
   f 25; 35
   g 64; 74
   h 39; 49
   i 17; 27
   j 10; 20

10 Less

Page 50 — Your Turn

1. a 84

Page 51 — Practice

1.

	Number	10 Less
a	90	80
b	14	4
c	66	56
d	82	72
e	75	65
f	99	89

1	2	3	4	5	6	7	8	9	10
11	12	13	14	15	16	17	18	19	20
21	22	23	24	25	26	27	28	29	30
31	32	33	34	35	36	37	38	39	40
41	42	43	44	45	46	47	48	49	50
51	52	53	54	55	56	57	58	59	60
61	62	63	64	65	66	67	68	69	70
71	72	73	74	75	76	77	78	79	80
81	82	83	84	85	86	87	88	89	90
91	92	93	94	95	96	97	89	99	100

2. a 44; 34
   b 78; 68
   c 39; 29
   d 83; 73
   e 50; 40
   f 24; 14
   g 61; 51
   h 39; 29
   i 12; 2
   j 97; 87

Place Value Review — Page 53

1. a 39 10 ~~5~~
   b ~~7~~ 18 27
   c ~~2~~ ~~3~~ 58
   d 90 ~~9~~ 19
   e 18 28 ~~8~~

2. a 34 c 56 e 55
   b 18 d 92

3. a

Tens	Ones
2	0

= 20

Answers

b

Tens	Ones
4	0

= 40

c

Tens	Ones
6	0

= 60

4. **a** 62 **c** 41
b 78 **d** 96

5.

	Number	Tens	Ones
a	17	I	●●●●●●●
b	85	IIIIIIII	●●●●●
c	34	III	●●●●
d	66	IIIIII	●●●●●●

6. **a** 20 **c** 40
b 49 **d** 66

7. **a** > **c** < **e** =
b = **d** > **f** <

8. **a** Check that the number is greater than 74.
b Check that the number is less than 89.
c Check that the number is less than 90.
d Check that the number is greater than 36.
e 84 = 84
f Check that the number is less than 14.

9.

	10 Less	Number	10 More
a	70	80	90
b	52	62	72
c	48	58	68
d	35	45	55
e	9	19	29
f	74	84	94

1	2	3	4	5	6	7	8	9	10
11	12	13	14	15	16	17	18	19	20
21	22	23	24	25	26	27	28	29	30
31	32	33	34	35	36	37	38	39	40
41	42	43	44	45	46	47	48	49	50
51	52	53	54	55	56	57	58	59	60
61	62	63	64	65	66	67	68	69	70
71	72	73	74	75	76	77	78	79	80
81	82	83	84	85	86	87	88	89	90
91	92	93	94	95	96	97	89	99	100

10.

	10 Less	Number	10 More
a	59	69	79
b	11	21	31
c	62	72	82
d	7	17	27
e	40	50	60
f	65	75	85
g	23	33	43
h	75	85	95
i	38	48	58
j	26	36	46

Answers

3. ADDITION

Addition within 10

Page 59 — Your Turn

1. **a** 9 **b** 8

Page 60 — Practice

1. **a** 9 **b** 6
2. **a** 7 **b** 13

Equal Sign and Plus Sign

Page 61 — Your Turn

1. **a** 7 + 1 = 8 or 1 + 7 = 8
   b 3 + 1 = 4 or 1 + 3 = 4

Page 62 — Practice

1. **a** yes
   b yes
   c no
2. **a** 3 + 5 = 8 or 5 + 3 = 8
   b 3 + 4 = 7 or 4 + 3 = 7

Draw a Picture

Page 63 — Your Turn

1. **a** 6 + 4 = ?

Draw 6 squares.	Draw 4 squares.	Count them all.
■■■■■■	+ ■■■■	= 10

Page 64 — Practice

1. **a** +
   4 + 3 = 7
   c  +
   5 + 1 = 6
   b   
   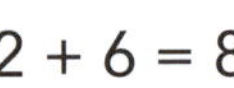
   2 + 6 = 8

2. **a** 8 + 3 = 11
3. **a** 10 **b** 16 **c** 5 **d** 11 **e** 8

Use Your Fingers

Page 66 — Your Turn

1. **a** 6 **b** 5

Page 67 — Practice

1. **a** 8 **b** 6 **c** 8
2. **a** 10 **b** 9 **c** 8 **d** 6 **e** 10

Count On

Page 68 — Your Turn

1. **a** 16

Page 69 — Practice

1. **a** 11 **b** 9 **c** 17 **d** 10 **e** 16 **f** 17 **g** 17 **h** 8
2. **a** 6 **b** 14 **c** 15 **d** 16 **e** 7 **f** 12 **g** 9

Make a 10

Page 71 — Your Turn

1. **a** 8 + 2 = 10

Answers

Page 72 — Practice

1. a 1 + 9 = 10
   b 4 + 6 = 10

2. a 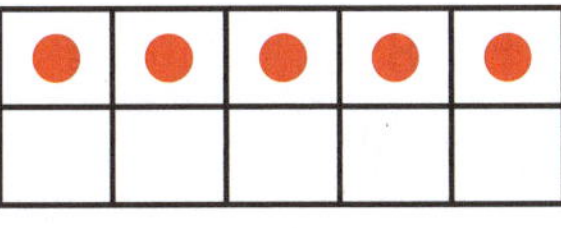

   b 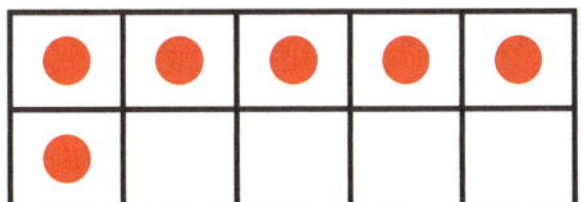

3. a 5 + 5 = 10
   b 1 + 9 = 10
   c 6 + 4 = 10
   d 8 + 2 = 10

4. a 6
   b 1
   c 3
   d 9

Use a Number Line

Page 74 — Your Turn

1. a 5 + 2 = 7

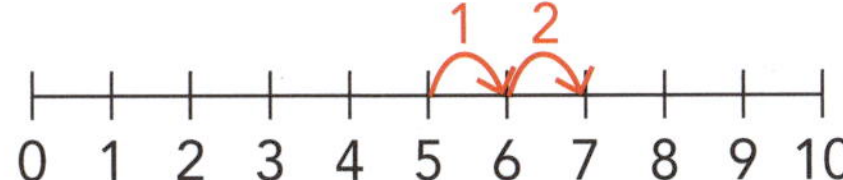

   b 9 + 4 = 13

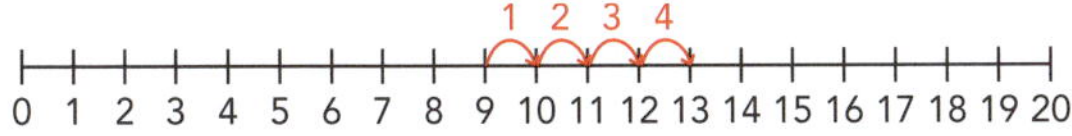

Page 75 — Practice

1. a 1 + 6 = 7

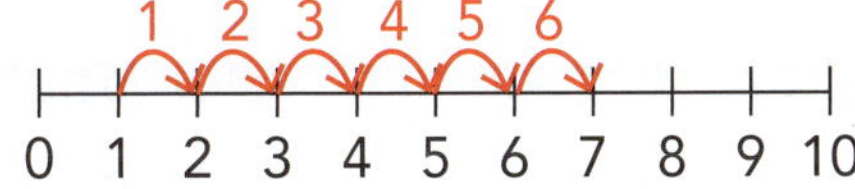

   b 4 + 1 = 5

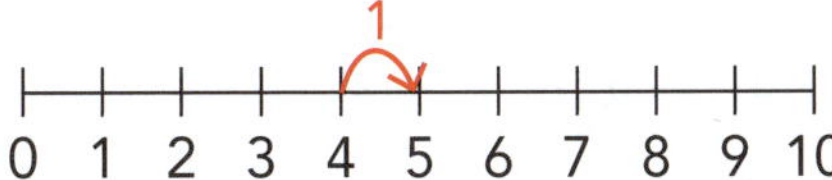

   c 7 + 2 = 9

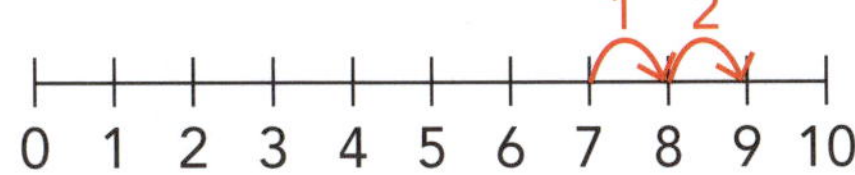

   d 2 + 5 = 7

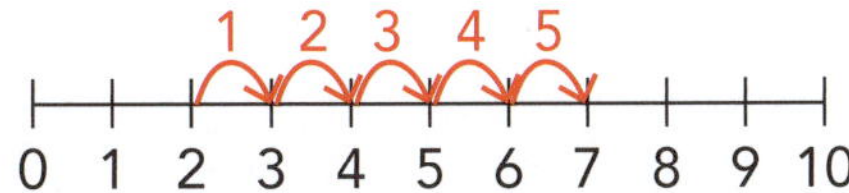

   e 5 + 5 = 10

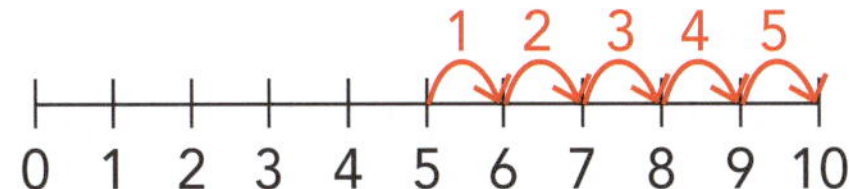

   f 6 + 3 = 9

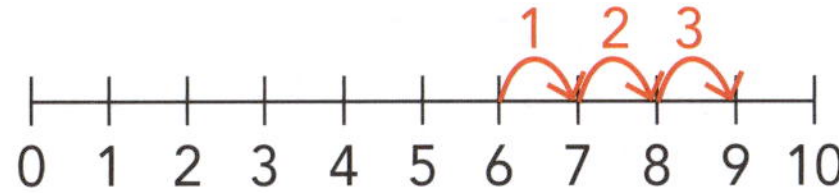

2. a 3 + 9 = 12

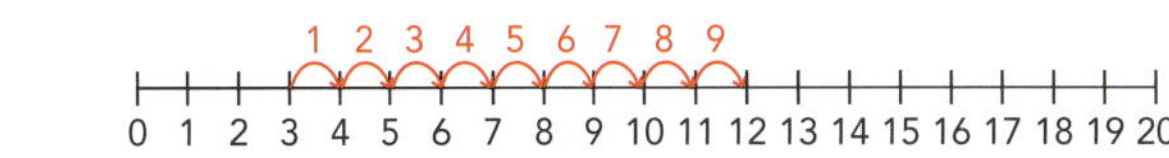

   b 7 + 6 = 13

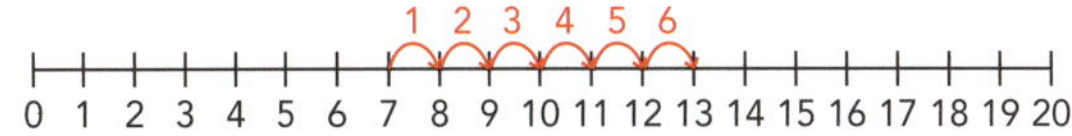

   c 8 + 8 = 16

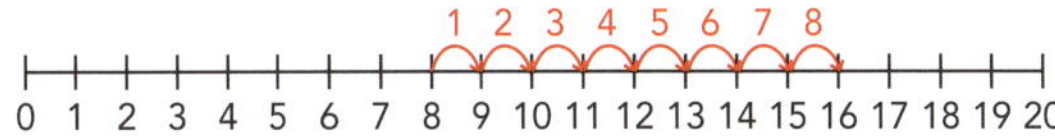

   d 9 + 6 = 15

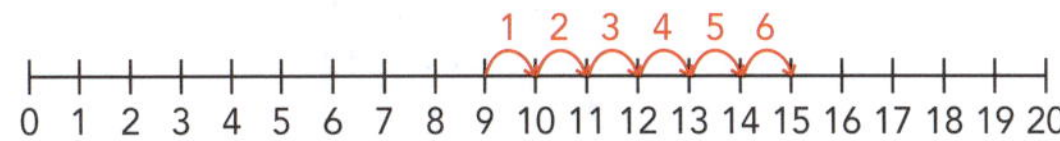

   e 5 + 7 = 12

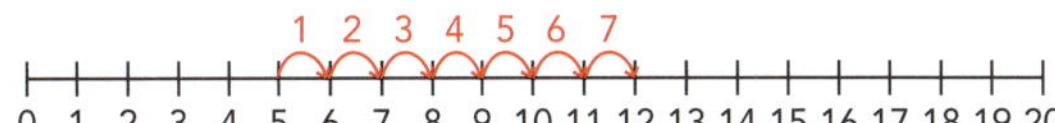

Tally Marks

Page 77 — Your Turn

1. a 3 + 3 = 6

   b 7 + 2 = 9

   c 4 + 8 = 12

Answers

Page 78 — Practice

1.

a	9 卌 ||||	15 卌 卌 卌	5 卌
b	13 卌 卌 |||	1 |	14 卌 卌 ||||
c	4 ||||	7 卌 ||	10 卌 卌

2. a $5 + 8 = 13$
   卌 卌 |||
   b $6 + 1 = 7$
   卌 ||
   c $2 + 2 = 4$
   || ||
   d $8 + 3 = 11$
   卌 卌 |
   e $9 + 3 = 12$
   卌 卌 ||

3. a $7 + 1 = 8$ 卌 |||
   b $1 + 5 = 6$ 卌 |
   c $4 + 3 = 7$ 卌 ||
   d $2 + 7 = 9$ 卌 ||||
   e $6 + 4 = 10$ 卌 卌
   f $5 + 8 = 13$ 卌 卌 |||

4. a 9 b 12 c 9 d 13 e 9

Strategy: Doubles

Page 80 — Your Turn

1. a 10 b 16 c 8

Page 81 — Practice

1. a 8 b 14 c 6 d 16 e 18 f 4 g 12 h 16 i 10

Add in Any Order

Page 82 — Your Turn

1. a 8; 8
   b 6; 6

Page 83 — Practice

1. a 5; 5 b 11; 11 c 6; 6 d 11; 11 e 13; 13 f 8; 8 g 11; 11 h 9; 9 i 15; 15

Addition: True or False?

Page 84 — Your Turn

1. a 3 + 5
   b 10 + 3

Page 85 — Practice

1. a Yes
   b Yes
   c No
   d Yes
   e No
2. a 7 + 7
   10 + 4
   b 3 + 4
   5 + 2
   c 10 + 0
   9 + 1
   7 + 3
3. a Check that the expression equals 14.
   b Check that the expression equals 6.
   c Check that the expression equals 12.
   d Check that the expression equals 5.
   e Check that the expression equals 11.
4. a–c Check that each set of expressions are equal.

Add 3 Numbers

Page 87 — Your Turn

1. a 14

Answers

Page 88 — Practice

1. a 12
   b 14
   c 10

2. a 2 + 7 + 4 = 13

   b 6 + 3 + 8 = 17

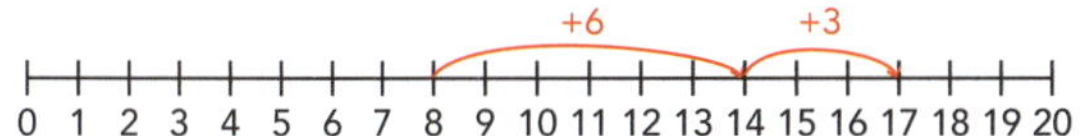

   c 5 + 6 + 1 = 12

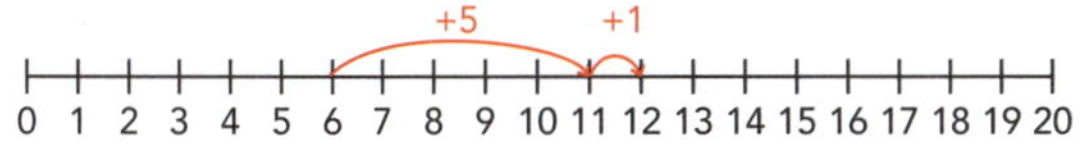

3. a (5 + 5) + 6
   10 + 6 = 16
   b (9) + 3 + (1)
   10 + 3 = 13
   c (2 + 8) + 1
   10 + 1 = 11

4. a 7 b 16 c 13 d 12

2 Digits Plus 1 Digit

Page 90 — Your Turn

1. a 79

Page 91 — Practice

1. a 87 b 79 c 99 d 35 e 68
2. a 98 b 88 c 78
3. a 68 b 49 c 36 d 58
4. a 29 b 69 c 77 d 58

2 Digits Plus Multiples of 10

Page 93 — Your Turn

1. a 45; 55; 65

Page 94 — Practice

1. a 64; 74; 84
   b 31; 41; 51
   c 76; 86; 96
   d 58; 68; 78
   e 53; 63; 73

Vertical Addition

Page 95 — Your Turn

1. a 47
   b 86

Page 96 — Practice

1. a 66
   b 39
   c 58

2. a

	3	6
+		1
	3	7

   b

	7	0
+		7
	7	7

   c

	5	5
+		4
	5	9

Make a 10 with 2-Digit Numbers

Page 97 — Your Turn

1. a

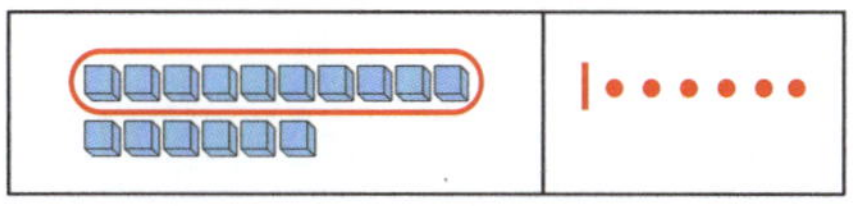

	|••••••

Page 98 — Practice

1.	a		|•
	b		|•••
	c		|

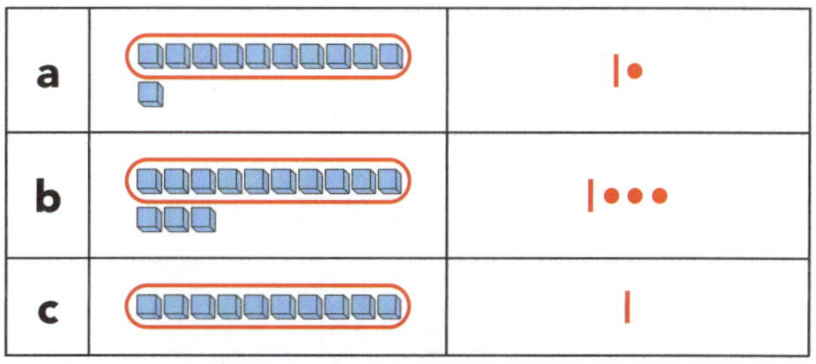

2.	a		||••
	b		|||||•••
	c		|||••••••••

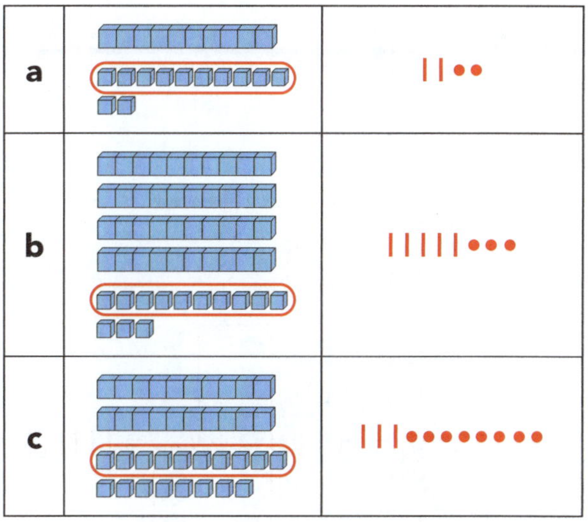

Answers

3.

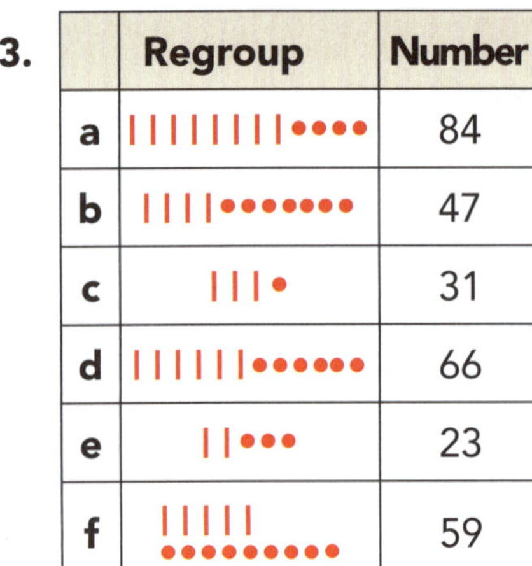

	Regroup	Number
a	|||||||| ••••	84
b	|||| •••••••	47
c	||| •	31
d	|||||| ••••••	66
e	|| •••	23
f	||||| •••••••••	59

Use Pictures to Make a 10

Page 100 — Your Turn

1. a

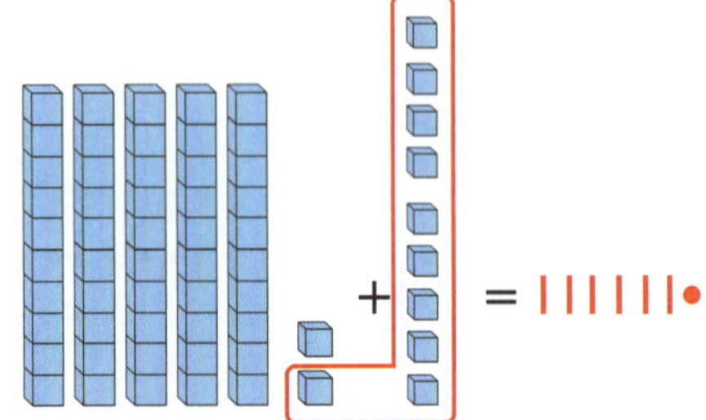

Page 101 — Practice

1. a

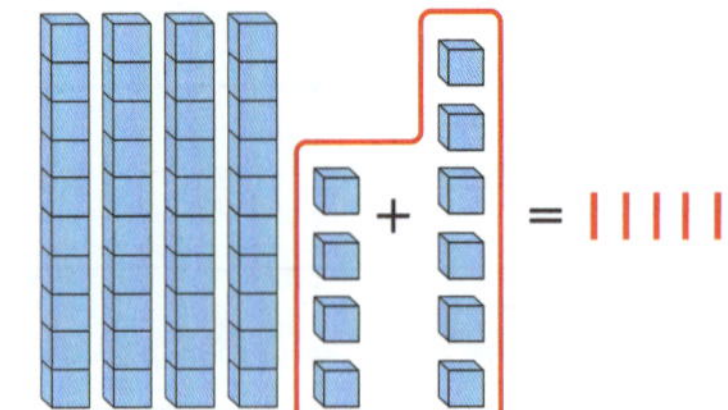

b

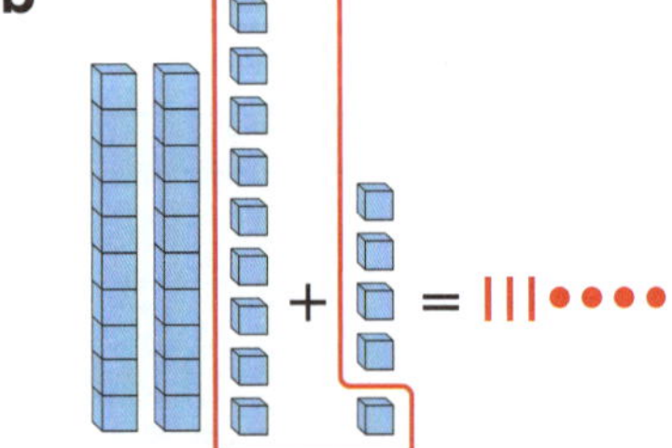

c

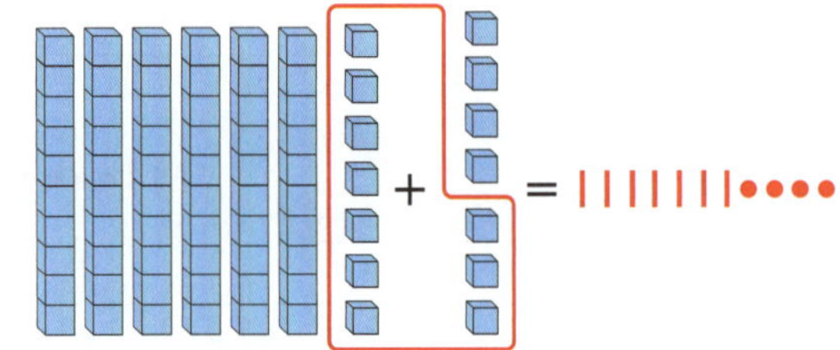

d

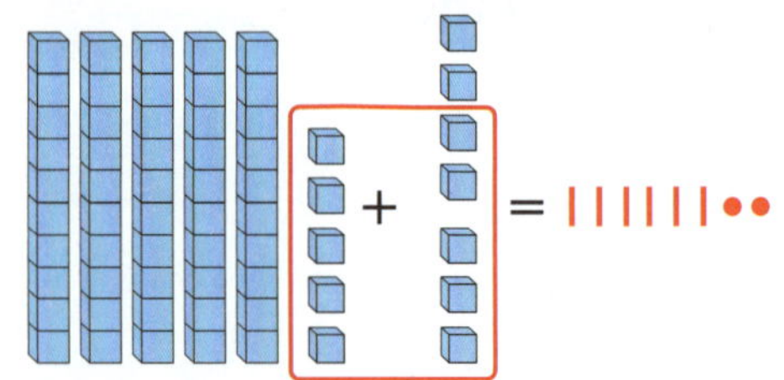

e

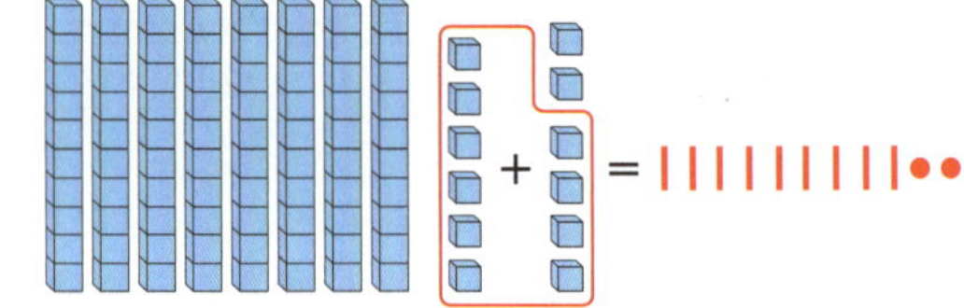

2. a 27 + 3 = 30

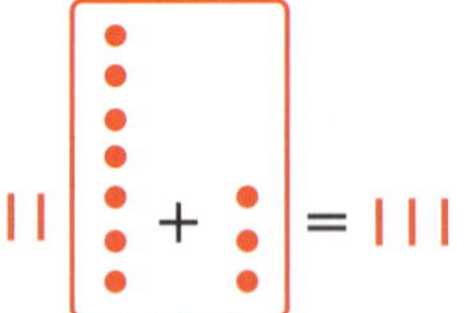

b 82 + 9 = 91

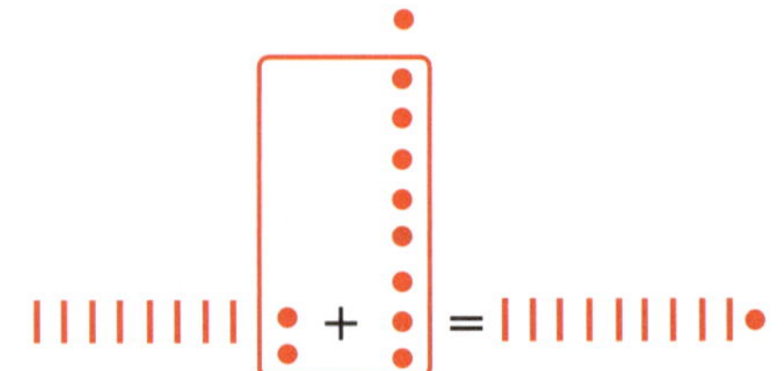

c 15 + 6 = 21

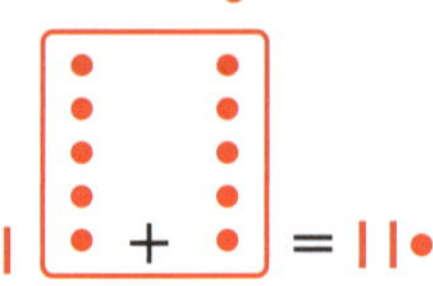

d 71 + 9 = 80

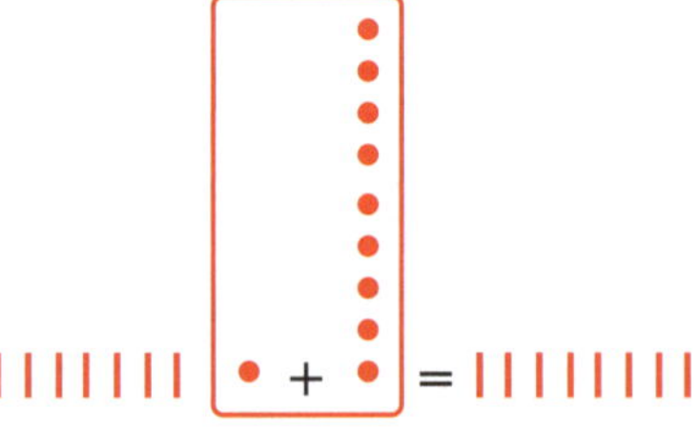

e 53 + 8 = 61

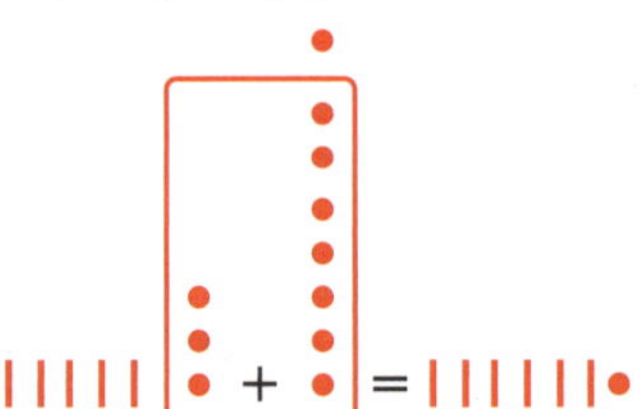

f 39 + 2 = 41

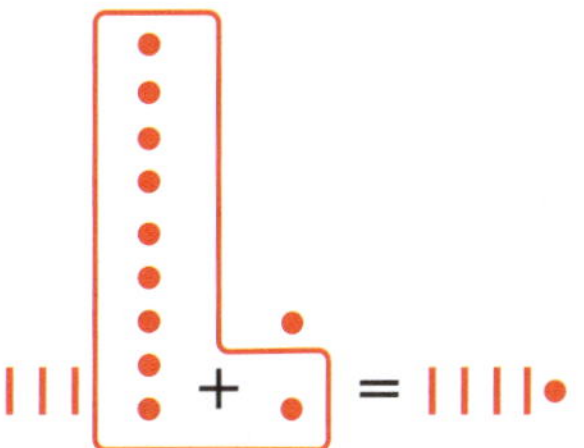

g 48 + 4 = 52

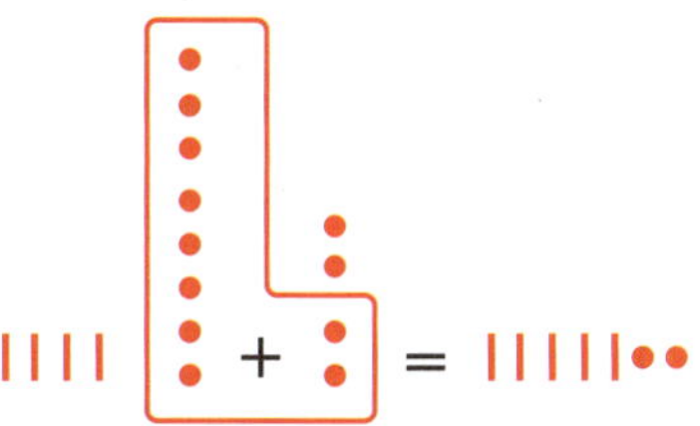

h 64 + 7 = 71

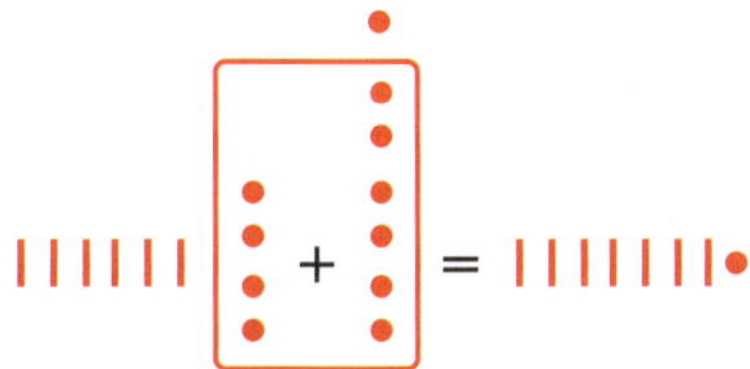

Use Numbers to Make a 10

Page 103 — Your Turn

1. a

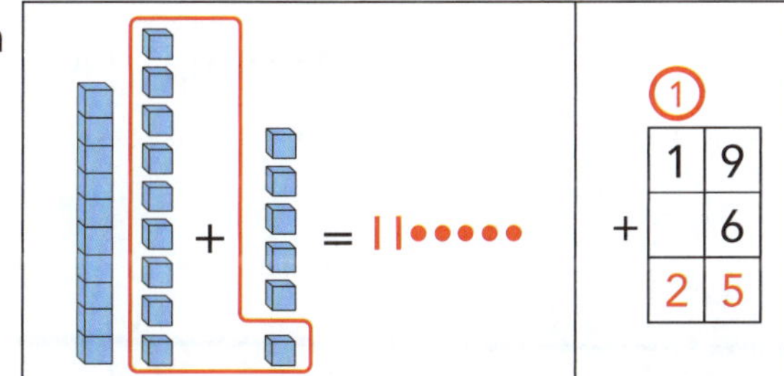

Page 104 — Practice

1. a
   b

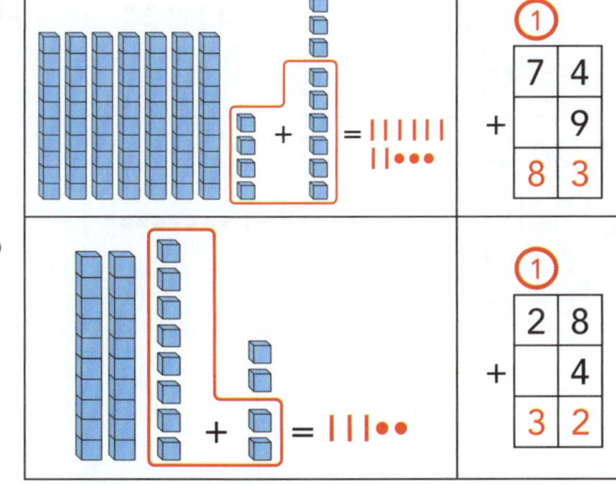

c

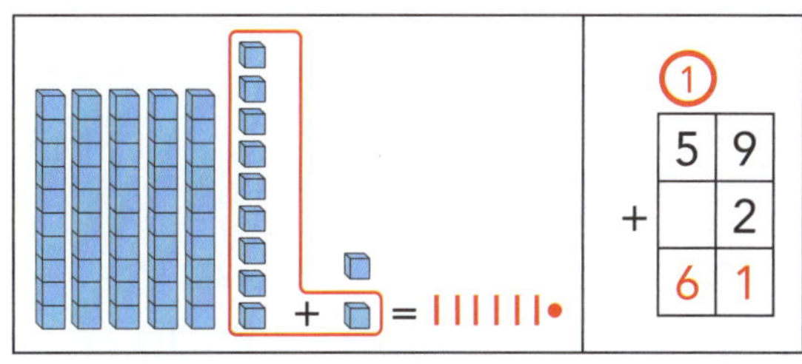

2. a

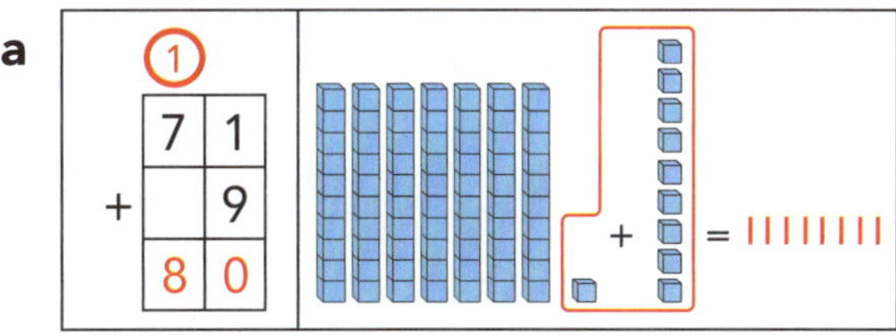

3. a

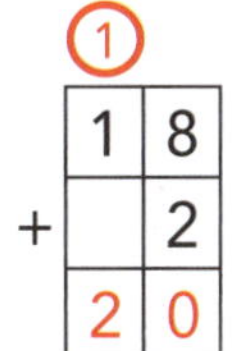

b

	1	
	7	4
+		9
	8	3

c

	1	
	3	9
+		6
	4	5

Addition Word Problems

Page 106 — Your Turn

1. a 5 + 4 = 9 cars

Page 107 — Practice

1. a 8 + 6 = 14 cookies
   b 9 + 8 = 17 books
   c 6 + 6 = 12 feathers
   d 3 + 5 = 8 fish
   e 7 + 4 = 11 bikes

Word Problems with 3 Numbers

Page 108 — Your Turn

1. a 8 + 2 + 6 = 16 straws

Page 109 — Practice

1. a 3 + 5 + 1 = 9 songs
   b 3 + 3 + 5 = 11 balloons
   c 6 + 5 + 3 = 14 plates

Addition Review — Page 110

1. a 11
   b 10
   c 5
2. a 4 + 7 = 11 or 7 + 4 = 11
   b 7 + 1 = 8 or 1 + 7 = 8

Answers

3. a 12
b 11

4. a 8
b 5

5. a 9 **b** 16 **c** 10 **d** 14

6. a 13 **b** 12 **c** 15 **d** 19

7. a 8 + 2 = 10 **b** 5 + 5 = 10

8. a 9 **b** 5 **c** 3 **d** 8

9. a 5 + 4 = 9

b 8 + 7 = 15

c 6 + 9 = 15

10. a 3 + 3 = 6

b 7 + 9 = 16

c 3 + 6 = 9

11. a 12 **b** 14

12. a Check that the expression equals 11.
b Check that the expression equals 6.
c Check that the expression equals 10.

13. a 14
b 11

14. a 3 + 5 + 6 = 14

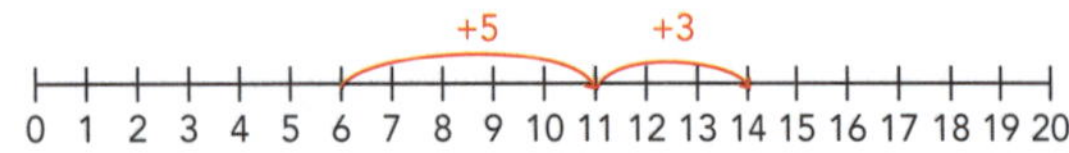

b 4 + 4 + 8 = 16

15. a 9 + 1 + 6
9 + 1 = 10
b 6 + 3 + 4
6 + 4 = 10

16. a 58 **c** 95
b 34 **d** 52

17. a 38 **c** 89
b 19 **d** 83

18. a 66; 76
b 67; 77
c 61; 71
d 88; 98

19. a

	7	1
+		7
	7	8

c

	9	3
+		3
	9	6

b

	3	5
+		2
	3	7

d

	6	4
+		5
	6	9

20.

	Picture	Regroup	Number
a			61
b			84
c			38

Answers

21. a 57 + 4 = 61

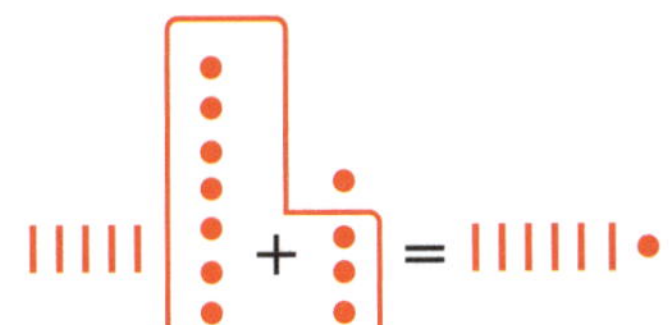

b 89 + 3 = 92

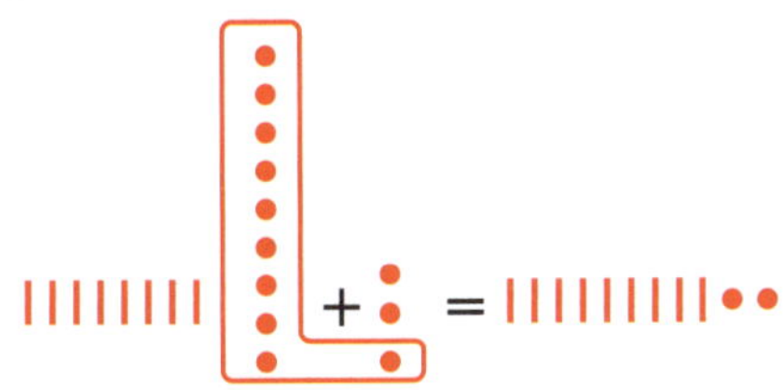

c 19 + 5 = 24

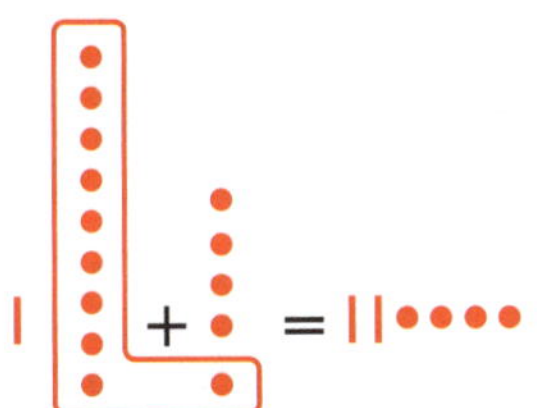

22. a

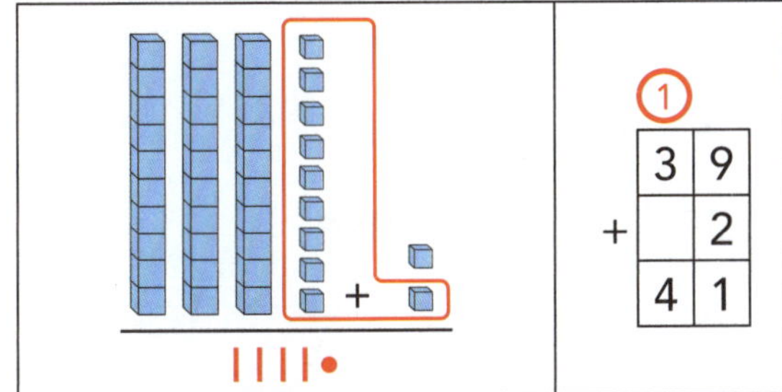

b

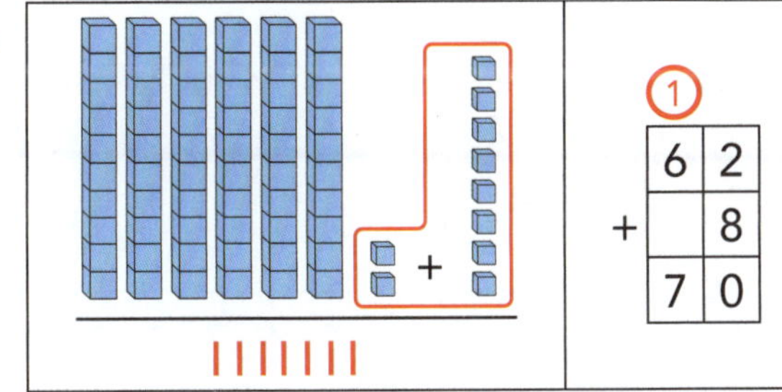

c

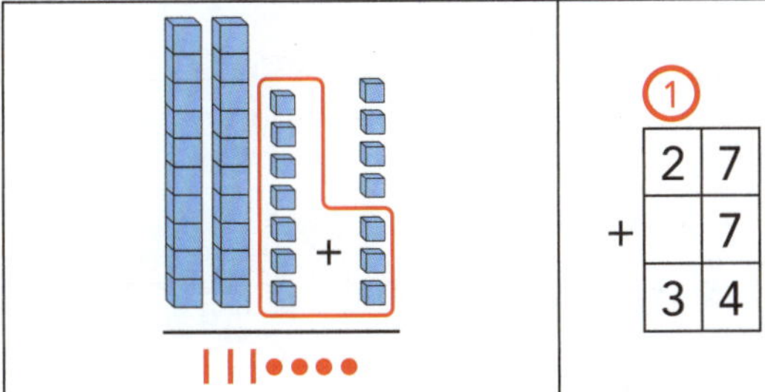

23. a

$$\begin{array}{r} {}^{1} \\ 44 \\ +\ 7 \\ \hline 51 \end{array}$$

b

$$\begin{array}{r} {}^{1} \\ 67 \\ +\ 3 \\ \hline 70 \end{array}$$

c

$$\begin{array}{r} {}^{1} \\ 76 \\ +\ 8 \\ \hline 84 \end{array}$$

d

$$\begin{array}{r} {}^{1} \\ 28 \\ +\ 5 \\ \hline 33 \end{array}$$

24. a 8 + 5 = 13 pieces of candy

b 5 + 3 = 8 people

c 8 + 6 = 14 apples

d 4 + 4 + 1 = 9 pens

e 6 + 2 + 4 = 12 flowers

4. SUBTRACTION

Model Subtraction

Page 120 — Your Turn

1. a 6

b 4

Page 121 — Practice

1. a 2 **c** 7 **e** 8

b 4 **d** 6

Equal Sign and Subtraction Sign

Page 122 — Your Turn

1. a 4 – 3 = 1

b 9 – 5 = 4

Answers

Page 123 — Practice

1. a $4 - 1 = 3$
   b $8 - 2 = 6$
   c $5 - 4 = 1$
   d $9 - 1 = 8$
   e $3 - 1 = 2$
2. a $9 - 7 = 2$ or $9 - 2 = 7$
   b $6 - 0 = 6$ or $6 - 6 = 0$
   c $5 - 4 = 1$ or $5 - 1 = 4$
   d $8 - 5 = 3$ or $8 - 3 = 5$

Draw a Picture

Page 124 — Your Turn

1. a 3
   b 4

Page 125 — Practice

1. a $9 - 3 = 6$
   b $14 - 7 = 7$
   c $15 - 9 = 6$
2. a 7
   b 4
   c 5
   d 9
3. a 4
   b 2
   c 6
   d 5
   e 8
   f 3
   g 1

Use Your Fingers

Page 127 — Your Turn

1. a 3
   b 6

Page 128 — Practice

1. a 1
   b 3
   c 4
2. a 4
   b 0
   c 8
   d 2
   e 3

Count Back

Page 129 — Your Turn

1. a 1

Page 130 — Practice

1. a 6
   b 8
   c 4
2. a $5 - 2 = 3$
   b $12 - 7 = 5$
   c $13 - 10 = 3$
3. a 1
   b 5
   c 4
   d 4
4. a 3
   b 8
   c 2
   d 5
   e 8

Use a Number Line

Page 132 — Your Turn

1. a $9 - 6 = 3$
   b $16 - 8 = 8$

Page 133 — Practice

1. a 0 1 2 3 4 5 6 7 (8) 9 10

   $8 - 6 = 2$

   b 0 1 2 3 4 5 6 7 8 9 (10)

   $10 - 5 = 5$

   c 0 1 2 3 (4) 5 6 7 8 9 10

   $4 - 1 = 3$

   d 0 1 2 3 4 5 (6) 7 8 9 10

   $6 - 3 = 3$

   e 0 1 2 3 4 5 6 7 8 9 10 11 12 13 14 (15) 16 17 18 19 20

   $15 - 5 = 10$

   f 0 1 2 3 4 5 6 7 8 9 10 11 (12) 13 14 15 16 17 18 19 20

   $12 - 4 = 8$

Answers

2. a $8 - 1 = 7$
   b $13 - 7 = 6$
3. a 3
   b 9
   c 4

Use Addition Facts

Page 135 — Your Turn

1. a 4
   b 6

Page 136 — Practice

1. a $9 - 8 = 1$
   b $5 - 3 = 2$
   c $10 - 3 = 7$
2. a $3 + 4 = 7$; $7 - 4 = 3$
   b $8 + 5 = 13$; $13 - 5 = 8$
   c $6 + 3 = 9$; $9 - 3 = 6$
   d $9 + 6 = 15$; $15 - 6 = 9$
   e $2 + 4 = 6$; $6 - 4 = 2$
3. a $12 - 2 = 10$
   b $11 - 3 = 8$
   c $8 - 7 = 1$
   d $7 - 3 = 4$
4. Possible answers:
   a $15 - 8 = 7$
   b $6 - 5 = 1$
   c $10 + 3 = 13$
   d $12 - 7 = 5$

Fact Families

Page 138 — Your Turn

1. a $4 + 8 = 12$
   b $12 - 8 = 4$
   c $12 - 4 = 8$

Page 139 — Practice

1. a $7 + 4 = 11$
   $4 + 7 = 11$
   $11 - 7 = 4$
   $11 - 4 = 7$
   b $9 + 1 = 10$
   $1 + 9 = 10$
   $10 - 9 = 1$
   $10 - 1 = 9$
2. a $7 + 8 = 15$
   $8 + 7 = 15$
   $15 - 7 = 8$
   $15 - 8 = 7$
   b $3 + 4 = 7$
   $4 + 3 = 7$
   $7 - 3 = 4$
   $7 - 4 = 3$
3. a 14 8 6
   $8 + 6 = 14$
   $6 + 8 = 14$
   $14 - 6 = 8$
   $14 - 8 = 6$
   b 6 5 1
   $5 + 1 = 6$
   $1 + 5 = 6$
   $6 - 1 = 5$
   $6 - 5 = 1$
4. a Check that the numbers have a sum of 12.
   b Check that the numbers have a sum of 4.
   c Check that the numbers have a sum of 11.

Subtraction: True or False?

Page 141 — Your Turn

1. a $12 - 2$

Page 142 — Practice

1. a no
   b yes
   c yes
   d no
   e yes
2. a $6 - 2$
   $5 - 1$
   b $10 - 4$
   $8 - 2$
   $9 - 3$
   c $5 - 2$
   $10 - 7$
3. a Check that the expression equals 4.
   b Check that the expression equals 9.
   c Check that the expression equals 3.
   d Check that the expression equals 5.
   e Check that the expression equals 5.
4. Check that expressions are equivalent.

Answers

Subtraction Within 10

Page 144 — Your Turn

1. **a** 7 **b** 5

Page 145 — Practice

1. **a** 7 **b** 4 **c** 1 **d** 2 **e** 8 **f** 4 **g** 1 **h** 1 **i** 2 **j** 4 **k** 0 **l** 7 **m** 5

Subtraction Within 20

Page 146 — Your Turn

1. **a** 9 **b** 5

Page 147 — Practice

1. **a** 12 **b** 7 **c** 15 **d** 9 **e** 9 **f** 9 **g** 10 **h** 10 **i** 9 **j** 9 **k** 10 **l** 6 **m** 6

Subtraction Word Problems

Page 148 — Your Turn

1. **a** 14 – 7 = 7 ladybugs

Page 149 — Practice

1. **a** 8 – 3 = 5 pies
b 15 – 5 = 10 markers
c 9 – 6 = 3 pillows
d 10 – 3 = 7 candles
e 6 – 1 = 5 batteries

Subtraction Review — Page 150

1. **a** 3
b 9

2. **a** 12 – 7 = 5 or 12 – 5 = 7
b 8 – 0 = 8 or 8 – 8 = 0
c 15 – 9 = 6 or 15 – 6 = 9

3. **a** 6 – 1 = 5
b 8 – 7 = 1
c 9 – 3 = 6

4. **a** 3
b 8
c 3

5. **a** 9
b 5
c 8

6. **a** (6 circled)
6 – 2 = 4
b (15 circled)
15 – 5 = 10
c (8 circled)
8 – 4 = 4
d (14 circled)
14 – 8 = 6

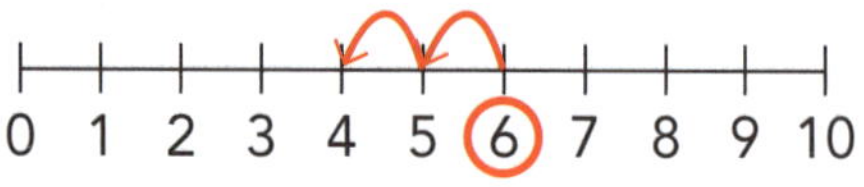

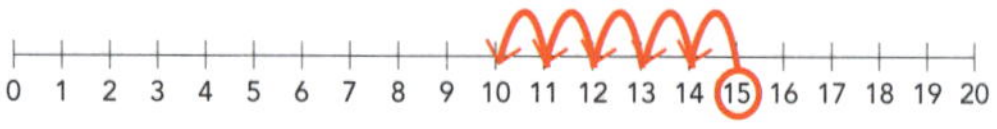

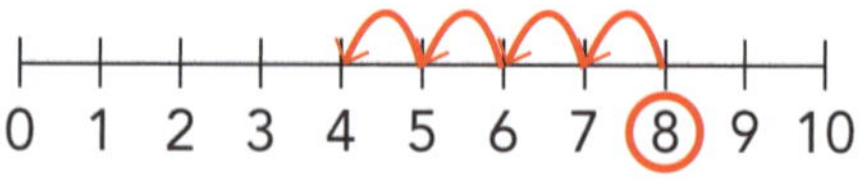

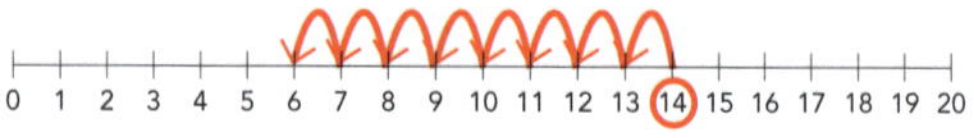

7. **a** 4 + 8 = 12 12 – 8 = 4
b 6 + 5 = 11 11 – 5 = 6
c 10 + 2 = 12 12 – 2 = 10
d 9 + 8 = 17 17 – 8 = 9

8. **a** 11 9 2
9 + 2 = 11
2 + 9 = 11
11 – 2 = 9
11 – 9 = 2

b 6 2 4
2 + 4 = 6
4 + 2 = 6
6 – 2 = 4
6 – 4 = 2

9. **a** Check that the numbers have a sum of 12.
b Check that the numbers have a sum of 6.

10. **a** Check that the expression equals 7.
b Check that the expression equals 6.
c Check that the expression equals 9.
d Check that the expression equals 3.

Answers

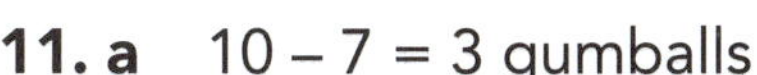

11. a 10 – 7 = 3 gumballs
b 12 – 5 = 7 cars
c 8 – 4 = 4 bees
d 8 – 6 = 2 buns

12.

a	8	**e**	8	**i**	3	**m**	4
b	4	**f**	10	**j**	6	**n**	12
c	2	**g**	8	**k**	2		
d	5	**h**	10	**l**	4		

5. MEASUREMENT

Compare Length

Page 156 — Your Turn

1. a

Page 157 — Practice

1. a

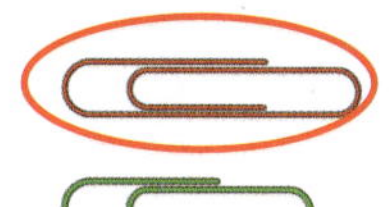

b

c

2. a

b

c

3. a

b

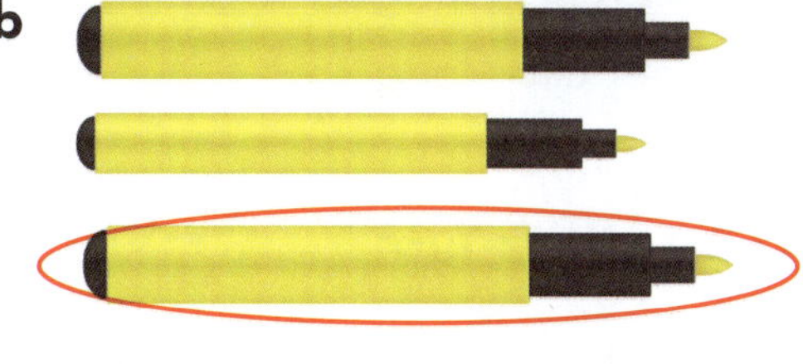

c

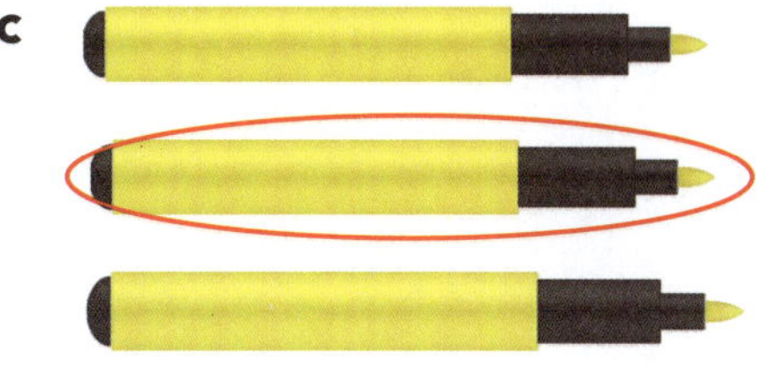

4. a 3, 2, 1
b 2, 3, 1
c 3, 2, 1

5. Check that the lines drawn are shorter and longer than the given lines.

Compare Weight

Page 159 — Your Turn

1. a

2. a

Page 160 — Practice

1. a heavier
b heavier
c lighter
d lighter

2. a about the same
b lighter
c lighter

Use a Unit of Length

Page 161 — Your Turn

1. a yes

Answers

Page 162 — Practice

1. **a** no **b** yes **c** no
2. **a** 2 paper clips long
   b 6 paper clips long
   c 6 paper clips long
   d 2 paper clips long

Measure in Inches

Page 163 — Your Turn

1. **a** 6 inches

Page 164 — Practice

1. **a** 5 inches
   b 3 inches
   c 4 inches
2. **a** 6 inches
   b 2 inches
   c 4 inches
3. **a–f** Check that students have drawn lines of the correct lengths.

Measurement Review — Page 166

1. **a** 3, 2, 1 **b** 1, 2, 3
2. Check that the arrows drawn are shorter and longer than the given arrows.
3. **a**

b

c

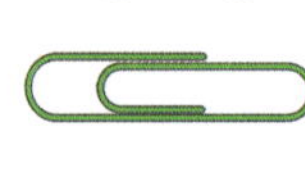

4. **a**

b

c

5. **a** no **b** yes **c** no

6. **a** 4 paper clips long
   b 8 paper clips long
   c 3 paper clips long
7. **a** 2 inches
   b 6 inches
   c 3 inches
   d 5 inches

6. DATA AND GRAPHS

Classify Objects

Page 169 — Your Turn

1. **a–b**

9 A 7 !
4 " " J R
T ? , 3

Page 170 — Practice

1. **a** 3
   b 2
   c 1
   d 3
   e 3
   f 3
   g 2
2. **a–d**

Picture Graphs

Page 171 — Your Turn

1. **a** pizza, sandwich, hamburger
   b 6
   c 8
   d 3

Answers

Page 172 — Practice

1. **a** It shows what type of pets people have.
   b 8
   c 5
   d 2
   e dog
2. **a** 10
   b 6
   c Weekend Activities
   d Students should choose one of the three activities from the graph.
   e park

Bar Graphs

Page 174 — Your Turn

1. **a** bus, car, walk
   b 4
   c 5

Page 175 — Practice

1. **a** 8
   b 3
   c Favorite Zoo Animals
   d elephant
2. **a** 10
   b 6
   c It shows people's favorite colors.
   d red

Questions About Graphs

Page 177 — Your Turn

1. **a** 3 + 5 = 8

Page 178 — Practice

1. **a** 3 + 7 + 3 = 13
   b football and baseball
   c 3 + 3 = 6
   d soccer
2. **a** 8 + 5 + 1 = 14
   b 8 – 5 = 3
   c pop
   d rock

Make Graphs

Page 180 — Your Turn

1. **a–b**

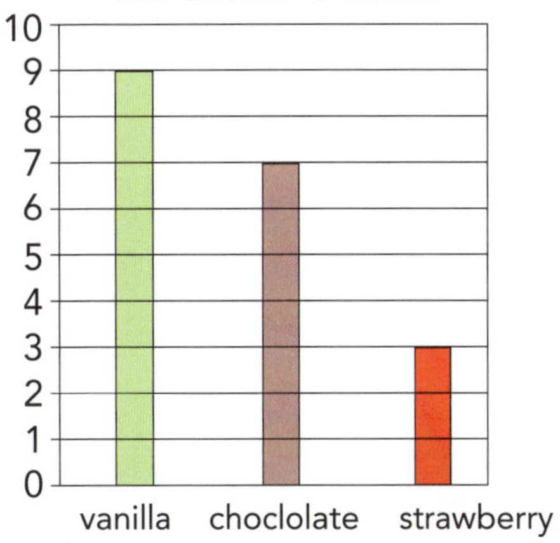

Page 181 — Practice

1. **a–d**

Shapes in the Classroom

squares	■ ■ ■ ■ ■ ■
triangles	▲ ▲ ▲ ▲ ▲ ▲ ▲ ▲
circles	● ● ● ● ●

2. **a–e**

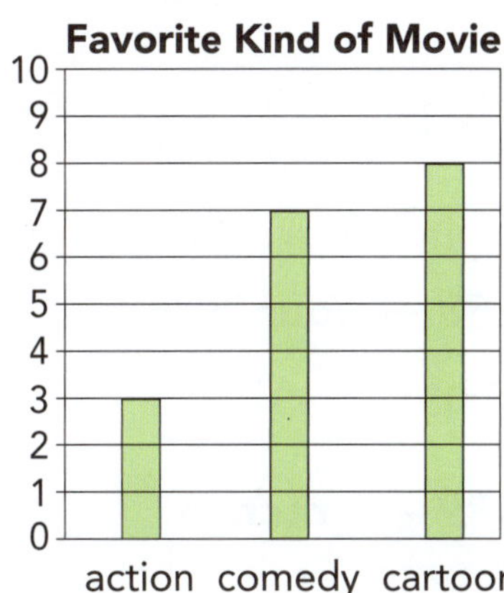

Data and Graphs Review — Page 183

1. **a** 3 **c** 3 **e** 2 **g** 1
   b 4 **d** 2 **f** 1 **h** 2

Answers

2. **a** water, juice, lemonade
   b 5
   c 5
   d 9
   e Check that students have chosen water, juice, or lemonade.
3. **a** 6
   b 8
   c 1
   d It shows people's favorite type of weather.
   e rainy
4. **a** music
   b 5 + 4 + 8 = 17
   c 5 − 4 = 1
   d 8 + 4 = 12
5. **a–e**

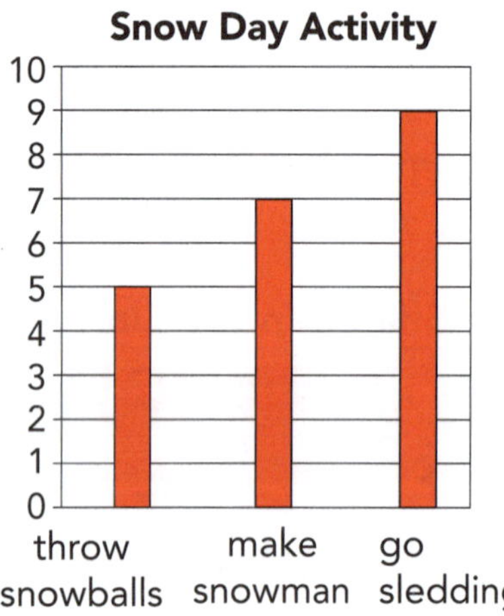

7. TIME

Time to the Hour: Analog Time

Page 188 — Your Turn

1. **a** 8:00

Page 189 — Practice

1. **a–c**

2. **a** 9:00 **b** 10:00
   c 2:00 **f** 7:00
   d 11:00 **g** 1:00
   e 8:00
3. **a** 1:00 **c** 12:00 **e** 6:00
   b 3:00 **d** 10:00
4. **a**  **d** 
   b **e**
   c 

Time to the Hour: Digital Time

Page 191 — Your Turn

1. **a** five o'clock
   b eight o'clock

Page 192 — Practice

1. **a** four o'clock **d** twelve o'clock
   b seven o'clock **e** three o'clock
   c nine o'clock

2. ●  

   a  

   b  

   c 
10:00

   d 
05:00

Answers

Time to the Half-Hour: Analog Time

Page 193 — Your Turn

1. a 9:30
   b 10:30

Page 194 — Practice

1. a 5:30 b 7:30 c 12:30 d 4:30 e 11:30
2. a 8:30 b 6:30 c 1:30 d 3:30 e 4:30
3. a

b

c

d

e

f

g

h

i

Time to the Half-Hour: Digital Time

Page 196 — Your Turn

1. a seven-thirty
   b ten-thirty

Page 197 — Practice

1. a twelve-thirty
   b four-thirty
   c ten-thirty
   d one-thirty
   e eight-thirty

2. 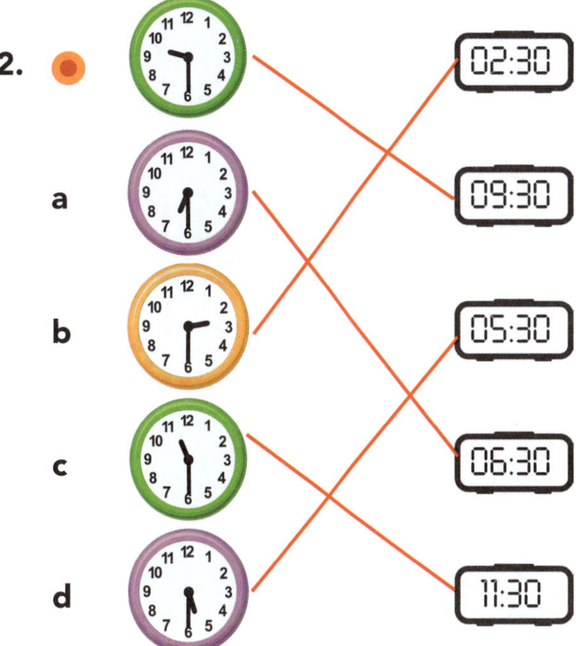

Time Review — Page 198

1. a 10:00
   b 2:30
   c 12:00
   d 6:30
   e 7:00
   f 3:30
2. a nine-thirty b one-thirty c four-thirty d eleven-thirty
3. 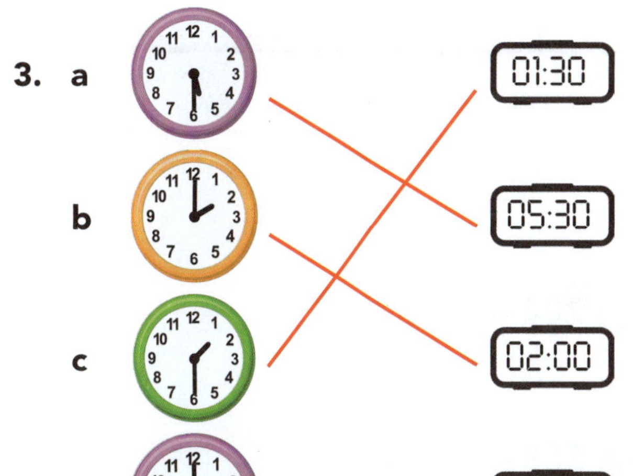

4. a 

b 

c 

d 

e 

f 

8. MONEY

Pennies

Page 200 — Your Turn

1. a 9¢ b 3¢

Page 201 — Practice

1. a      

b      

2. a 13¢ b 6¢

3. a 

b 

Nickels

Page 202 — Your Turn

1. a 15¢ b 25¢

Page 203 — Practice

1. a

b

2. a 30¢ b 40¢ c 10¢

3. a 

b 

Dimes

Page 204 — Your Turn

1. a 20¢ b 40¢

Page 205 — Practice

1. a 

b 

2. a 20¢ b 50¢ c 70¢

3. a 

b 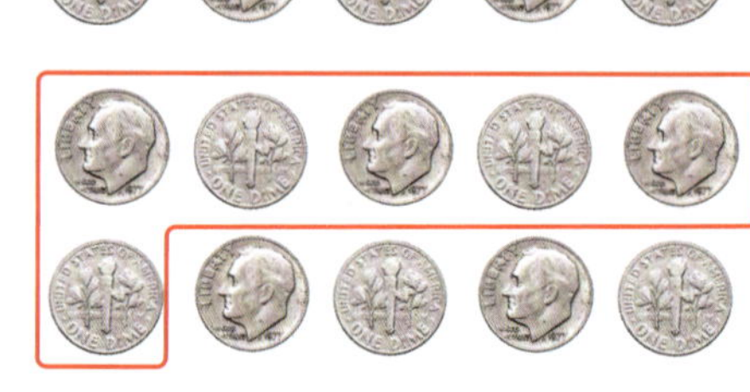

Quarters

Page 206 — Your Turn

1. a 50¢ b 75¢

Page 207 — Practice

1. a    

b 

c    

2. **a** 25¢ **b** 75¢

3. **a**    

b   

Make a Dollar

Page 208 — Your Turn

1. **a** 100

Page 209 — Practice

	Picture of coin	Name of coin	Value	How many in a dollar?
a		nickel	5¢	20
b		dime	10¢	10
c		quarter	25¢	4

2. **a** no **b** yes **c** yes

Money Review — Page 210

1.
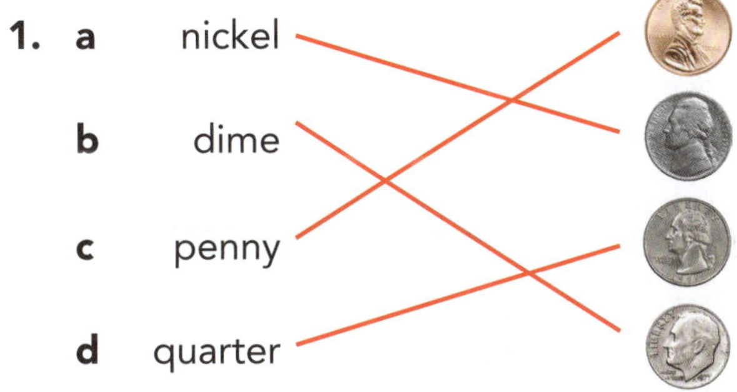

2. **a** penny
b quarter
c dime
d penny
e quarter
f nickel

3. **a** 10¢
b 10¢
c 4¢
d 70¢
e 45¢
f 100¢ or $1.00
g 30¢
h 75¢
i 50¢
j 25¢
k 15¢
l 100¢ or $1.00

9. SHAPES

Positions

Page 212 — Your Turn

1. **a** above

Page 213 — Practice

1. **a** beside
b between
c in front of

2.
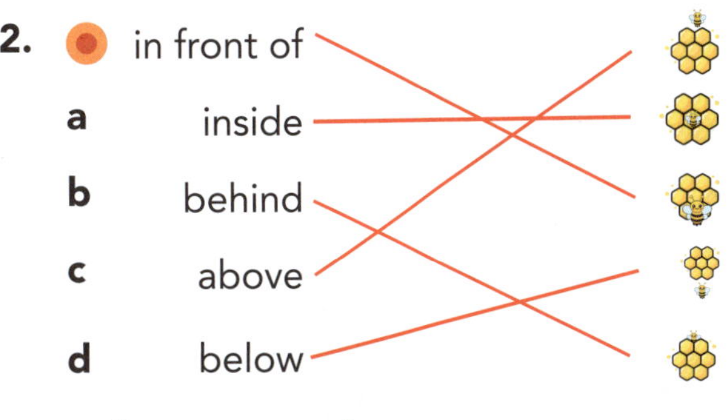

3. 
a–f

Sides and Vertices

Page 215 — Your Turn

1. **a** 4 sides; 4 vertices

Answers

Page 216 — Your Practice

1. a 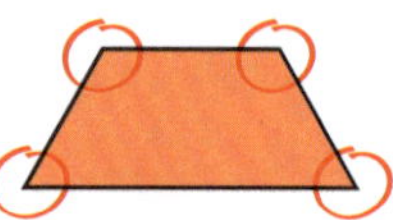

   c 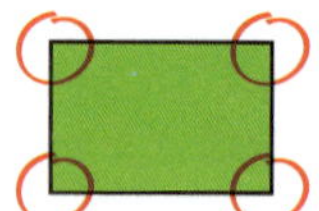

   b 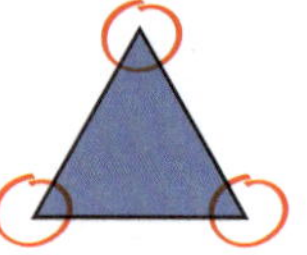

2. a 

   c 

   b 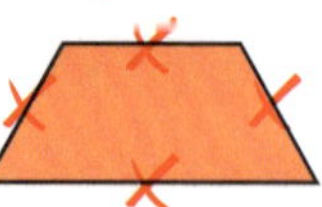

3. a 4
   b 0
   c 4

Attributes

Page 217 — Your Turn

1. a Possible answer: It is green.
   b It has 4 sides.
   c It has 4 vertices.

Page 218 — Practice

1. a It has 3 vertices. It has 3 sides. It is pink.
   b It has 4 vertices. It has 4 sides. It is green.
2. a 4 sides
   b 4 vertices
   c 4 equal sides

2D and 3D Shapes

Page 219 — Your Turn

1. a 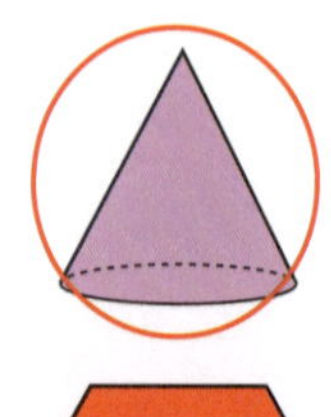 

   b 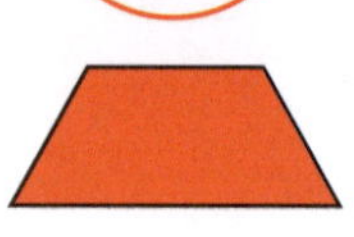 

Page 220 — Practice

1. a rectangle
   b trapezoid
   c circle
   d square
2. a sphere
   b cube
   c cone
   d cylinder
3. a 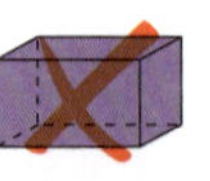 

   b 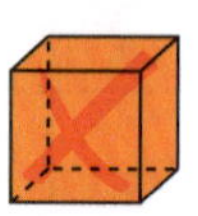 

   c 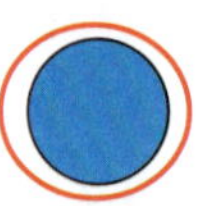 

   d 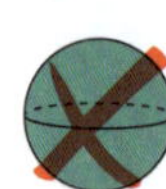 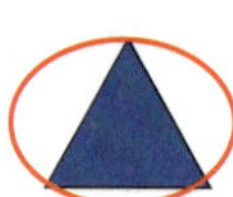

4. Answers may include:
   2D shapes are flat.
   They have length and width.
   3D shapes are solid.
   They have length, width, and height.

Make Shapes

Page 222 — Your Turn

1. a 

   b 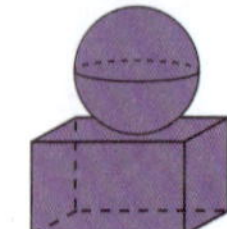

Answers

Page 223 — Practice

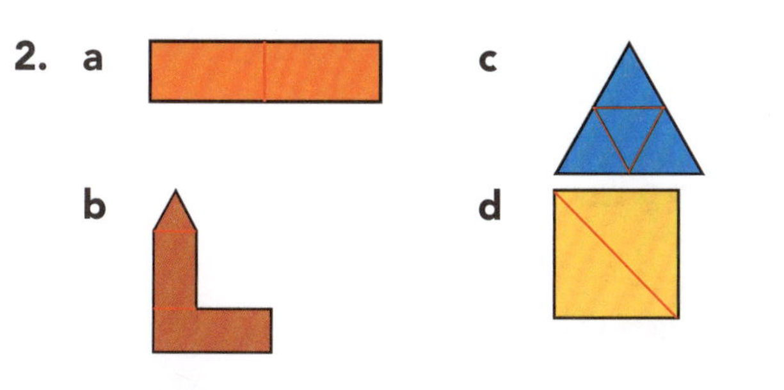

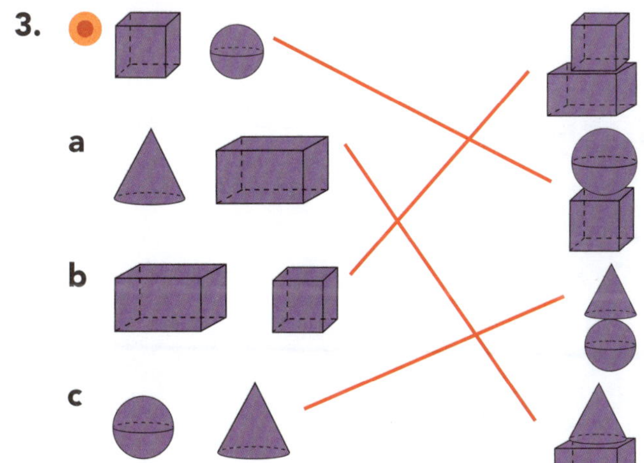

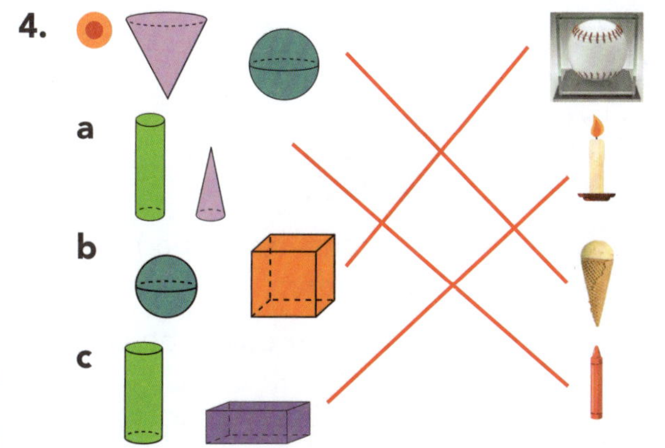

Shapes Review — Page 225

1. a in front of
   b between
   c above
   d between
   e inside
   f beside
   g beside

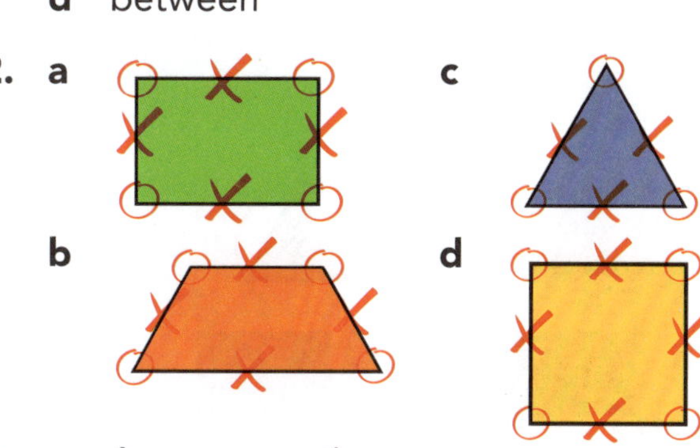

3. a 4 square vertices
   b 3 sides
   c 4 sides
   d 4 square vertices

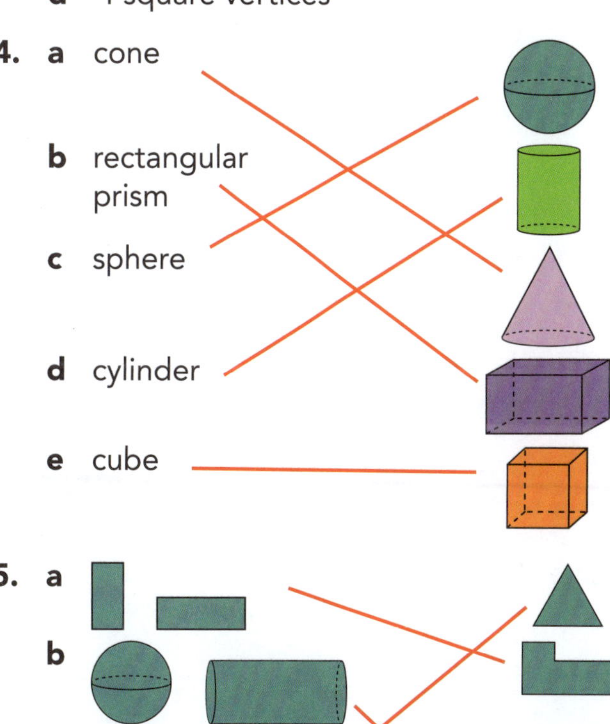

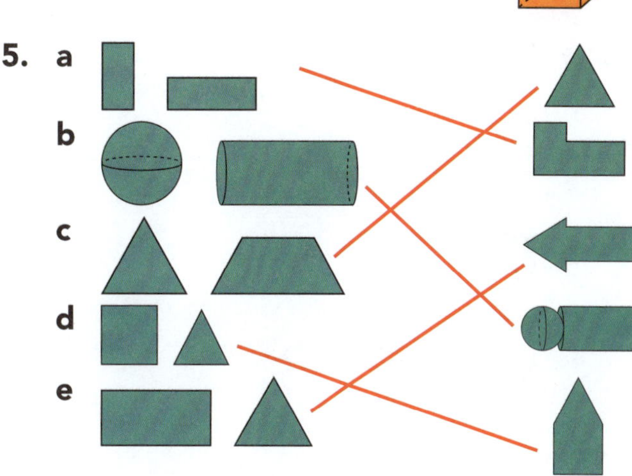

Answers

10. FRACTIONS

Equal Parts

Page 228 — Your Turn

1. a yes b no

Page 229 — Practice

1. a 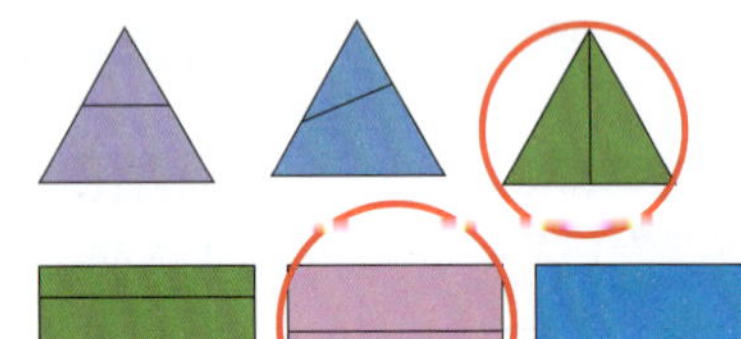

   b 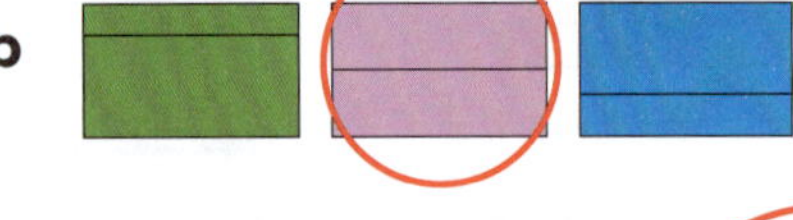

   c 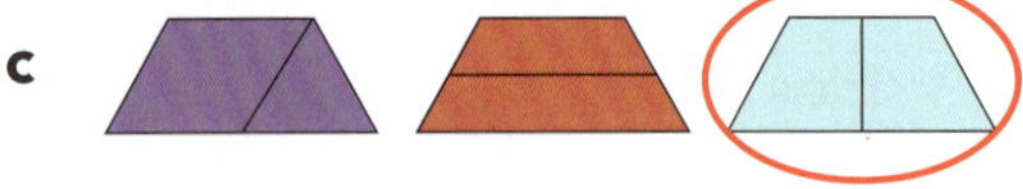

   d 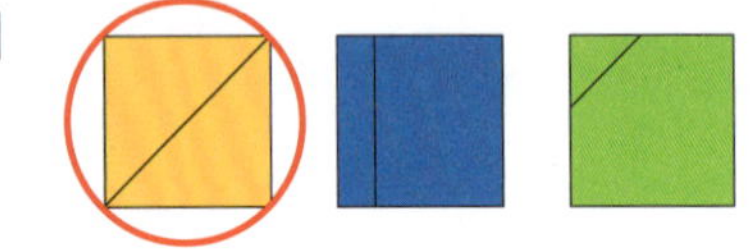

2. a yes
   b no
   c no
   d yes
   e yes

Halves

Page 230 — Your Turn

1. a   b  

Page 231 — Practice

1. a 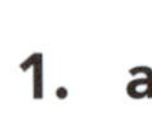 

   b 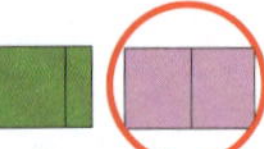

   c 

2. Possible answers:

   a 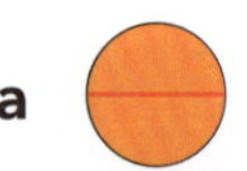

   b

   c 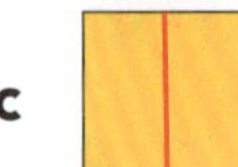

3. a 

   b

   c Possible answers:

Fourths

Page 232 — Your Turn

1. a 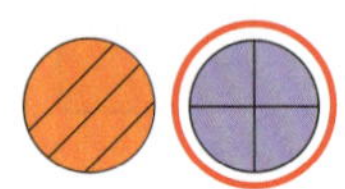

   b 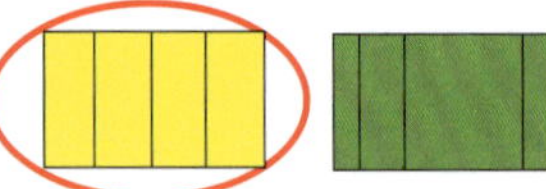

Page 233 — Practice

1. a 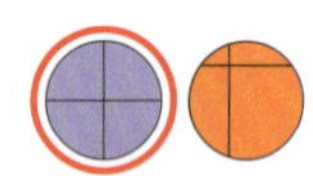

   b 

   c 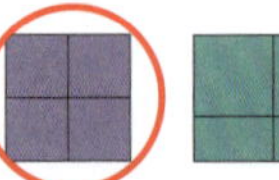

2. Possible answers:

   a 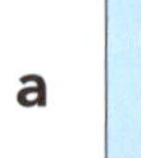 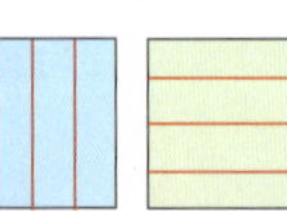

   b 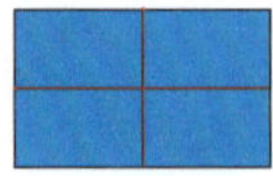

3. a Check that students have shaded all fourths in the square.

   I filled in 4 fourths to color the whole.

Answers

Fractions Review — Page 234

1. **a** yes

b no

c yes

d yes

2. Possible answers:

a 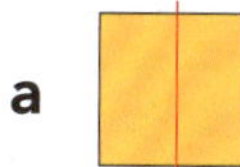

b 

c 

d 

3. Possible answers:

a 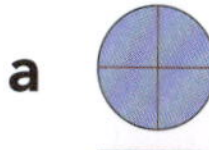

b 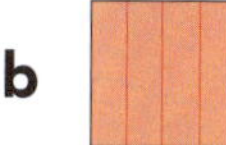

c

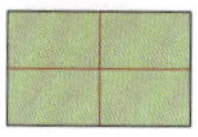

4. **a** Check that students have shaded both halves in the square.

I filled in 2 halves to color the whole.

b Check that students have shaded all fourths in the circle.

I filled in 4 fourths to color the whole.

Notes